Retrospecta 39

Contents

Letter from the Dean

It is a pleasure to add my letter in my first year as dean to Dean Stern's letter at the completion of his final year as dean of the Yale School of Architecture. *Retrospecta*, our annual publication of student work, is an appropriate place for the brief thoughts of the deans, and for the detailed representations of the students' work. This issue, *Retrospecta 39*, covers the work done in academic year 2015–2016, Dean Stern's eighteenth year leading the school and is a testament to his commitment to architectural education. To quote him, "We welcome the challenge of the future, confident that our approach does not insist on what to think, but on how to think."

At YSoA we teach a broad variety of courses, seminars and studios that educate our students in the diverse, multifaceted, historic, technological, environmental, aesthetic, cultural and social aspects of the discipline and profession of architecture. The work herein reveals our students' creativity and intelligence. It is a reflection of their commitment to engaging and shaping architecture, and Architecture, in its broadest cultural sense.

Deborah Berke
Dean and William Henry Bishop
Professor of Architectural Design

Letter from the Dean

This is a year of changes for the Yale School of Architecture. Some exciting—the upcoming takeover of the dean's chair by Deborah Berke—some historical—the school's 100th anniversary—and some tragic—the passing of our dear friend and colleague Zaha Hadid. As we look to the future and reflect on the past as a school and community, YSoA maintains its commitment to pedagogical pluralism, where all views are not accepted blindly but instead dissected critically. This school is a place of friction where we are each made better by peers and friends we often don't agree with, where conversations break the borders of dogma, and where we each develop a more rich and diverse view of architecture.

Moving forward, Yale's history of excellence will continue to provide the framework for an educational institution where thinking, doing, and making exist concurrently and perpetuate new and challenging forms of discourse. Our school's commitment to education and how it supports the profession gives me great confidence that we will continue to be both critical and relevant, even as society and technology change at an increasingly rapid pace.

As the profession is forced to address new and outstanding problems, the school remains dedicated to offer a far-reaching and inclusive dialogue through its diverse faculty, extensive international programs and established reputation as a leader of effective professionals.

It is with much gratitude towards the steadfast commitment of my colleagues and continued excellence of our student body that I conclude my final year as dean of the Yale School of Architecture. With great confidence in her abilities, I welcome our new dean, Deborah Berke, to Rudolph Hall.

Robert A.M. Stern
Dean and J.M. Hoppin Professor
of Architecture

Rather than highlighting distinct architectural philosophies, this issue is a continuous narrative of serendipitous juxtapositions. *Retrospecta 39* is our opportunity to celebrate these relationships that color Rudolph Hall.

Dimitri Brand
James Coleman
Amanda Iglesias
Jeongyoon Song

July 21, 2016
Editors' Letter

Deborah Berke Interview

Retrospecta 39:
What do you see as the primary role for a dean of a 21st century architecture school?

Deborah Berke:
To be inclusive, supportive, well-read, knowledgeable, and open to new ideas.

R39:
In your opinion, where will Yale in particular position itself in the greater landscape of architectural education?

DB:
How about the things I just said? [*laughter*] Yes, that's the answer.

R39:
How do you think architecture positions itself in relationship to social issues now, in comparison to when you graduated?

DB:
It's a hard and complicated question. I think in many ways my generation was much more focused on social issues. Coming out of the sixties—the war in Vietnam, the Civil Rights Movement, and the rise of the feminist movement—there was a highly politicized air at the time. I'm younger than that but that mood was still in the air. I think the architecture pendulum went all the way in the other direction and [architecture] completely removed itself from all social issues, and now the pendulum has swung back. I think in part the swing is motivated by the collapse of many American cities, rapid climate change, and issues that include all of the built environment. I'm happy with the pendulum swinging back to the concern about social issues, or at least the acknowledgement that the built environment plays a role in righting some of the social wrongs that exist.

R39:
How do you think your career would have differed if you graduated in 2016?

DB:
I'd have a lot more varied and broad skillset and tools available to me to manipulate form.

R39:
What is the university's role in advancing the critical dialogue that surrounds architecture?

DB:

I think the university's role is very broad, and architecture's role as a "capital A" art form, discipline, and profession is part of a larger cultural discussion.

But it's also part of a larger discussion about social issues, historical issues, and intercultural relationships. I feel that there really isn't a study at a university that doesn't touch on architecture in its broadest definition: as the built environment, the city, the landscape, planning, architectural history, etc.

R39:
How has research and writing affected your practice as an architect?

DB:
Well, I'm not a writer. I am primarily interested in the built environment not created by architects and the influence that has on architecture. I read about it, I take photos, I sketch when I travel. I look at the forms created by non-architects and try to understand what is their inspiration, impetus, and goal relative to my own work. I'm not a scholar on the subject. I'm a keen observer.

R39:
Part of Dean Stern's legacy is his cocktails and his after-review gatherings at his admittedly decadent apartment. Do you have any plans for you own soirées?

DB:
Well I like to party, I like to drink, but I don't like martinis. We will continue to have parties. I think architecture is inherently social in a very positive way.

The exchange of ideas is assisted by food and drink. I want to continue the exchange of ideas in a comfortable form.

The celebratory discussions have become part of the history of the school and part of who we are. I'm going to continue that, but it won't always be about the martinis.

R39:
Will you have a Lichtenstein in your apartment?

DB:
No. [*laughter*]

R39:
What does it mean to be the head of an office and the head of an architecture school?

DB:
I don't know yet; this is only day two. Well, this job at the Yale School of Architecture has always been held by a practitioner. In this job, you practice architecture and you run a school that teaches future practitioners, but I like a very broad definition about what it means to be a practitioner. Can you ask me that question next year? I know plenty of people have done it before me at Yale, so it seems doable.

R39:
What are your thoughts on the prevailing architecture review structure here at Yale and beyond?

DB:
I think the review structure where a student pins the work on the wall, presents it, and stands there to receive commentary, in broad-stroke description, is a good tool. Because in fact, as an architect, one has to know how to present work to others, hear what they're saying, and respond accordingly. That being said, a tight wall of too many people is a physical barrier to the participation of everybody standing behind them. We often have too many people on the jury so everybody gets a sound bite and there is no conversation. So I will be looking to change the physicality of it so it's literally more porous and penetrable and reduce the number of people. So what students hear is an exchange of ideas rather than a series of bullet points.

R39:
What concerns you most about architectural education?

DB:
The sheer number of things that have to be learned to be an architect in the limited amount of time available. There is just so much to learn. To do it well takes care, focus, and attention.

R39:
Are you optimistic?

DB:
Oh yeah. If I wasn't, I wouldn't have said yes to the job.

R39:
What's on your agenda for this week?

DB:
I am going to look at the budget for next year and try to wrap my head around it. It's a really complicated thing. I do answer my own e-mails, so I am going to answer some e-mails, and I am leaving here this evening to have dinner with my husband in New York [after] day two of sitting in this room.

Rome: Continuity and Change

Design & Visualization

Miroslava Brooks
Brennan Buck
Joyce Hsiang
George Knight
Bimal Mendis

This intensive five-week summer workshop takes place in Rome and is designed to provide a broad overview of the city's major architectural sites, topography, and systems of urban organization. Examples from antiquity to the present day are studied as part of the context of an ever-changing city with its sequence of layered accretions. The seminar examines historical continuity and change, as well as the ways in which and the reasons why some elements and approaches were maintained over time and others abandoned. Hand drawing is used as a primary tool of discovery during explorations of buildings, landscapes, and gardens, both within and outside the city. Students devote the final week to an intensive independent analysis of a building or place.

Tess McNamara 1
Christopher Leung 2
Matthew Bohne 3
Gina Cannistra 4
Anna Nasonova 5
Robert Yoos 6

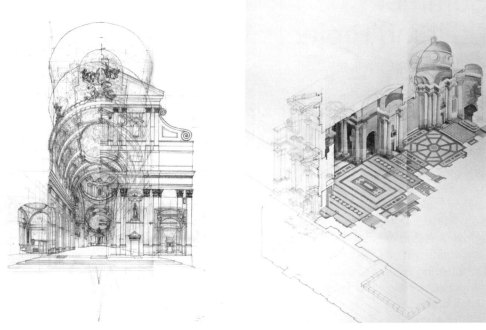

2

5

3

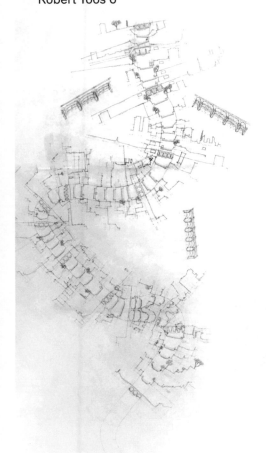

1

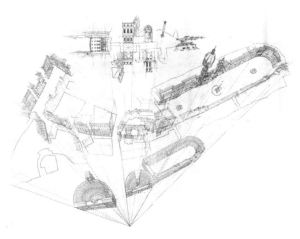

4

6

Summer
Building Project
Design & Visualization

Kyle Bradley
Adam Hopfner

Since 1967, the Yale School of Architecture has offered its first year students the unique chance to design and build a structure as part of their graduate education. Unique among architecture schools, this program is mandatory for all members of the class. The Building Project results in a single-family house in an economically depressed neighborhood.

The late Charles W. Moore, who headed Yale's Department of Architecture (later the School of Architecture) from 1965 to 1971, founded the First-Year Building Project in collaboration with faculty member Kent Bloomer. Moore saw that getting out of the studio and building something would have several benefits for the students. As a believer in simple tectonics and basic technologies, he hoped students would be inspired by the mechanics of building.

The earliest projects were outside of New Haven, and included community centers in Appalachia and a series of camp buildings in Connecticut. Reduced budgets in the 1970s and '80s, as well as increasing pressure on student schedules, led to a scaling back of the program and projects, which included several park pavilions confined to the New Haven area.

More recently, a focus has been placed on affordable housing. The houses allow students the experience of working with a client and the opportunity to respond to the challenges of affordable housing and urban infill. Many students arrive at school with a desire to include socially responsible work in their future professional lives. Having the opportunity to participate in the design and construction of such building projects often reinforces their convictions.

Visualization IV

Design & Visualization

John Blood
John Eberhart

This seven-week intensive course introduces Building Information Modeling (BIM) alongside manual drawing to expand each student's analytical and expressive repertoire. Fundamental techniques are introduced through short exercises and workshops leading toward a sustained study of an exemplary precedent building.

Quantitative analysis is pursued through both assembly modeling and visual dissection of both the programmatic spaces and functional elements. Observational and imaginative manual drawings allow for a reconstruction of the design process and reestablish the thought patterns that formed the building's design priorities. These discoveries then are represented through interactive multimedia presentations to describe the building assembly and its design ambitions.

Guillermo Castello, Justin Lai, Alison Zuccaro 7, 8

Alexis Hyman, Margaret Marsh, Danielle Schwartz 9

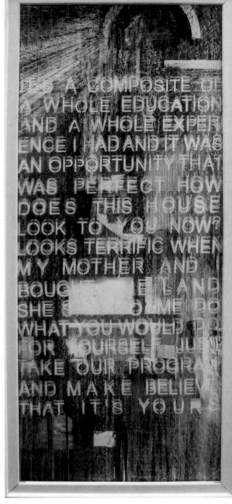

9

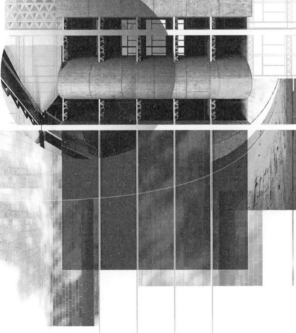

7

8

Stig Andersson
Empowerment of Aesthetics

Timothy Egan Lenahan Memorial Lecture

This is only one half of the total understanding of the phenomenon. The other half is the sense experienced. These two together are the entire and complete description of the garden. It is both the rational—the factual listing of parts: a scientific explanation of the material structure—and a sense perceived—the felt subjective feeling—that give us a deeper insight into the phenomenon. These two are complimentary and form together a complete description of the phenomenon. What we sense is not describable in the same language as the rational documentation. It is not a language that we can speak and it relates to the method used for the physical layout of the garden. It is a method based on intuition that balances form and emptiness.

The Architectural Surface

History & Theory

Anthony Vidler

This seminar examines and debates the theoretical controversies surrounding the material and conceptual properties of the architectural surface. The course is conceived as a series of case studies of buildings and projects—supported by readings in philosophy, psychoanalysis, and historiography—discussing the role of the surface historically and today. Themes include smooth and rough (Alberti, Romano); solid geometries (Ledoux, Boullée); historicist tableaux (Piranesi, Soane); frames and skins (Labrouste, Paxton); smooth and rough (Le Corbusier); containers and wrappings (Koolhaas, SANAA); topologies (Lynn, Schumacher).

The Flat Bed Fresco
Daphne Binder

The disjunction between surface plane and pictorial plane in the fresco is also evident in Diego Rivera's mural. It is important to note that Rivera's work is not considered here a transitional moment in fresco painting (not to say that it couldn't). Rather, as its name suggests, the fresco provides a unique moment in which the muralist has decided to play with the conventions of the fresco, rendering its apparatus apparent to the viewer. Immediate affinities emerge between the two paintings: the perspectival construction of the fresco from a heightened vantage point—visualized in "Making a Fresco." Rivera's actual perch on the scaffold, the location of the first floor scene [is] at an elevated level, the margins of the murals—similarly constructed as corner pilasters—obscure the very moment when illusionary space and 'real' come together.

At the same moment fresco painting conventions are found, Rivera manipulates them. Unlike Da Vinci, Rivera does not construct an elevated perspective; instead the perspective is constructed from our vantage point, the viewer, and recedes into the shallow depth of the mural. Nor do we find the picture plane and the surface plane as before. While the picture plane seems to be right in front of the scaffold, in searching for the surface plane we look at the illustration of the fresco, of the laborer, behind the scaffold. The depicted central figure's flatness is accentuated by a similar flatness in the appearance of sky to the left and right. So much so that the opening behind the draftswomen seems more like a blue opaque plane than a window. Rivera has thereby contained the entire scene of the mural within the bounds of the scaffold, sandwiched between the picture plane on the one side and the surface plane on the other. In "Making a Fresco," Rivera has increasingly narrowed the space of illusionary depth, a space that Steinberg will argue will collapse completely in the context of Rauschenberg's work.

Teleologies of the Architectural Surface via Borromini
Adil Mansure

This suggests an open, proto-parametric logical system that can sustain the constant redefinition of form, space, volume, order and meaning. This openness also anticipates that not every aspect of the church would be worked out completely in any given stage of its evolution.

In the algorithm … as the column diameter attains a particular value, it leads to the elimination of a set of columns. Inversely, the columns are willed into existence by values of specific parameters rather than only classical principles of columns. On further increasing the values of the diameter, the remaining pairs of columns coalesce into apses and the lozenge morphs into a lobed octagon—the first figure drawn by Borromini. … The interchangeability of the elements redefines their fundamental genetic properties and their functional/structural roles in the scheme.

These modifications were driven by questions of urbanity and the building site; and also by intensive formal properties of columns and apses. By reverse engineering the implicit code …a pseudo-algorithmic intuition in Borromini's design process and thinking emerges. His artistic intelligence itself functioned algorithmically and parametrically. With animated algorithms, not only can all the possible iterations and generative potentials in the design process be computed but also visualized. The animations represent a form of spatial dynamism that is created not only by rhythmic elements on a surface but as a result of a kinetic design process manifest spatially as effectively unstable, fragile and tenuous conditions of the architectural surface.

Architectural Theory II: 1968–Present

History & Theory

Anthony Vidler

This course is a survey of theoretical and critical literature on contemporary architecture. It explores the texts of postmodernism, post-structuralism, and critical and post-critical discourses, as well as current debates in globalization, post-humanism, and environmentalism in the architectural discipline from 1968 to the present.

The Abattoir Construct Complex
Gregory Cartelli

Looking back on their installation from 1991, the Smithsons wrote that their recent thinking on pavilions had resulted in the idea of the 'fragment of an enclave' which they proceeded to define through the relations between the idea of the *study* and of the *desert*, concluding that perhaps the "only easily defensible enclave is again the *desert.*"[1] To make this retroactively applicable to *Patio and Pavilion* is not a difficult task. The eponymous *Pavilion* "was a three walled 'shed', or shanty house, with a corrugated plastic roof."[2] It was, importantly, not fully enclosed. It existed as a permanently fractured structure, a 'fragment of an enclave.' The *Patio* "was sand… surrounded by a wall of semi-reflective aluminum-clad plywood with a doorway that allowed for visitor access."[3] Easily, the *Pavilion* is the *study* and the *Patio* the *desert*, if not for more than their material similarities. Confusing boundaries between the two were the semi-transparent roof of the pavilion and the semi-reflective aluminum fencing of the patio.

In the Smithsons' words from 1980 (moving again from end to beginning), capriciousness was introduced through these permeable and refractive elements (the plastic pavilion roof and the sand patio) which allowed for the interventions by their collaborators, artists Nigel Henderson and Eduardo Paolozzi, to be embedded and seen through.[4] Additionally, the reflective walls were said to "include every visitor as an inhabitant."[5] While collaborator is an apt description, the Smithsons refer to Henderson and Paolozzi as inhabitants (1980) and occupants (2000) both. The first term implies a normative use of the building as a shelter, while the second is unorthodox and points to a subjugation, and potential misuse, of the built environment by a human element.

1. Importantly, it is specifically the desert that is figured here as a contrast to the study. The desert, as both the iconic smooth space and rhizome of Deleuze and Guattari, is figured by Rebeca Solnit in 1996 as "a test site for the last few decades of critical theory," and it is noted by Catrin Gersdorf that as "the desert exists in the dominant cultural imaginary as a huge, dangerous space full of nothing, it can be easily converted into an ideal location for planning, practicing, and executing operations. On the other hand, the residual signs of such activities…remain there, out in the open for anyone to see. …because of the desert's specific geology and climate, it will take an extraordinarily long time to cover up, as it were, the ruins and relics of human occupation and activity." Alison Smithson and Peter Smithson, "The Nature of Retreat," *Places Journal* 7(3) (1991), 19.

2. Ben Highmore, "Rough Poetry: Patio and Pavilion Revisited," *Oxford Art Journal*, 29(2) (2006), 271.

3. Ibid.

4. Alison and Peter Smithson, "The 'As Found' and the 'Found,'" in *The Independent Group: Postwar Britain and the Aesthetics of Plenty*, ed. David Robbins, (Cambridge: The MIT Press, 1990), 201.

5. Alison Smithson and Peter Smithson, *The Nature of Retreat*, 19.

Preservation: the Contemporary Paradigm of a Former Architecture
Jack Lipson

This conversation manifested itself in the postwar period, as the special interest of history, ruination and lost cultural imagery became a leading factor in the active preservation methodologies used throughout the '60s and '70s. Today we see an ease of accessibility to our collectively valued monuments through immense levels of unprecedented tourism—an industry that thrives off of the seemingly broad strokes and declarations that many nations willfully embrace: that every object, building, and moment is worth preserving for display. Alike the visual propaganda that Piranesi shared with the north, glorifying the ruins of a destroyed Rome, we too flock towards the remains of past civilizations. We see the world's economy thriving as cities seem to trade in their ambitions for innovation with capital efforts to remain in stasis—and for those that continue to build, it is within the grasp of an agenda which anticipates preservation. In his manifesto featured in *Preservation*, [Rem] Koolhaas writes that "through preservation's ever increasing ambitions, the time lag between new construction and the imperative to preserve has collapsed from two thousand years to almost nothing. From retrospective, representation will soon become prospective, forced to take decisions for which it is entirely unprepared."[1] With that provocation, and through understanding the lineage of discourse surrounding preservation theory, we must ask the question: what is the role of the preservationist as the act of preservation becomes a prospective and integrated component of the architect's vision? Or for that matter, what is the role of the architect once their contribution is stripped of innovation and reduced to pragmatic restoration?

1. Cronocaos. Biennale, Venice. 29 August–21 November 2010. New Museum, New York. 7 May–5 June 2011. *Journal of the Society of Architectural Historians* 71.2 (2012). Web, 122.

Architecture and Books
Design & Visualization

Luke Bulman

For architects, the book has been a necessary (if not essential) tool for clarifying, extending, and promoting their ideas and projects. This seminar examines the phenomenon of the book in architecture as both an array of organizational techniques (what it is) and as a mediator (what it does). Arguably, outside of building itself, the book has been the preferred mode of discourse that architects have chosen to express their intellectual project. Because lasting impression relies partially upon durability of message, the book remains the objet par excellence among media. This seminar is part-lecture, part-workshop, where the experience of making a series of books helps to inform the development of ideas about the projective capacity of the book. Through case studies, the first portion of this seminar examines the relationship book production has with a selection of contemporary and historical practices, including each project's physical and conceptual composition as well as how each project acts as an agent of the architect within a larger world of communication. The second part of the seminar asks students to apply ideas in a series of three book projects that emphasize the book as an instrument of architectural thinking.

Kristin Nothwehr 10
Wes Hiatt 11, 12
Anny Chang, Andrew Dadds, Ethan Fischer, Richard Green, Wes Hiatt, Cynthia Hsu, Karl Karam, Jizhou Liu, Anna Nasonova, Kristin Nothwehr, Madison Sembler, Dima Srouji 13

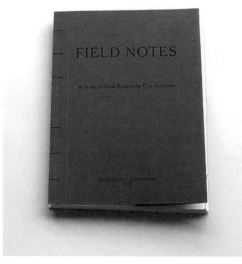

10

11

12

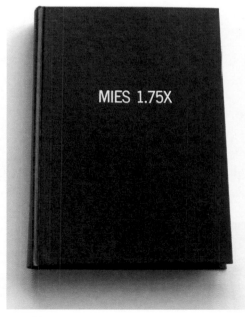

13

Pier Vittorio Aureli

Design & Visualization
Advanced Studio

with Emily Abruzzo

14

15

This studio is about the most obvious topic in architecture: the architecture of domestic space. We depart from a simple yet crucial question: what is domestic space? And most importantly, why has domestic space historically become such an important—if not crucial—reference for our way of living? Far from accepting housing as a natural way of being, we are interested in questioning its architectural nature as a historically constructed domain in which issues such as subjectivity, gender, ownership, and class play a fundamental role. This year we are further radicalizing this approach by focusing on the *house* as a multifarious apparatus that links together form, gender, construction, ownership, and subjectivity as one systemic domain. The goal of the studio is to put forward an idea of architecture where *form* has a chance at agency within the housing domain. While form in

architecture is always the product of specific political forces, it is also the edge against which new forces and subjects can recognize themselves. More specifically, the studio will focus on the nature of domestic space when the latter has been put under the pressure of extreme (and artificial) regime of scarcity such as in the recent dramatic housing crisis that is affecting cities such as New York or San Francisco. Following last year's brief, we imagine a scenario where 100,000 new houses (or more) will be built in San Francisco in the next few years. Facing such a task, we see the architectural project as the production of examples in the form of prototypes, rather than the crafting of singular artifacts. However, we believe that even though the issue of shortage is an important component of the answer to the current housing crisis,

it cannot be reduced to a mere quantity problem. The question of housing can be properly answered only if we enter its political core—that is, the organization of reproductive labor as the fundamental and yet largely invisible support of society. With the best possible intentions, architects have tried to propose new horizons for the family apartment, playing with double levels, with different distribution patterns, with new models of furniture. However, we have hardly ever criticized the basic articulation of living spaces into a predetermined set of rooms. Taking the room as the first element of a project for living space allows us to see the question of housing on completely different terms from the ones we normally work with. The very presence, form, position and quality of furniture and objects is an integral part of the project of the room this year, precisely

17

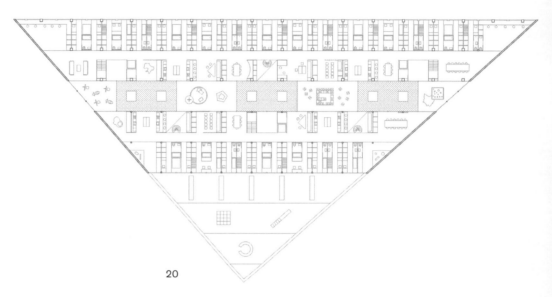
20

18

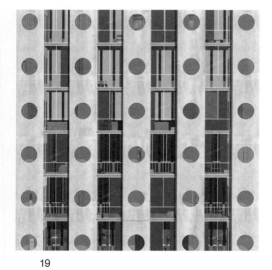
19

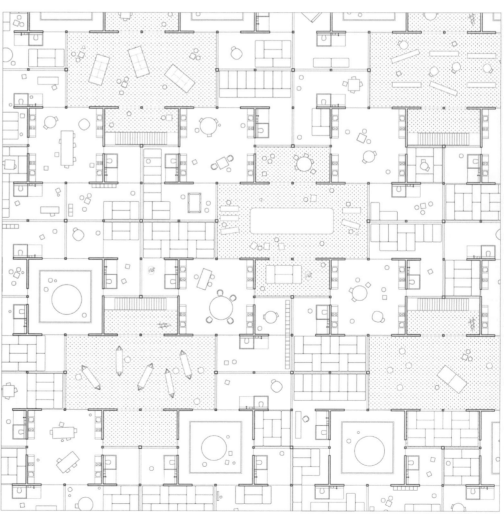
21

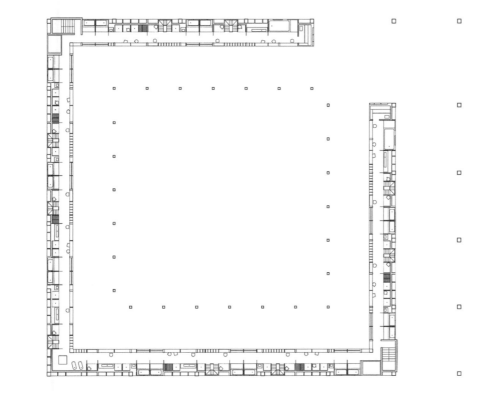

because furniture is not a neutral element but rather a powerful way to characterize (or de-characterize) the room. Ultimately, to imagine a city made of rooms for individuals or groups of people means to reject the model that sees the city as an agglomeration of nuclear families.

Excerpts from *Home is a Four Letter Word: 100,000 Homes for San Francisco*, published by the studio.

Background

The morphology of the urban and political form of San Francisco is defined by a continual cycle of expansion and contraction. The opposing forces of expansion and contraction have not defied the establishment of a synthetic urban whole; in fact, this dialectical tendency characterizes the very nature of the city and defines the unique political and urban project that is San Francisco. The Bay Area's extreme topography denies isotropic urbanization of the territory. Settlement of the city's hills was not possible until the development of modern transportation technology; even the density today of the slopes remains very low. An equally powerful force of opposition are the city's grassroots movements. Demographically diverse activist movements were particularly effective in preventing uncontrolled urban renewal in the middle of the twentieth century. Despite their initial success, anti-development policy has incentivized the preservation of the city's status quo, stifling contemporary development and causing severe lack of affordable

housing in the city. The nostalgic ethos of preserving the image of the city is denying San Francisco's diverse population their right to the city, and denies inhabitance to the precarious worker who is the original character of the city.

Site Strategy

To create 100,000 houses for San Francisco is not a scheme to expand the city, but rather to retrofit the existing fabric while providing greater density through specific prototypes. Therefore, we focus on soft-sites and entire neighborhoods that lack density: retrofitting is based on specific strategic criteria that take advantage of available under-utilized land and existing infrastructural necessities such as public transit corridors along Divisadero and 16th street; empty under underdeveloped areas such as SoMa and Dogpatch; and areas that are often considered 'full' such as the Sunset District, which is in fact a low density suburban neighborhood. Deploying structures in parking lots, empty corner lots, gas stations, under-used waterfront areas, and postindustrial sites, a figure emerges from the city: not a master plan, but a system of proximities.

Seven Prototypes

These seven prototypes for communal living aim to challenge the current domestic landscape made up of single-family houses and apartments. The goal of these prototypes is twofold: to prove that despite the image of a 'dense city,' San Francisco has a lot of unused land,

and to offer accommodations that encourage living beyond home-property. Crucial for all the prototypes is the issue of land use. We propose 100,000 homes for the sites that lack density or a clearly defined use—vacant urban lots, neglected sites, residual parcels or areas occupied by low-rise buildings such as warehouses. All these sites could be leased or obtained at lower rates from public or private owners through special planning agreements. Time-limited building permissions could be granted in exchange for a controlled rental rate. In terms of typology, the pro-posed 100,000 houses aim to minimize individual space and maximize collective space. The criteria is pursued with different degrees of intensity: from realistic reforms of the typical household to radical challenges of traditional domestic spaces such as the removal of the bedroom or the personal bathroom. In terms of building and construction, the goal is to largely rely on prefabrication and use of industrial building components. These criteria aim to offer a generous living and working space while reducing costs as much as possible.

Andreas De Camps 14, 15
Luke Anderson, Dante Furioso (Feldman Nominees) 16
Jessica Angel, Dorian Booth 17, 20
Ali Naghdali 18
Daphne Binder, Alicia Pozniak 19
Anna Meloyan 21
James Kehl, Vittorio Lovato 22

Building Project

Design & Visualization
First Year Studio

Andrew Benner
Peter de Bretteville
Adam Hopfner
Amy Lelyveld
Joeb Moore
Alan Organschi

Since 1967, first year students at the Yale School of Architecture have worked collaboratively to design and build a structure as part of their graduate education. Unique among architecture schools, the Jim Vlock Building Project is a required component of Yale's curriculum. The Building Project has focused on the design and construction of houses in New Haven's economically distressed neighborhoods. This year's brief targets a 1,000 square foot house located in New Haven's West River neighborhood. Students are challenged to develop a cost-efficient and flexible design that addresses the unique challenges facing similar sliver sites in New Haven and other urban environments across the country. During the first half of the spring semester, students work individually, each developing a prototype for the dwelling. A portion of these initial schemes are selected for further development, and the class is divided into teams, each team tasked with creating a final design proposal. At the end of the semester, one project is chosen and the entire class works together to build the selected design.

Critics
Andrew Benner (AB), Deborah Berke (DB), Phillip Bernstein (PB), Kyle Bradley (KB), Turner Brooks (TB), Peter de Bretteville (PdB), Leslie Gill (LG), Adam Hopfner (AH), Everardo Jefferson (EJ), Amy Lelyveld (AL), Joeb Moore (JM), Petia Morosov (PM), Herbert Newman (HN), Alan Organschi (AO), Alexander Purves (AP), Julie Savin (JS), Robert A.M. Stern (RAMS), Beka Sturges (BS), Amy Wrzesniewski (AW)

Jonathan Molloy 23, Ziyue Liu 24, Dylan Lee 25, Claire Haugh 26, Timon Covelli 27, Alexis Hyman 28, Andrew Busmire 29, Caitlin Baiada 30, Laura Quan 31, Jeongyoon Song 32, Alexandra Karlsson-Napp 33, Robert Smith Waters 34, Jack Lipson 35, Christian Golden 36, John Holden 37

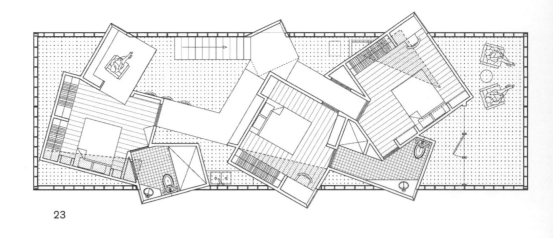

23

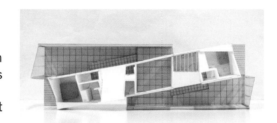

24

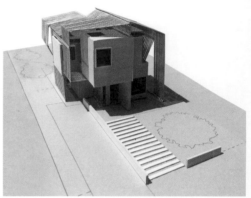

28

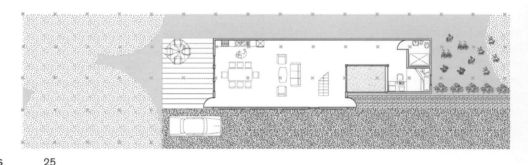

25

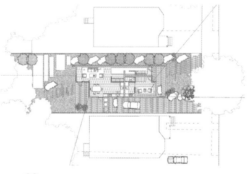

26

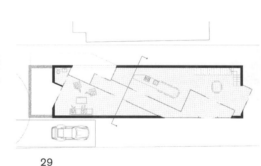

29

27

30

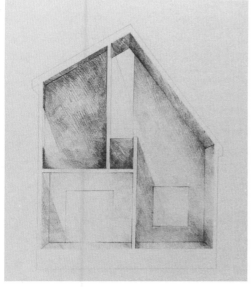

31

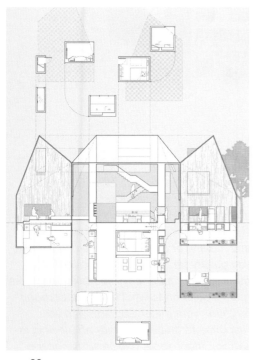

32

35

33

36

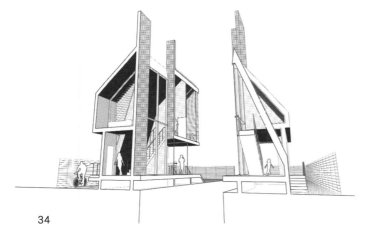

34

37

Team A 38, 39

Abena Bonna, Christian Golden, Justin Lai, Dylan Lee, Stephanie Medel, Jeongyoon Song, Pierre Thach

TB: *I really like the way you celebrate its tininess. It becomes the tiny house on the block and I think it takes on a kind of power as a result of that. It's not in between—everything is ambivalent, in between a small house and a normal house. The one emaciation that I really don't appreciate is you could've swollen the living room. I think that's the one place in the plan that is a disaster.* RAMS: *Artistically, either the gable this way or that way would have been better. Now it looks like something from LOT-EK—a prefabricated unit, whereas they could have been an eloquent neighborly gesture.* AP: *The issue I have with this is the dimension of its living spaces on the ground floor, which I think is just intolerable. At least allow some kind of usability because you're walking through it as well.* RAMS: *Is it legal to bring these [dormers] down to the ground? Then why not bring them to the ground?* AO: *Because they are really fighting some dimensional stuff and the square footage…* RAMS: *Well… you know … [laughter] Get rid of the porch on the second floor. This is not a house for retirement people of the leisure class. They do not have time to sit on a porch—I don't have time to sit on a porch so how do they have time to sit on a porch?* LG: *Each one of us is modifying it to adjust it either to be dimensionally more palatable or thinking about infill strategies but you've got all of us.* HN: *There's a joyousness about the way you've made this and presented it and the fact that the plan is the whole site plan. It's not just solving a problem.*

39

Team B 40

Dimitri Brand, Denisa Butazu, James Coleman, Hyeree Kwak, David Langdon, Julie Turgeon

RAMS: *What about the elevation of your house? The house should have something to do with the language of the street. An interesting attention would grow up by having a different expression for these light monitors, which is I think what you have. A device Kahn used, Aalto used, Sir John Soane used. You're not the first ones to do it. But you don't have the one intersecting with the other or engaging with each other, which would enrich the composition, not making it so diagrammatic which I think it is now, creating a street façade which is wisely hid behind that tree.* DB: *For me the success of this scheme is its beautiful simplicity which is then compromised by a lot of stuff going on on the second floor, which I don't think is helping you.* RAMS: *Domestic architecture is about closets.*

[laughter] *Where's Joeb? Would you say that closets are very important in domestic architecture?* JM: *Yes, but I wouldn't make them the theme.* RAMS: *I hate sleeping and looking at closets.* Denisa: *I don't think you qualify for this house.* [laughter] BS: *I think it's very hard to try and take on a more radical position to what the neighborhood is. I think your initial diagrams and your response to that initial study about what is extraordinary about this particular space, and making that big open floor are just incredibly strong. There's some evident struggle with the representation and the form-making but I think there's a conceptual clarity that everybody has remarked on.* RAMS: *I think most people don't wish to have their private world exposed to the public street. First off, the traditional house on this street is elevated above the street, three steps or whatever, which means that automatically you can't really look into the depth of the house, even if there are no curtains.* AO: *Make it do more.*

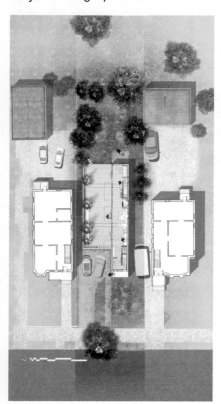

38

40

Team C 41, 42

Claire Haugh, Zachary Hoffmann, Margaret Marsh, Danielle Schwartz, Matthew Shaffer, Phineas Taylor-Webb

TB: *I think the entry sequence is really nice, elegant and protracted, in a good way. I like the way you come in the door and have living room and kitchen. A really disgustingly stupid practical comment: I wonder what I would do if I was coming back home with my two daughters' smelly, enormous hockey bag of equipment. Where do I go? That's not clear.* LG: *With a small house you set up a clear objective to use a variety of spaces in different ways and to, in a sense, always anticipate the on/off switch of how someone could begin to use or reuse something. I like the fact that the efficiency moves up from a landscape idea into a utility and storage idea. You have to have a lighter touch with your built-ins; at a certain moment you want the sense of release from the density of the pour.* RAMS: *I think that, more important* than the color, which could be changed at any time, is your horizontal proportionality for the windows. [They] seem completely at odds with anything on the street and not terribly beneficial to your own design with the central gable, which needs to be addressed in some way on the façade.* DB: *You denied us the pleasure of talking about the outside [and the experience of] putting a door one story up a staircase; what is it like up there? How much space do you need to park yourself, [drop off] your hockey equipment, and to unlock the door?* JM: *The large tree at the sidewalk is in the center. I completely agree with Deborah's points about the awkwardness with the interior, but [the tree] would have helped if it was dotted and lightly put in there.* PM: *I encourage you, if this moves forward, to think about how the materiality can be a lot more playful with that ceiling surface because right now it just feels very blunt to me and I think that there's a kind of beautiful layering vertically and horizontally of spaces.*

41

42

Team D 43, 44

Melinda Agron, Audrey Li, Gentley Smith, Robert Smith Waters, Alexandra Thompson, Dylan Weiser, Samuels Zeif

RAMS: *Two things I find a little troublesome. One, the observation that you push the house back so that it would not be in the horse-blinders of the two houses. It doesn't seem to me that you took any advantage of that, since you have no windows that look to the sides. The other is the extra living room. It isn't much of a useful room and is exactly like the room above it for the tenant. You could have had a door from the street right into the tenant's apartment, and then you eliminate the outside stair. You've been here in the winter. You must know what a nightmare that would be.* BS: *Somehow in the overall argument, this idea of openness along the ground floor is not being captured. I think your façade is not in any way speaking to this notion of openness, even a prioritization of the owner experience. I think trying to make the courtyard space on the south is a valiant effort. I don't feel 100% convinced that it is a success. I get it, and it's provocative.* TB: *As someone who hates renderings, these are very seductive.* HN: *I think though that the capitulation to the front door and street front is antithetical to the interiority that you are striving for in your various renderings. By the time you* get a powder room in there, you've lost the functionality of the space. Explore pushing the building even further back on the lot and using the courtyard as your entry point.* AP: *I like the idea of continuity of space on the ground floor. For that reason, I would argue for the tenant upstairs. I just don't understand why you'd break the wall on the ground floor. It makes an extremely unpleasant condition inside. It seems against the clarity of the proposition. You don't want to divide the house longitudinally.* RAMS: *Beka said that all of the drawings are so nice and consistent. I beg to differ. These drawings are for a very elegant house getting ready for Architectural Digest. They do not look like a New Haven house for a Scrabble [playing] family. I'm not saying you have to play down, but you have to be realistic as to what kind of life would occur.* HN: *There's a great nourishment that's been given to the courtyard in terms of details which are programmatic. But there is an ambivalence, an indecisiveness about what is the character of the house on the street. It's undernourished. It has to make up its mind.* RAMS: *For a lot of people who are stuck at home—they are older, they aren't well—a porch shaded from the intense sun, open to the street, is a wonderful asset. Why not use that asset? Every house always looks like it's been undernourished, underfed.*

Team E (Selected design) 45–47

Patrick Doty, Kevin Huang, Alexis Hyman, Jonathan Molloy, Ron Ostezan, Meghan Royster, Misha Semenov

RAMS: *I think it's a very nice design though your elevations are horrible. I question whether you can have a green roof on a modestly wood-framed structure but I'll leave that to Adam to figure out. The double height space over the dining room I find to be a waste of space and it's like being at the bottom of a well. You could have created another bedroom and, in the current configuration, I think the tenant would appreciate having another bedroom. I'm only speculating, but I don't imagine your parents want to make sure you're doing your homework from some remote location a floor above. If you're going to use an aesthetic argument, we could talk about it.* DB: *Can you describe why this building is clad in vertical siding? You've elected to do a gable-ended façade on the street where there are other houses and your attitude towards how you clad it really does mean something. I think your ground floor plan is beautiful and the composition of your elevations is not yet refined.* LG: *It's hard culturally to celebrate small in America and I think your first floor plan does that in a very successful way. Even though the scale of the larger rooms is quite diminutive, by understanding how you've created transitional spaces and slippage spaces, you break down the scale of a larger grouping to an idea of the entire floor. You've tried to embrace this larger space and give it a sense of gravity. You've done that, and also have given it a sense of seclusion. I commend you on that. I think the first floor plan has an incredibly light touch. It's really sophisticated.* RAMS: *I wish I could be so enthusiastic as my colleagues. I think your living room is very difficult to furnish. To sit on a sofa at the bottom of a stair does not strike me as a nice relationship. There isn't even a place to put a table on the side for a lamp, or a drink, or whatever. I think there's an enormous amount of circulation around that kitchen. How many people are cooking in this kitchen? I think it's a lot of wasted space, frankly. I'm not dazzled.*

43

44

45

47

46

Building Project

Team F 48, 49

Timon Covelli, Ian Donaldson, Daniel Fetcho,
Amanda Iglesias, Suzanne Marchelewicz,
Adam Meis, Francesca Xavier

LG: *I think its innovation comes from its
internal organization and from understanding this as a prototypical building that
could be placed many different places and
locations. [It] is, in a way, trying to marry a
very particular American idea of what living
is into very compact zones and spaces, and
that's where I see its success.* TB: *I really
like it because it's a normal house with
these odd enormous growths coming out of
it, which bring the small scale house into the
scale of the street and the bigger buildings
all around it. I think that's a very clever thing.
Like dwarfs with huge heads, it's a small
guy with big features. I think that's a very
inventive way of pushing the spaces around
it. I do think the bottom floor main space
is a little claustrophobic.* BS: *Do you need
a counter? I know conceptually you need
the counter, but I do think it's crowding the
space.* DB: *I think the counter just needs
wheels. You show four different floor plans
for upstairs, why not just be able to slide it
away?* EJ: *I wish there were more windows
for more light to come into that centralized
space, but you do already have the skylight.
That roof has to be somehow looked at.
Maybe it doesn't have to overlap so much;
it can just touch the edge and come down,
[be] more volumetric.* RAMS: *You don't
want to make the house a roadmap on the
outside for what's on the inside.*

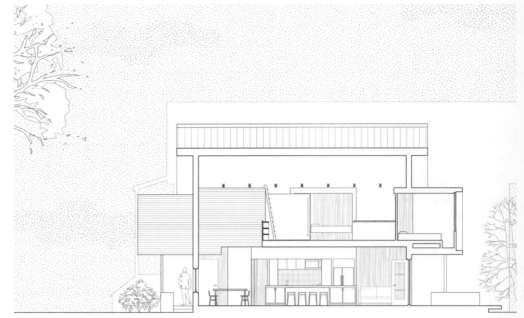

49

Team G 50, 51

Azza Abou Alam, Guillermo Castello,
Spencer Fried, Alexandra Karlsson-Napp,
Xiaomeng Li, Ziyue Liu, Laura Quan

LG: *I think your building is anything but
subtle. Then when you gave the argument
of the scale of your building and the
relationship to this inner block, you had
me. I fully understand what your challenge
was, what your sense of efficiency was, and
how you understood this building to fit into
its context. I feel like the building is too tall
right now.* RAMS: *If you're going to do a
house or a building that's based on an idea
of modular regularity of bays, you just can't
add things on. Le Corbusier said that that
shouldn't be done in 1925. "That is too easy,"
is what he said. Trés facile. That is what the
problem is here. It's not subjected to the
discipline that you, at first glance, think is
there. You show more skill with fenestration
than anybody so far today, although the
fenestration sometimes is large pieces of
glass that may not exactly be in the budget
of low-income housing. How do you frame
these, are they steel frames or wood? The
thing that upsets me is not the flat roof,
because you could put a hipped roof on a
cube and it would fit with the same rigor,
but this wing sticking out, is compositionally*
a catastrophe. BS: *You allow the neighborhood to continue to exist in the successful
spatial way it has existed and this becomes
an out-building that actually is extremely
elegant. It's kind of a covert act of grace in
the neighborhood; that's really strong.*
RAMS: *Architecture is not just one thing.
A good building has to have an internal,
compositional logic. Your building, if you
get rid of the front wing, would have a
compositional logic. It's basically a square.
Or it could be a rectangle. But it's neither.
It's like a one-clawed lobster. You better
hope [the tree] lives.* Spencer: *Why wouldn't
it?* RAMS: *Why wouldn't it? Well have you
ever heard of Dutch Elm Disease?* Spencer:
Old trees have a lot of value to cities.
RAMS: *They're the ones that die. Elm trees
die from Dutch Elm Disease.* AO: *This
may be a cultivar that is particularly robust
and therefore should be protected.*
RAMS: *I'm interested in architecture as a
principle. I know now I sound like Peter
Eisenman. I think this is not done for the
principle. I think this is done from taste.
I've been around too long, okay? As a
work of taste or composition, it's not very
good because it's not disciplined. It's not
subjected to the rigor that you set out to do.
If you don't do that, you just end up in
Dwell Magazine, frankly.*

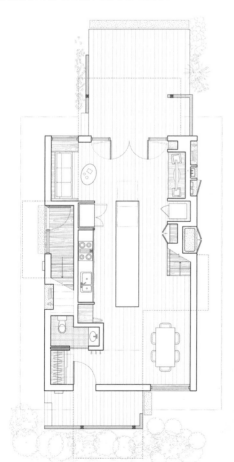

48

50

51

53

Team H 52, 53

Caitlin Baiada, Valeria Flores, John Holden,
Hunter Hughes, Jack Lipson, Larkin
McCann, Alison Zuccaro

RAMS: *Aren't most of the houses horizontal
clapboarding or shingles? I don't know any
houses, except Yale houses, that are always
stuck in vertical wood siding. Houses, or
buildings in general, don't usually, or don't
need to, change materials on every side
to express something about the context.*
DB: *It sounds very detailed, focused-in
and minor, but the horizontal siding would
have allowed you to strike the datum of the
symmetrical doorway, strike the datum at
the top of the windows, strike the datum
that's at your eave height, and use the
language, which is so great, because you're
playing off that incredibly simple façade and
basic dormer.* LG: *I felt like two elevations
were also some of the most deliberate
elevations we've seen today; the front
elevation and the side elevation, are where
you really begin to understand how the
house might be occupied. But you're also
balancing a dialogue between the rhythms
of the surrounding buildings. To me that's
where you're working very successfully.*
RAMS: *Some of this is getting down to the
small strokes, so to speak, but it's a terrible
room. Just awful. And the way you have your
bed here, this pour soul will never be able to
change the bed linen. I think you could
have done much more around it to pick up
some of the vocabulary of the neighborhood and really embrace the neighborhood.
Forget about being a modern architect
and be an architect.* BS: *It's too literal of
a solution to not have a window on that
back façade; it's fighting the kind of delight
in light that is otherwise operating in this
project. I think that you lost your concept a
little bit in that moment.*

52

Building Technology

Technology & Practice

Adam Hopfner
Alan Organschi

This course examines the role of material and procedure in the formation of architecture and the physical, logistical, and environmental constraints and demands that shape the processes of construction. In the first half of the term, a sequence of lectures surveys the conceptual concerns and technological factors of building. Corresponding construction examples and case studies of mid-scale public buildings introduce students to the exigencies that so often influence decision making in the technical process and inflect (and potentially enrich) design intention—regulatory requirement, physical and environmental stress and constraint, procedural complication, labor and material availability and quality, energy consumption, and ecological impact. The course seeks to illuminate the ecological considerations as well as the materials, means, and methods that are fundamental to the conception and execution of contemporary building.

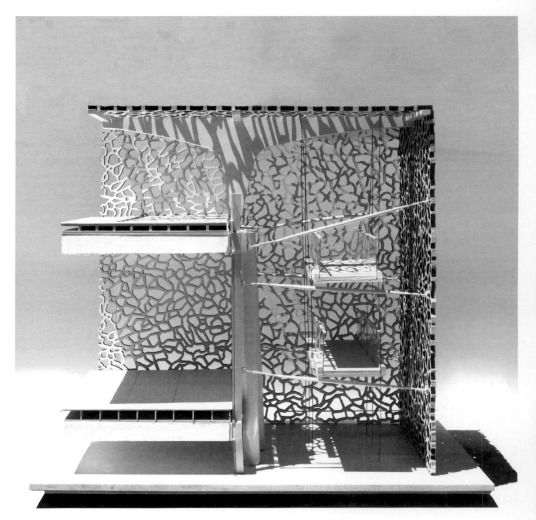

54

55

53

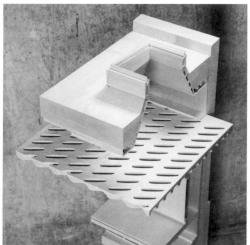

56

The Chair

Design & Visualization

Timothy Newton

The chair has been a crucible for architectural ideas and their design throughout the trajectory of modern architecture. The chair is both a model for understanding architecture and a laboratory for the concise expression of idea, material, fabrication, and form. As individual as its authors, the chair provides a medium that is a controllable structure, ripe for material and conceptual experiments. In this seminar, students develop their design and fabrication skills through exploration of the conceptual, aesthetic, and structural issues involved in the design and construction of a full-scale prototype chair.

57

58

60

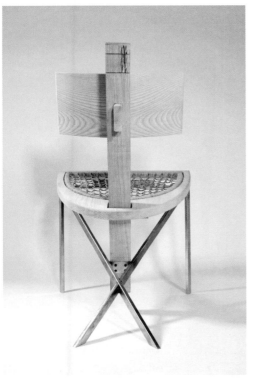

59

61

62

63

65

66

67

64

68

Construction of Exactitude: Classicism and Modernism

History & Theory

Karla Britton

This seminar examines the theme of exactitude as a design and constructional theoretical method in the creative processes of seminal architects over the past one hundred years. Conceived to readdress the concept of the classical in architectural thought and practice (understood not as style but as a rational process of distillation, clarity, economy, and syntax), the seminar emphasizes how fundamentals derived from this mode (unity, composition, proportion) have shaped the work of leading modern architects. Concepts addressed are the universal, the tectonic, permanence, cultural continuity, and the vocation of the architect. Representative practices are contrasted with other methodological modes that stem from the organic, the decorative, the parametric, and the local. Works studied include those by architects, historians, literary figures, artists, and theorists such as Perret, Garnier, Le Corbusier, Valéry, Nietzsche, Said, Calvino, Mies, Scully, Niemeyer, Kahn, Vidler, Frampton, and Eisenman.

Gina Cannistra 69
Michael Harrison 70
Garrett Hardee 71

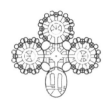
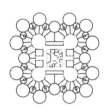

70

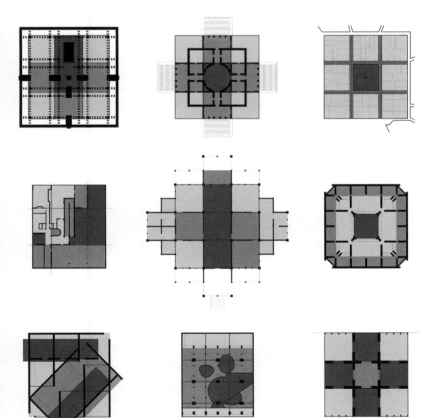

69

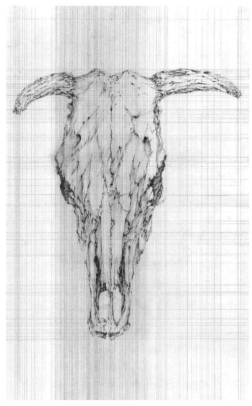

71

Contemporary Architectural Discourse Colloquium

History & Theory

Eeva-Liisa Pelkonen

Organized by second-year M.E.D. students in collaboration with the director of the M.E.D. program, this year's colloquium investigates the powerful yet often invisible roles of gender in the built environment. In public and private spaces, the gendering of spaces reinforces cultural norms and is therefore inscribed in the production of spaces. This colloquium asks students to consider how different spaces—exterior and interior—are organized and articulated to reflect and determine gender relations within the built environment. The course explores these particular notions of space through different media, specifically film, photography, and art, and against the larger background of activism, labor, class identity, and urban culture, among others. Through conversations with emergent theorists, historians, and practitioners, and engagement with different media, students are challenged to consider how gender politics are (re)produced across various cultural and physical landscapes, and how an excavation of gender might highlight potential for spatial or professional intervention.

Craft, Materials, and Digital Artistry

Technology & Practice

Kevin Rotheroe

This course reviews materials and manufacturing processes especially suited for digitally crafting aesthetically unique architectural components and surfaces. Cross-fertilization of digital and conventional modes of making is emphasized, as this approach often enables economically viable opportunities for creative expression. This is a hands-on, project-based seminar addressing fundamental theoretical issues in the transformation of ideas into material reality via representations, hand-operated tools, and CNC-automated forming devices.

Ethan Fischer 72
Shreya Shah 73
Maxwell Mensching 74

74

72

73

Craft, Materials, and Digital Artistry

Credentials:
The Professions
of Urbanizing

Urbanism & Landscape

Todd Reisz

As the close of the 1960s found cities in Europe and North America designed into obsolescence, urbanization unfurled with conviction in other parts of the world. The following decade could have been an era of true global expansion for the architectural and planning professions; however, there are many examples of where they were dismissed in favor of other enterprises, namely large-scale engineering companies and so-called technical and management service providers. The products of these urbanizing professions set in motion the global rules for and expectations of modern notions of the city. This seminar identifies and pursues case studies of expansive infrastructural projects in such places as Turkey, Pakistan, Iran, Iraq, Saudi Arabia, and the United Arab Emirates.

75

Design
Computation

Technology & Practice

Michael Szivos

Computational machines, tools once considered only more efficient versions of paper-based media, have a demonstrated potential beyond mere imitation. This potential is revealed through design computation—the creative application of the processes and reasoning underlying all digital technology, from e-mail to artificial intelligence. This seminar introduces design computation as a means to enable architects to operate exempt from limitations of generalized commercial software; to devise problem-specific tools, techniques, and workflows; to control the growing complexities of contemporary architectural design; and to explore forms generated only by computation itself. Topics include data manipulation and translation, algorithms, information visual-ization, computational geometry, human-computer interaction, custom tooling, generative form-finding, emergent behavior, simulation, and system modeling.

77

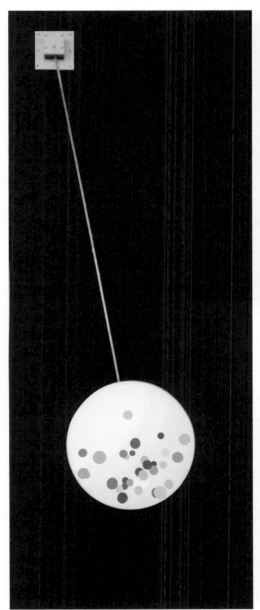

76

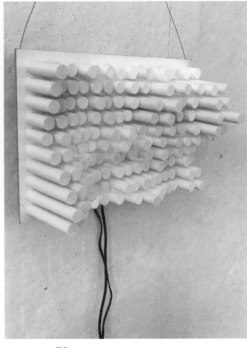

78

James Schwartz 75
Guillermo Castello, Zachary Hoffmann, Alexandra Karlsson-Napp 76
Maxwell Mensching 77
Tess McNamara 78

Diagrammatic Analysis

Design & Visualization

Peter Eisenman

If architecture today can be said to be witnessing a paradigm shift similar to what took place between modernism and post-modernism in the 60s and 70s of the last century, how is it possible to understand the nature of that shift and where it might be going? There are many explanations of what happened in the past in the time of such shifts; one of those explanations concerns a term used by the Russian formalist Victor Shklovsky called 'baring the device.' The critic Rosalind Krauss used this term to help explain how one might understand any such future shifts. What Krauss argues is that within any paradigm there appear anachronistic manifestations that logically don't quite fit into the then-existing paradigm, which in fact are, in retrospect, the signals for a future paradigm. Krauss' argument, initially following from Shklovsky, is that the device is something that inhibits a direct transparent representation between a sign and its object. This inhibition dams up transparency and forces a kind of opacity on the object. Because of this opacity, the attention is shifted from mimetic representation to the experience of the being of the object. This damming up supposedly reveals the cognitive ordering, the inner structure and workings of an object. But as Krauss points out, this inherency of the device to the object was perhaps only true of the modernist paradigm. As modernism began to shift, it was realized that many times these devices were the early signals of a shifting paradigm. This seminar attempts to uncover the nature of such devices in architecture, whether as diagrams or some other form of cognitive ordering. The argument is that such ordering is necessary, no matter the style, site, or program, for something to be called architecture.

Maison de Verre
Stephen McNamara 79
Museum Moderner Kunst
James Coleman 80
San Cataldo Cemetery
Jack Lipson 81

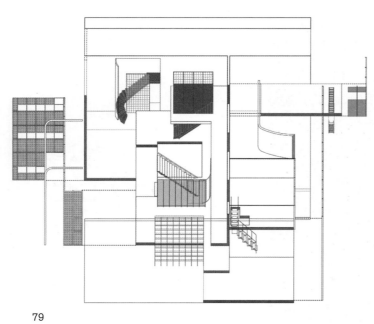

79

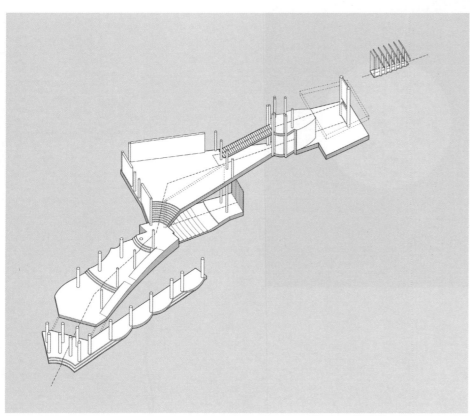

80

81

Disheveled Geometries: Ruins & Ruination

Design & Visualization

Mark Foster Gage

Architectural ruins index the total failure of individual buildings, technologies, economies, or, at times, entire civilizations. The irony of late capitalism is that now these failures, through their ability to generate vast amounts of capital through tourism and regional identity, are more financially valuable than ever. Architecture is unique in this quality—that evidence of its total failure can now be among its more profitable assets. Architectural education encourages the study of the design, construction, and the maintenance of buildings, but the study of their ruination and decay—despite the potential value and use of such considerations—is a topic rarely addressed. This course researches these topics of ruination and architectural ruins—what produces them? What defines them? How do they impact individuals, cities, and civilizations on levels from the visual and formal to the philosophical and psychological?

  Matthew Bohne 82
  Valeria Flores 83
  Nasim Rowshanabadi 84

83

84

82

Drawing Projects

Design & Visualization

Turner Brooks

Students investigate a particular subject through the media of drawing for the entire term. There is a weekly evening pin-up with group discussion of work in progress.

Rashidbek Muydinov 85
Aymar Mariño Maza 86
Dakota Cooley 87
Matthew Kabala 88

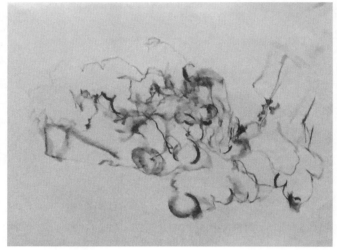

87

85

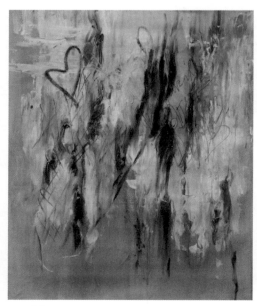

86

88

Keller Easterling

Design & Visualization
Second Year Studio

This fourth core studio, an introduction to the planning and architecture of cities, concerns two distinct scales of operation: that of the neighborhood and that of the residential, institutional, and commercial building types that typically constitute the neighborhood. Issues of community, group form, infrastructure, and the public realm,as well as the formation of public space, blocks, streets, and squares are emphasized. The studio is organized to follow a distinct design methodology, which begins with the study of context and precedents. It postulates that new architecture can be made as a continuation and extension of normative urban structure and building typologies.

Critics
Emily Abruzzo (AB), Naomi Darling (ND), Keller Easterling (KE), Rosetta Elkin (RE), Andrei Harwell (AH), Jesse LeCavalier (JL), Tim Love (TL), Bimal Mendis (BM), Alan Plattus (AP), Alexander Purves (APu), Elihu Rubin (ER), Aniket Shahane (AS), Rosalyne Shieh (RS), Jonathan Sun (JS), David Waggonner (DW)

Elaina Berkowitz, Madison Sembler 89
Our intervention in the site is simply to use what's already there—truck access—to support the need for more fresh food to the families in the area who have to travel almost two miles to the nearest grocery store. The space under the overpass will be illuminated, providing a sense of safety to the families nearby, and a sense of curiosity from those passing by on the train.
AP: *There's a sort of Highline syndrome that is taking over the world of urban open space where if it's cool enough, people will come regardless of how difficult it is to get there and I'm not sure Bridgeport is quite there yet.*

Wilson Carroll,
Rashidbek Muydinov 90
The project builds upon incremental community-led steps to imagine a holistic change for the city of Bridgeport. The first of four defined steps is painting the regions of the street and the unused, adjacent lots to indicate an alternative use. As the public's awareness grows, community centers are established from vacant gas stations. The next step connects each of the centers with continuous bike lanes and intermediate pocket parks. The last step includes new developments, public and private. The Painted Mile serves as a retention network for storm water.
TL: *There is a tension in your proposal between the artfulness of it and the other more insidious idea of turning the city into a diagram. It would be interesting to be less utopian and more dystopian.*

89

90

Exhibitionism: Politics of Display

History & Theory

Joel Sanders

Since their inception in the eighteenth century, art museums—prestigious buildings commissioned by those who wield power and influence—have behaved like cultural barometers registering changing attitudes about the role cultural institutions play in society. Looking at museum buildings from the inside out, this seminar traces the evolution of this building type through an in-depth analysis of its key architectural elements: gallery, interstitial (circulation, assembly, retail) and infrastructure (security/climate control) spaces, and site. This seminar explores how the spatial and material development of these tectonic components both mirrors and perpetuates changing cultural attitudes about aesthetics, class, power, wealth, nature, leisure, gender, body, and the senses as seen through the eyes of artists, architects, critics, collectors, and politicians.

Vittorio Lovato, Caitlin Thissen 91
Erik Freer, Madelynn Ringo 92

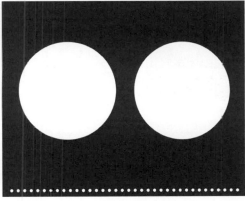

92

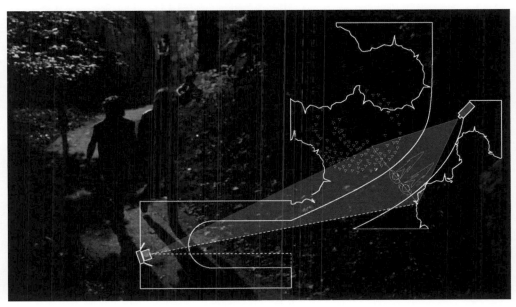

91

Kersten Geers

Design & Visualization
Advanced Studio

with Caitlin Taylor

93

94

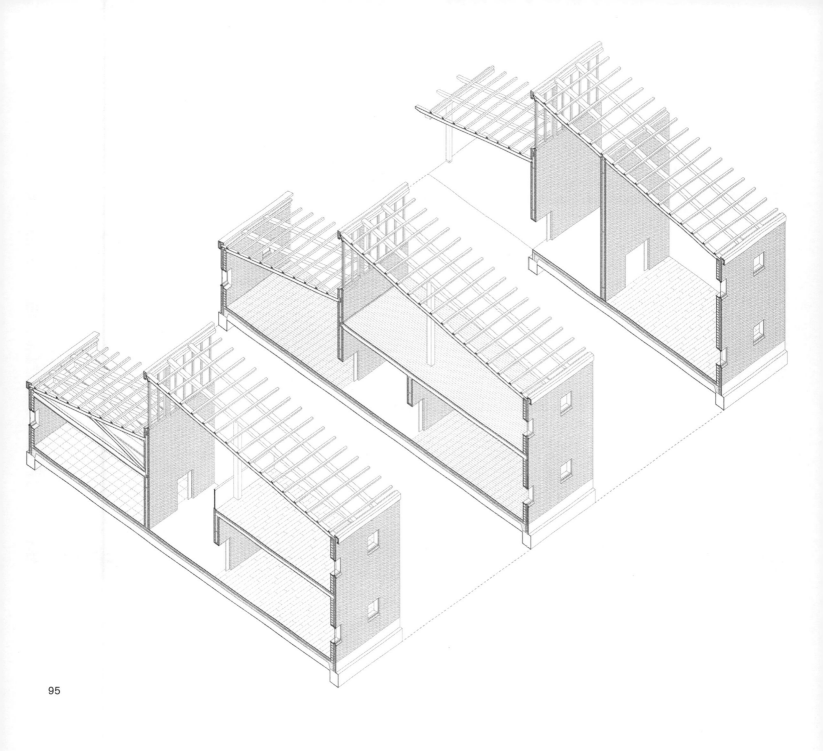

95

'Almost Classicism' starts where Neo-Palladian left us. It starts in full conviction that the current project in the United States has to focus both on the countryside and on an attempt to reintroduce some kind of commons. We feel the best way to illustrate this is to start where the commons has left us, what used to be called 'the village.' We would argue, though, that the relatively small investment in the commons of such places outweighs the benefits in that it might be able to bring back a sense of hierarchy and, who knows, a sense of belonging to the American field. Starting with a set of simple and perhaps related buildings that replace the outlived infrastructure of today—city halls, police stations, fire stations, schools—we hope to present a portrait of the village of tomorrow—not as some kind of weird tech dream but rather as a few elements to anchor the increasingly pulverized life we live in. The new land once conquered transforms into the (un)even covered field.

    Critics
Pier Vittorio Aureli (PVA), Eva Franch (EF), Kersten Geers (KG), Sharon Johnson (SJ), Michael Meredith (MM), Hilary Sample (HS), David Van Severen (DVS), Robert A.M. Stern (RAMS), Caitlin Taylor (CT), Enrique Walker (EW)

    Anthony Gagliardi 93
Francesco Dal Co stated "after all, isn't kitsch the ultimate mask of the banal, the sublime of the obvious." This project argues in a kitsch manner that the village has not changed: the suburban commons is family and what already exists. One increasingly invisible part of the family is the grandparent sent to an assisted living home. These facilities are islands relegated to the borders of cities, where their immobile residents are surrounded by everything they need but nothing they can reach. This project proposes a large-scale assisted living facility, in the form of a fractured square, which frames the eclectic and comprehensive amenities of a suburban intersection.

EW: *I suspect your project is most successful, not within the frame, but that these buildings have a back and they act as a background to this world.* MM: *You produce a very interesting* Rear Window *situation. It seems to me a theatrical model of urbanism. If you go from Serlio to Koolhaas, there's always a stage after metaphor. Delirious city and delirious subject, generic city and generic subject: they produce each other. They're caught in this stage/actor relationship. Today that relationship is pushed in some other way. That relationship has loosened the actor in the stage.*

96

Meghan Lewis 94
My project takes on the basic program of a co-op, including
the machinery storage and silos, yet also positions itself as the
communal and commercial center of [the town of] Coin and
the surrounding area. The co-op must negotiate two scales: the
agricultural machines, ever increasing in size, and the scale of
the town and humans. The project negotiates this challenge
through assuming a large footprint with a lightweight form and
two façades, giving equal weight to both human and machine
program. The two façades reflect its dual nature, facing outwards
to the industrial fields and inwards to the town.
PVA: *The Palladian diagram is almost there. What was iconoclastic
about his architecture was for the first time after the fall of the
Roman Empire, a classicist architecture was built in the countryside.
It was considered very rustic and uncivilized territory. So once you
move to this iteration, that kind of classicism is gone. I would like
you to take a position on this choice: how [do] you undermine the
classicist language of architecture?* EF: *I'm not sure the loggia
versus the field does enough of an exploration or disruption of what
we understand as symmetry. As we have phenomenal versus literal
transparency, we could have a phenomenal symmetry in which it
would not be about just producing a symmetry, but producing a
symmetry which engages with the movement and the ways in which
the bodies relate to the functions of the buildings.*

Sofia Singler 95, 96
This project, an agricultural co-operative school, anchors knowledge back in the village. The school liaises with state-funded
initiatives such as the Iowa Youth Institute Food Program that offer
subsidies for agricultural learning centers to partner with
existing public schools. This agricultural school offers students
at Clarinda High School the opportunity to learn the basics of
small-scale farming for credit. Like a furrow in the fields, the
school marks a line between large-scale industry and small-town

community, and sows the seeds for local, collective agricultural
production in the village.
PVA: *I like the project because it is a thesis. There is a clear intention which tries to counter one of the biggest problems we have
with agriculture, that in the 20th century, to be a rural worker was
something to be emancipated from. One way to emancipate oneself
from being a rural worker was to study. So there is a misconception
that to be a good worker is to lack a certain knowledge. However,
working has its own very important knowledge and we are giving
up this knowledge to large corporations which are industrializing
everything out of our control.* SJ: *I find the rendering very nostalgic
and it seems counter to the contemporary non-architecture
approach. You're very intentional in your renderings but I think they
tell a different story than your plan and sections.* Sofia: *That sense
may come from the fact that the renderings are hand-drafted.*
MM: *They're hand-drafted? You are nostalgic!*

Kristin Nothwehr (Feldman Nominee) 97
The architectural proposal began with the landscape, which is
experienced as utterly horizontal, yet dynamic—constantly rising
and falling as crops are grown and harvested. This moving
datum corresponds exactly to the unique labor cycles of farmers,
who experience periods of intense activity, followed by months of
relative quietude. The architecture is meant to respond to
this movement, establishing its own horizon that is concealed
and revealed as the fields rise and fall around it. A single entrance
to the building leads to a vast interior, which is the territory of
machinery and logistics. Those arriving by car, however, process
into the smaller square nested within the larger perimeter, or
what I'm calling the commons. This commons becomes a space of
transition and respite between the home and the field.
PVA: *You gave a very thought-out technical explanation, but I would
like to talk about the symbolic aspect of your design choices.
The most outstanding is the mixing of the typology of the barn with*

that of the courtyard. These are very different archetypes and it's interesting, for example, when Palladio reinvented the barn (we call his houses 'villas' but they were, in fact, barns), he actually avoided the courtyard. He never used that archetype and the reason for that, I think, is he didn't want his villas looking like monasteries. You perceive your project from the outside as a barn, but then inside you have a courtyard and I was wondering how you could elaborate that friction. This is a very interesting tension in your project which to me seems to symbolize the elephant in the room: that is, on one hand, the industrial tendency of agriculture, and on the other, an attempt to reclaim agriculture as a commune where people share their own ethos, their own understanding of each other as coworkers rather than owners. KG: I think there are two barns in this debate. The barn as the prototypical image of the old American barn which returns in White Noise if I'm not mistaken. Then there is a barn as factory, a big covered space or canopy. EF: What I find fascinating about your images is that the building poses itself as an

object in a field in which the horizon is always that which dictates the movement of bodies through this entire landscape. So the fact of producing a building is a fantastic space because that's not necessarily what people are able to experience. So this is a state of exception in the landscape that one is able to experience here as a subject within a field. I think the building understands itself in the landscape scale but the moment we start to understand how things behave it becomes difficult. Maybe these children, instead of playing on the grass, play on the grain, creating a new landscape by which not only the workers are going there to share space of production and collection, but also citizens that might be somewhere else in the field. I'm confused by the formal resolution of those desires, but I have to say I love this image and I love it as a building. So how do we reconcile those spaces of decision making with objects that are beautiful but are not solving, or addressing, or constructing a new landscape?

Kersten Geers
Architecture Without Content

I am talking about our architecture but also perhaps about what we feel that architecture could still be about.

For that reason, the rather preposterous title *Architecture Without Content* speaks to the way we increasingly start to see the possibilities of architecture and how to express what we are doing

in the office. *Architecture Without Content* started as a set of reflections on the architecture of the 'big box.' In many different studios we had been thinking over the last couple of years whether it is possible to take the big box as a phenomenon, a very big building, and a container of many things, seriously.

Could we actually research together with the students in different places if we could find a possible track, or scenario, through economy of means?

… So you could argue from that perspective that architecture in all its simplicity and technicality has a very specific tectonic originality and is also about what it contains implicitly, as perhaps suggested in *Architecture Without Content*. So if *Architecture Without Content* contains many things it somehow leaves that aspect of it in a relative disconnect.

Frank Gehry

Design & Visualization
Advanced Studio

with Trattie Davies

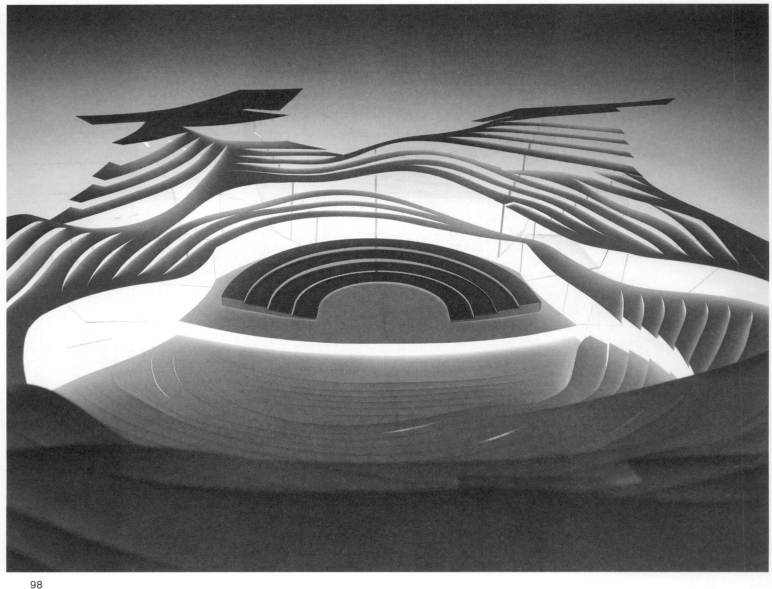

98

This studio takes on the challenge of designing a new concert hall for Barbican Centre to replace Barbican Hall, currently a subterranean 1,949 seat theater, hosting classical and contemporary performances, home to the London Symphony Orchestra and the BBC Symphony Orchestra. The new site for the hall will provide an opportunity to radically re-imagine the role of the Concert Hall within the Barbican Centre, responding to changing audience expectations for the arts and visibly addressing the ambition for the Barbican to serve as a cultural quarter, engaged and equally welcoming to residents.

Critics

Frances Anderton (FA), Deborah Berke (DB), Trattie Davies (TD), Sam Gehry (SG), Nicholas Kenyon (NK), Hans Kollhoff (HK), Meaghan Lloyd (ML), Victoria Newhouse (VN), Toshihiro Oki (TO), Niko Pont (NP), Esa-Pekka Salonen (ES), Patrik Schumacher (PS), Kazuyo Sejima (KS), Robert A.M. Stern (RAMS), Craig Webb (CW)

Winny Tan 98

PS: *I feel very tempted to suggest a different placement of the hall into a frame because I feel there's an obfuscation somehow. What if you take this beautiful creation, rather than kind of packing it in and hiding it, maybe just creating a plinth that pops?* HK: *Public space to me has a certain value that is beyond our intentions as architectural designers. It's given to us by hundreds of years of urban development.* FG: *The Romans didn't do that.* HK: *The Romans respected heritage very much. But for certain moments, they cut through it.*

Anne Ma 100

RAMS: *What happens when there is an intermission, and people come out of the hall, how do they 'refresh' themselves?* Anne: *Are you talking toilets or bar?* [laughter] RAMS: *It's a good question… I was trying to heighten the conversation. But it seems so hermetically sealed—so much about the internal environment and not much about the city around it.*

TD: *I wonder if your plans make it look more like it's all one thing, you know, even with a line around it, rather than a collection of parts.* RAMS: *You're tyrannizing the poor concert-goer into this organic field.* Anne: *Where do you want them to go… exactly?* RAMS: *I'm missing a connection to the city.* HK: *If you look at the model, it is there. The building relates the program to the life of the city… it's there. One can imagine that it's a building that people would flow through, and might go out.*

Chris Hyun 101

NK: *You'd have to do a bit of work on where people are expected to come from. Are they going to come from the train station? Are they going to come from those pedestrian routes? Because [with] more people that come from the train station direction you'd want a sense of welcome at the top of the building.* NP: *I agree there needs to be enough parking spaces. And they will be underground. Thinking about our subscribers, a lot of them are elderly people.*

A lot of people come by public transport actually. I think in terms of streams of people approaching the hall, this will be the route. HK: *It's a crucial question because you explained there's a certain lightness. The model shows gigantic sized rocks. So it becomes a question of the materialization if this seems to be light or not. And also it should be all about acoustics but that needs some research and needs some precision in your argument.*

Richard Mandimika 103

NK: *There is a difference between asymmetrical and unbalanced.* DB: *I would love for you to have been passionate about asymmetry... but you're hesitant about it.*

Jessica Elliott 104

RAMS: *You said you were a musician, but you need to think about the concert-goer's point of view. The plans are so diagrammatic compared to everything else. I think they are really undercooked.* FA: *Your influences here are sort of organic and rocky, certainly not urban or [for] Munich. Was there any kind of local influences that found their way into the project?* NP: *From a promoter point of view, I think it's probably ambitious to have that many seats actually behind the stage. I hear that the most expensive seats in the hall are for their experience, and are actually two or three rows behind that stage because that's where people who are prepared to spend the most money want to sit because it's so exciting.*

John Chengqi Wan 105

VN: *When does [form] become arbitrary? This form is so completely indeterminate. Why is it this form and not so in another part of it? The final piece feels a bit*
amorphous, perhaps. PS: *I want to address this question of arbitrariness or amorphousness of some of the formal results. I think it is a wonderfully creative and furtive project with so many stimulating studies. A lot of them don't have the element of unresolvedness. It becomes kind of menacingly chaotic.* DB: *I think where this building fails is for the same reason Patrik was saying, and that is that when you follow the rules you've made for yourself, like the continuous surface, that is where you succeed and when you fail to short-hand it is when you stop obeying your own rules.*

Shayari De Silva 106

DB: *What's the process that gets you from the outside where you understand this amazing collection of surfaces, to the inside where you experience this amazing collection of surfaces? On the one hand you don't want to give it all away. On the other hand, you've created a series of things that are kind of banal and don't deliver on the promise from the street.* PS: *The correlation between the ceiling rhythm and the zones— do you think they should just be indifferent or should the ceiling together with that plateau generate a kind of zone and space? What is the relationship between the two? At the moment it seems they are indifferent to each other.* NP: *I like this pod idea specifically from a pragmatic point of view, thinking about the large subscription audience, which is a typical thing for Munich. I must sound sort of stupid and boring and shallow in comparison to these aesthetic conversations, but it comes to: how do you sell your subscriptions? How do you price tickets? How do you generate this general*
feeling of subscribers who actually meet each other every three or four weeks? So there's a special connection between these people, and I think this is a very, very nice way of supporting this.*

Shuangjing Hu (Feldman Nominee) 107

HK: *I think it would be so important to be able to look into the space from the garden. How you would get light in is a different story. [Whether] you even need daylight is another question. And with the concept of an urban park which should be with the site very well, there's a beautiful garden, where people want to stay and relax and do whatever they want.* PS: *It's a very contemporary [idea] because I think a lot of us might want to participate in something that we might not want to risk being locked in for three hours. I'm serious! It's not only for concert events, it's for conferencing and this opening up [enables] being participative.*

Isaac Southard 108

DB: *I kind of buy your argument... I don't like the way you're using the word landscape, but I see this as a giant built piece. I love this building and I really love the plan—it seems to have both asymmetry and balance at the same time. I just think your building is too big to be the piece of topiary in the city you want it to be. Except at that one axial moment and the one very long oblique moment from the train, I can never get far enough away from it to take the kind of picture you show there of that ancient topiary. It needs to be smaller to be its more compelling self.*

Jared Abraham 99
Jack Bian 102

99

Gehry, Frank

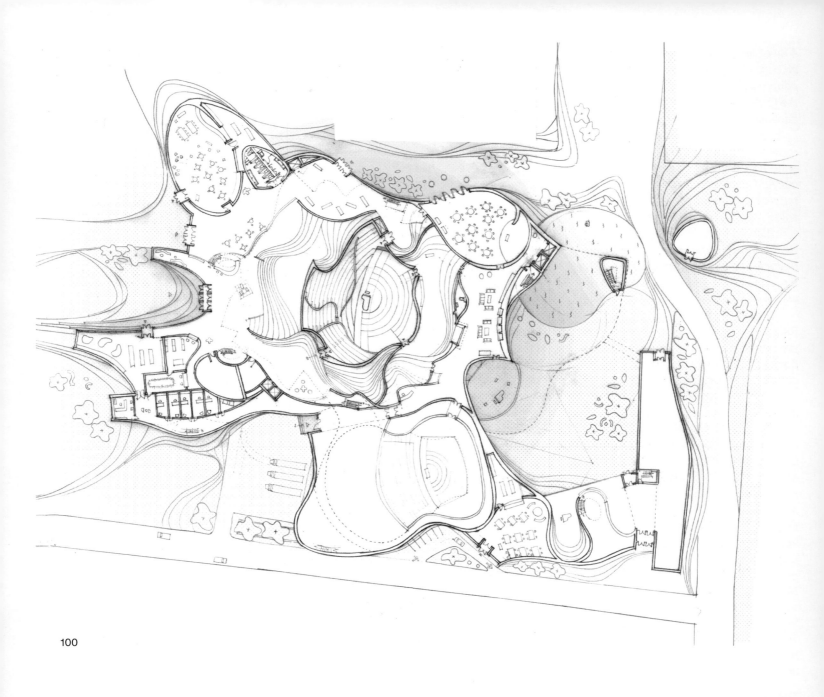

100

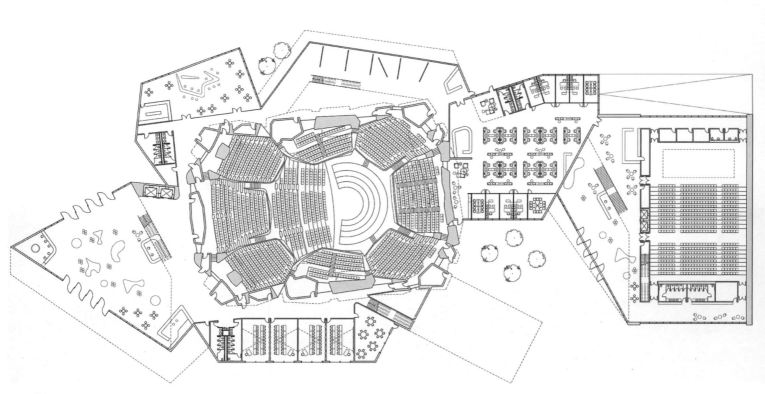

101

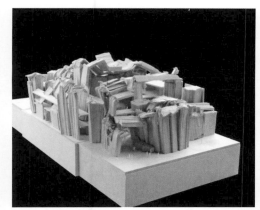

102

105

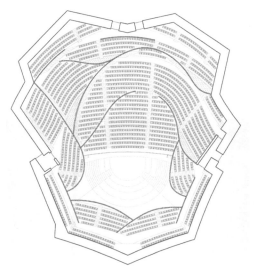

103

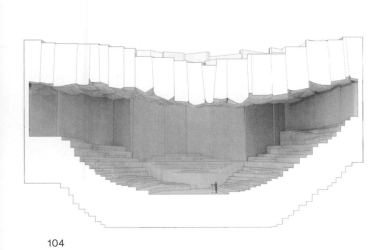

104

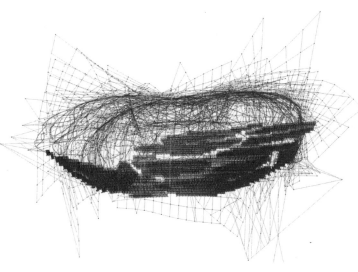

106

Gehry, Frank

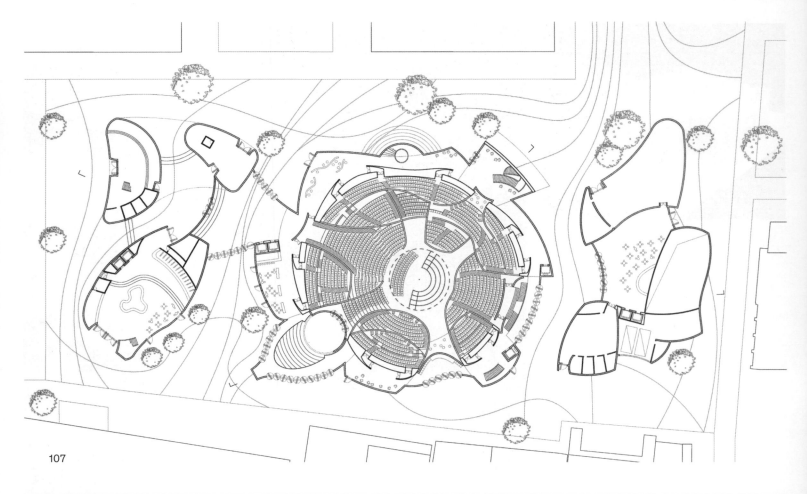

107

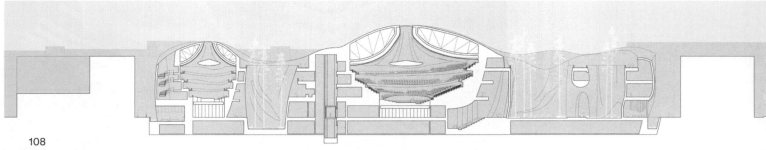

108

Ghost Town

Urbanism & Landscape

Elihu Rubin

"Ghost Town" is an interdisciplinary graduate seminar that draws from architectural history, urban planning, the politics of preservation, tourism, collective memory, nostalgia, and, ultimately, sustainability. The premise is that the production of the ghost town in the mythology of the American West contains tools for understanding the investment cycles, built environments, and redevelopment patterns in cities more broadly. We all live in ghost towns, even in what seem to be thriving cities. They are places where the tensions between occupation and displacement, stasis and change, resilience and adaptation, and memory and anticipation set the parameters of our daily lives. The seminar split into two teams and produced two different ghost town interventions in New Haven. The first group examined the afterlives of the mostly empty New Haven Clock Company building on Hamilton Street, producing a map, zine, and image projection installation in the space. The second group produced and installed a series of "historical wayfinding signage" exploring the rhetoric and memory associated with the Oak Street Connector, New Haven's mid-century urban redevelopment highway project.

Oak Street
Hannah Novack, Madison Sembler, Matthew Zuckerman 109

New Haven Clock Factory
Francesca Carney, Dante Furioso, Casey Furman, Claire Haugh, Luis Salas Porras, Robert Yoos, Alison Zuccaro 110

"IT WAS A SACRED SPOT. A WORLD. A UNIVERSE."

–SID BRUSKIN, REFLECTING ON HIS CHILDHOOD HOME ON OAK STREET

#OakStreetHistoricalSociety

109

110

Sean Griffiths and Sam Jacob

Design & Visualization
Advanced Studio

with Jennifer Leung

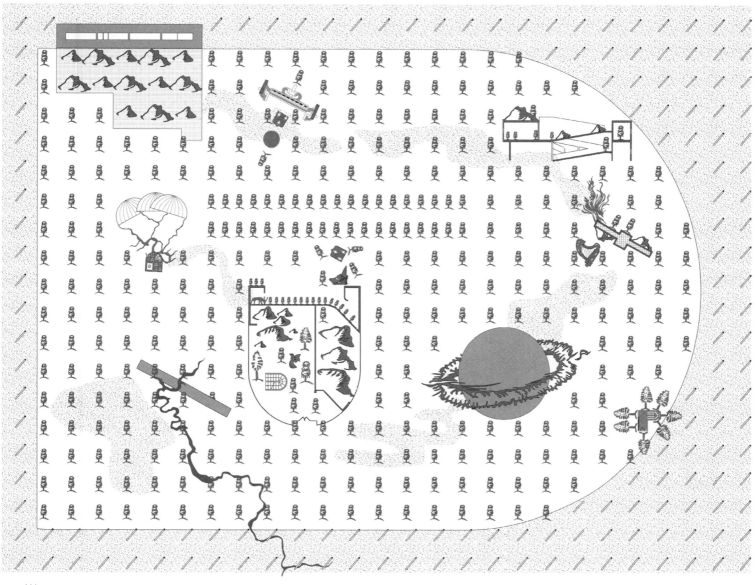

111

What is the minimum number of lines you need to make architecture? Peckham is London's latest cultural hot spot, the opposite of minimalist. It's full of stuff. It's chaotic. It's messy. It's vibrant and its rough edges are in danger of being smoothed out by the forces of 'regeneration.' Its economic engines are the often marginal commercial activities of locals and immigrants who, together with a thriving artistic community, have generated unique patterns of use and a scattergun streetscape. Peckham contains the maximum number of things. The project will be an investigation of how to accommodate the maximum number of things amongst the minimum number of lines. The project's program is a place of exchange—perhaps a market place, perhaps an educational institution, perhaps a business hub, perhaps a mash-up of these things.

Critics

Diana Agrest (DA), Beatrice Galilee (BG), Sean Griffiths (SG), Ariane Lourie Harrison (AH), Jeffrey Inaba (JI), Sam Jacob (SJ), Keith Krumwiede (KK), Jennifer Leung (JL), Surry Schlabs (SS), Patrik Schumacher (PS), Oliver Wainright (OW), Mark Wasiuta (MW)

Andrew Dadds 111–114

Early artifacts and gridscapes deploy themselves in Peckham. The project becomes a world enveloping contradictory things: spa and meat market, gallery and residential spaces, self-referential proportions, and calligraphic ribbon windows all come together in a polyphonic world about representation and architecture. MW: *You're trying to find narrative pieces that fit together but also produce startling disjunctions. I imagine that's a struggle—so it's hard not to think of experimental writers and how they solve that through systems in which they tried to figure out how to propose those disjunctions. There's something about the grid in your project that can absorb any type of disparity and produces a set of associations, even though you have a precisely sampled set of associations.* SS: *Sitting this close to it, I see echoes of the calligraphic line and it seems deliberately placed there. It seems ordered but absolutely unpredictable. The Corbusian stair appears repeated— it becomes typographic, even hieroglyphic and the juxtaposition of this against the more ornamental flourishes of the calligraphy is really formally brilliant.*

Griffiths, Sean and Sam Jacob

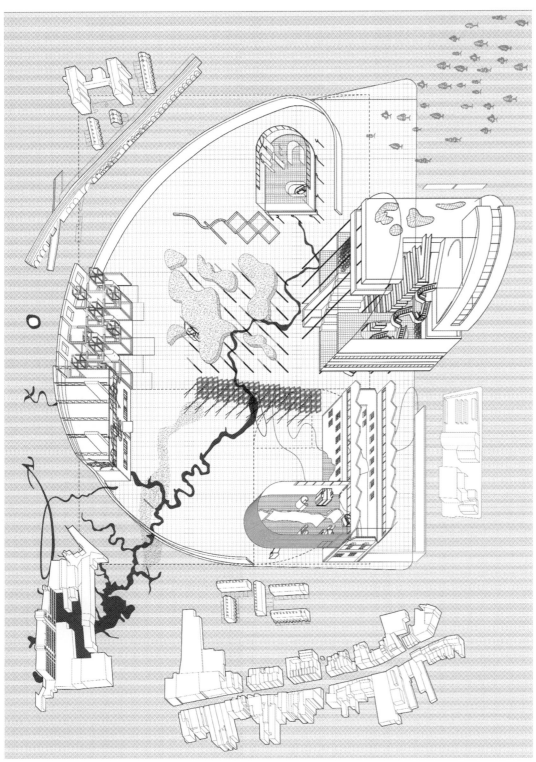

112

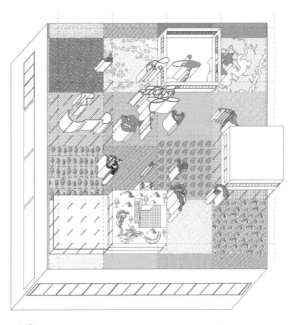

113

Griffiths, Sean and Sam Jacob

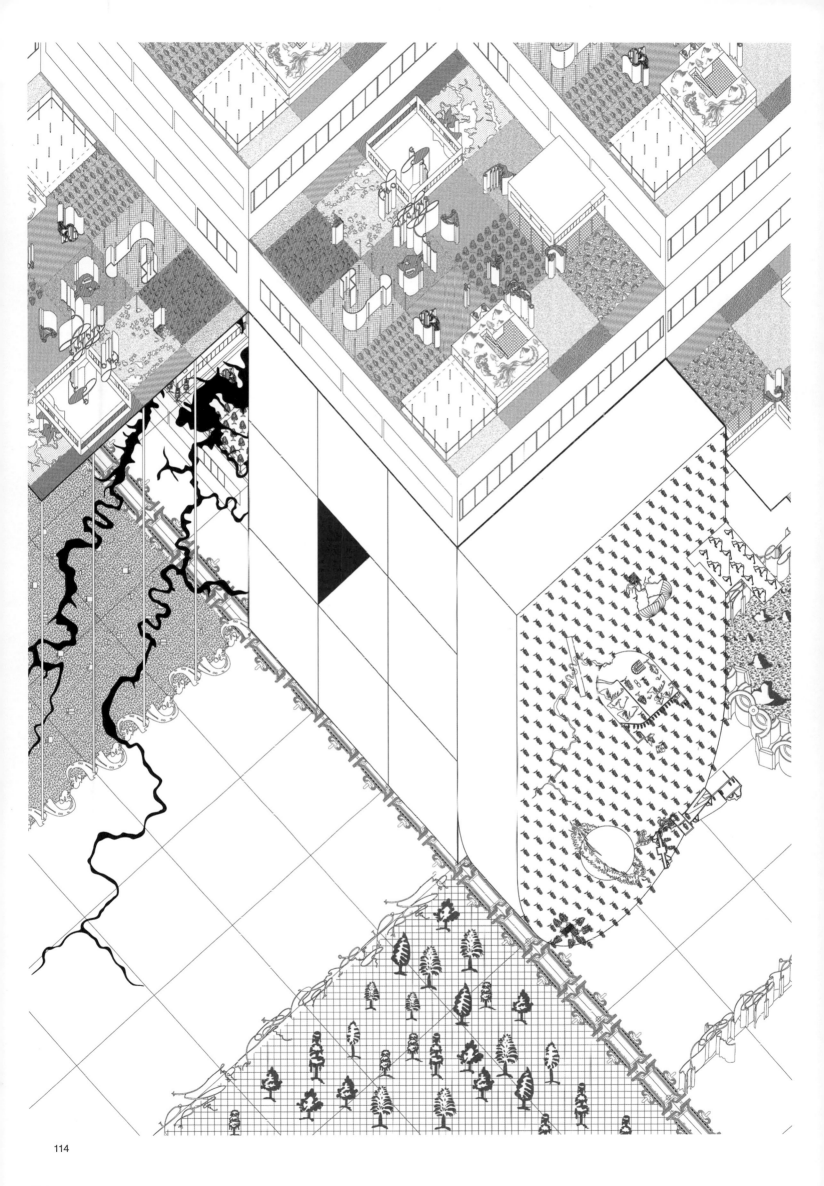

51
Griffiths, Sean and Sam Jacob

115

116

Griffiths, Sean and Sam Jacob

Cynthia Hsu (Feldman Nominee) 115, 116

The program is a place of commercial and cultural exchange: a curious mash-up of an art gallery wrapped around a market place. The project explores how lines can generate different textures and how they are capable of defining boundaries of program and space, influencing one's experience of the objects that inhabit them. JI: *I think the enfilade overdetermines the project as being about a single grid meeting rather than the overlap. I don't have a problem with the fact that there's no section there except for the fact that the enfilade—the opening and the linearity of it—seems to diminish all the other potentials that the plan has.* MW: *Isn't the emphatic insistence on the grid the project? The grid of the wall is so clearly the Robert Irwin project in glass form that it's hard to know whether the project is that—a series of planes of glass and your movement through it, or the object that sits in front of it. I think that's the curiosity. I don't think you can read this as a conventional museum. The ambiguity between market and art somehow has to operate according to a logic of the vitrine or the hanging sausage. You can't do what you're doing here—you're not going to hang the paintings— Stella or Jasper Johns—on the glass walls, are you? You're going to put objects in rooms. So it's a complex set of staging for the encounter of what an aesthetic space is versus commercial space and they're all framed identically through the glass.*

Luis Salas Porras 117

This set of speculative drawings and built works explores the translation of drawn architectural lines into graphic systems that organize 2D and 3D space. This graphic, essentialized space becomes the site of exchange between frame and content, drawing and mass, the abstract and the real. SS: *What's missing is the process of actually making this, of actually drawing the line. One of the things that's most fascinating about line work is the framing and spatial rhyme—the virtualized process*

118

of making structure, which I'm sure was a big part of your process. MW: *Suzanne Briet famously described the difference between a thing in the world and a document. The analogy it issues is that an antelope in the wild is a thing but in a zoo is a document. It seems like your project. As we shift by it, suddenly the thing it frames appears differently: it's not an abstract line but one that articulates all types of distinctions between what is valued and what is seen as perceptually and culturally significant. This thing is the minimal framing mechanism for differentiating objects.*

Matthew Bohne 118–120

The project explores the drawing of adjacent, converging, and isolated fields, which produces an ambiguity in drawing that addresses the spatial indices of architecture. The project explores the line as a fragment, capable of defining density, atmospheric and material, minimum and maximum. Various lines wander, respecting some edges, disobeying others, simulating the configuration and dissolution of material. The use of various types of projections allows for simultaneous views, the articulation of flat objects and the collapse of perceived dimensional objects. SS: *You've thrown the term 'ambiguous' around a lot as well. There's good ambiguity and bad ambiguity. Good ambiguity has the both/and generosity—a bad ambiguity just results in confused disorientation. I don't mind the disorientation but you do veer a bit into bad ambiguity.* AH: *There's such a meticulous investigation of lines and thicknesses. I see this as atmospheric architecture that is crystalizing as you make it. It's a formation. You're using the techniques of drawing to actually sculpt the space of the building— very different from how we typically use drawing.* MW: *There is a strange anachronism in the drawings in the way they try to replicate techniques and different reproduction technologies than those that have been actually used to produce them. What do you want us to read in this process? Is this a system of conscription notation or is it atmospheric?*

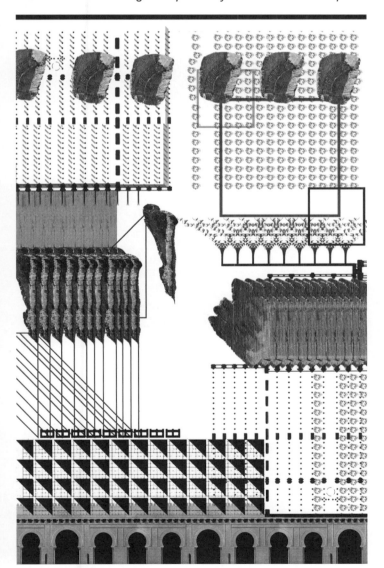

117

Griffiths, Sean and Sam Jacob

119

Griffiths, Sean and Sam Jacob

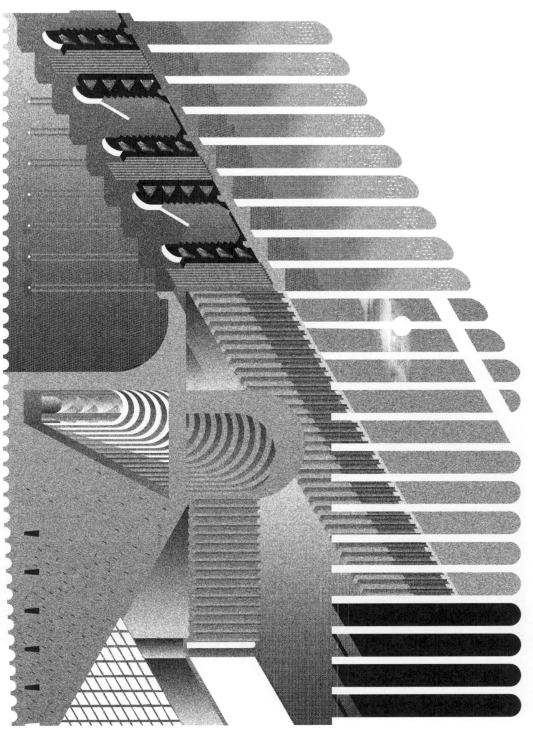

120

Griffiths, Sean and Sam Jacob

Zaha Hadid and Patrik Schumacher

Design & Visualization
Advanced Studio

with Lasha Brown and Simon Kim

121

The underlying premise of the studio is the current historical tendency toward high density urban concentration. The socio-economic background for this is given by the high intensity communication requirements of a Post-Fordist network and information society. Economists speak of agglomeration economies, but we all feel it in our bones: we have to join the major urban centers—and locate ourselves as central as possible within them—to ensure our connectedness and thus productivity. Remaining provincial is not an option. The studio design methodology will exploit the analogy of a multi-author urbanism with a multi-species ecology. Consider the way the various features and creatures within a natural environment coalesce to create a complex variegated order on the basis of rules (laws of nature) that establish correlations between the various organic and inorganic subsystems that make up a natural landscape. The topography correlates with the path of the river, the river together with topography and sun orientation differentiate the flora, and the differentiation of the flora—together

with river and topography—shape the differentiation and distribution of the fauna, which in turn impacts back on the fauna and thus often also on rivers and even the topography. Correlations and thus inference potentials are being established in all directions, and give information to those who want to navigate such a landscape. The key here is the build-up of correlations and associations. Each new species of plant or animal proliferates according to its own rules of adaptation and survival. For instance, the moss grows differentially on the terraced rock surface in certain shaded slopes. A population of a certain species of birds then might settle on these slopes accordingly. In the same way our studio envisions the build-up of a densely layered urban environment via differentiated, rule-based architectural interventions, that are designed via scripts that form the new architectural sub-systems, just like a new species settles into a natural environment. This process delivers rich navigable diversity. Each new architect/author can be uniquely creative in inventing the rules of his or her project and

participate in its own unique way in the build-up of a variegated, information-rich urban order. The analogy also extends to the navigation in rule-based environments: the urbanite's intuitive orientation within an urban environment functions as analogous to animal navigation in a natural environment.

Critics
Lasha Brown (LB), Evan Douglis (ED), Marc Fornes (MF), Joseph Giovanni (JG), Sean Griffiths (SG), Mariana Ibañez (MI), Simon Kim (SK), Jeffrey Kipnis (JK), Sulan Kolatan (SK), Ali Rahim (AR), Patrik Schumacher (PS), Brett Steele (BS)

Lisa Albaugh, Benjamin Bourgoin, Jamie Edindjiklian, Roberto Jenkins, Justin Oh (Feldman Nominees) 121–125 London's skyline can be thought of as a collage city—where the unique individuality of each tower prevents each from engaging with the urban scale of its surroundings. This divergent urban order is neither unique to London nor a condition that will diminish without careful and direct intervention. This project seeks to address this collage condition by creating a

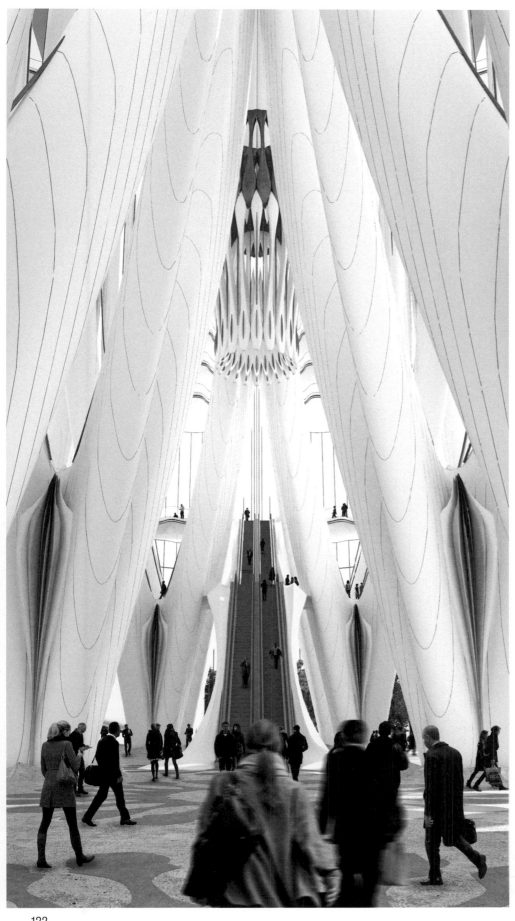

complex that is at once individual and collective as a field of pencil towers blending seamlessly with one another, creating a new and iconic urban order as an archetype for London's continued growth. The project is organized into four main components: a high-density tower, a mid-rise neighborhood, a train station that bridges the two, and a park landscape that mediates between the existing viaduct and the various access points throughout the site. The blending of four distinct architectural typologies addresses a diversity of urban functions—from living, working, recreation, to transportation. Respectful of its greater surroundings, this proposal creates a distinct sense of place in the city of London, a significant contribution to her public realm for pedestrians and city alike.

SG: *Your presentation was absolutely brilliant. Absolutely terrifying. The only bit missing at the end was "Dubai, the place where dreams come true." You've covered the landscaping. It's much more coherent than anything I've seen today—you've thought about how it integrates into the city. But I can't escape the fact that there would be riots in the streets if people tried to do this. I know this area really well. It's a site of massive conflict. This whole site is the subject of huge debate—people up in arms about stuff that's happening, which is rather modest compared to what you guys are proposing here. But all this stuff about parametric... why do they have to be so huge?* JK: *Patrik, it is our responsibility to teach, to insist, to force not even our constituencies but our victims to recognize that we're responsible for a whole lot of resources and effects. The people who have a right to weigh in here are not just the loud-mouths that live here. We're going to take the total effect—the consequences of our labors—and measure them to the best benefit. Now, you can say [there are] three value systems in architecture and I think it's important to bring all three to the table. You can do the greatest good for the most number of people, which is a legitimate way to do it. You can do the greatest diversity with the greatest coherence, which is an important way to think—and you can also do a bag of abject creativity. All three of those are on the table and none can be made collaboratively with another. All three have a place within the practice but you cannot pick one and dismiss the other two. And that's what you [Griffiths] are trying to do.* PS: *My view is that these are not things that you can solve in your ivory tower. This is what the market computes through prices.* AR: *But for the first time, in many years, he's talking about diversity. He's not talking about parametric homogeneity; I've never heard him talk about that. Let's encourage that because that's the next step in the development work.*

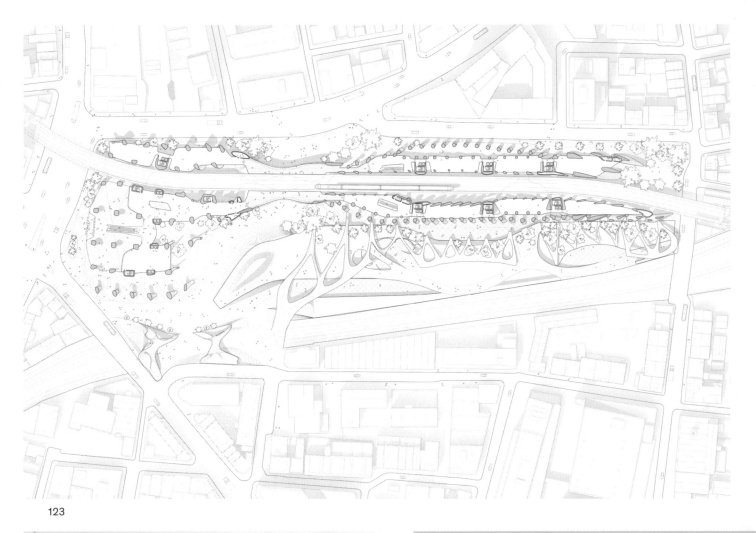

123

124

125

Hadid, Zaha and Patrik Schumacher

Today our world is much diminished by the loss of a great architect and a great person. Before I introduce this evening's speaker I will take—with your permission—a few moments to reflect on the sudden death of Zaha Hadid—my friend and our colleague. Zaha saw her studios as laboratories, as experimental workshops. They were also master classes that by the force of her personality, by the intensity of her commitment to the art of architecture, and of course by dint of her remarkable talent—made them unrivaled. Those studios were unforgettable learning experiences. Those of us who have worked with Zaha as a colleague—or as a student—respected her, for her unstoppable intelligence, her take-no-prisoners commitment to excellence, and her warm humanity. I ask that we pause for a moment or two, in quiet contemplation, to honor a great architect, friend, and mentor, Zaha Hadid. —Robert A.M. Stern

Andrei Harwell

Design & Visualization
Second Year Studio

This fourth core studio, an introduction to the planning and architecture of cities, concerns two distinct scales of operation: that of the neighborhood and that of the residential, institutional, and commercial building types that typically constitute the neighborhood. Issues of community, group form, infrastructure, and the public realm,as well as the formation of public space, blocks, streets, and squares are emphasized. The studio is organized to follow a distinct design methodology, which begins with the study of context and precedents. It postulates that new architecture can be made as a continuation and extension of normative urban structure and building typologies.

Critics
Emily Abruzzo (EA), Naomi Darling (ND), Kathleen Dorgan (KD), Keller Easterling (KE), Rosetta Elkin (RE), Alexander Felson (AF), Deborah Gans (DG), Kian Goh (KG), Javier González-Campaña (JG), Andrei Harwell (AH), Denise Hoffman (DH), David Kooris (DK), Jesse LeCavalier (JL), Tim Love (TL), Bimal Mendis (BM), Alan Plattus (AP), Alexander Purves (APu), Todd Reisz (TR), Elihu Rubin (ER), Joel Sanders (JS), Surry Schlabs (SS), Aniket Shahane (AS), Rosalyne Shieh (RS), Jonathan Sun (JS), David Waggonner (DW)

Elizabeth Nadai, Georgia Todd 126
This project revives Bridgeport's waterfront identity by establishing a web of interconnected, pedestrian-friendly public realms, redefining Bridgeport's relationship with water as the physical paths and performative public squares gradually take shape.
JC: *If you think about Rome with the obelisks, they work as an excuse to reorganize the city. I'm not suggesting that you plow new boulevards through Bridgeport, but you can think subtly that rather than the single lines of waterway, what is the secondary level of connection?*

Andrew Padron, James Schwartz 127
By re-centering on the river, the downtown rediscovers its historic orientation while providing the city with a resource. Civic and public anchors such as recreational facilities, a new central library, and public market continue pedestrian axes that bridge existing governmental or thriving downtown communities from Main Street across the Pequonnock River to the East End's own vibrant East Main Street.
KG: *On one hand that is clear: the aspects of climate change and flooding enables us to rethink ground planes in the city. At the same time, there's not enough specificity about where it's actually going to flood, and what you are doing with the floods.*

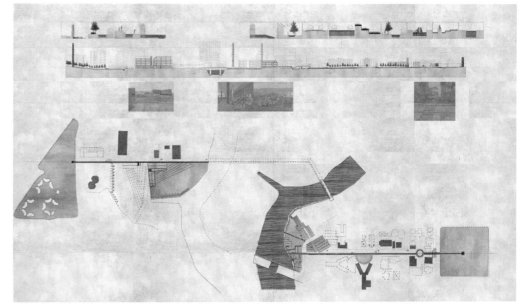

126

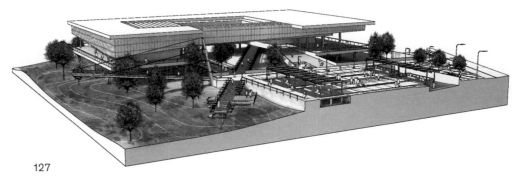

127

History of British Landscape Architecture: 1600 to 1900

Urbanism & Landscape

Bryan Fuermann

This seminar examines chronologically the history of landscape architecture and country-house architecture in Britain from 1600 to 1900. Topics of discussion include Italian and French influences on the seventeenth-century British garden—military landscaping, the Palladian country house and British agricultural landscape, Capability Brown's landscape parks, theories of the picturesque and of the landscape sublime, Romanticism and the psychology of nature, the creation of the public park system, Arts and Crafts landscape design, and the beginnings of landscape modernism. Comparisons of historical material with contemporary landscape design are made.
Michelle Gonzalez 128
Sarah Kasper, Isaac Southard 129
Madelynn Ringo 130
Anthony Gagliardi, Pearl Ho 131

128

OBSERVATIONS
ON
SEVERAL PARTS OF ENGLAND,
PARTICULARLY THE
LINES AND SURFACES

ROUTHLAND & KASPER

129

130

131

Justin Hollander
The Promise of Neuro-Architecture

Eero Saarinen Lecture

We construct stories as part of how we experience places. I'm going to talk about the Villa Lante, in Bagnaia, Italy. It was developed in the Mannerist style, and there was some sense of folly. They didn't really take the enterprise very seriously. So there are some jokes hidden in here. In fact, the whole thing is really a narrative. When you arrive, you arrive at the beginning of a story. … So the reason that stories work so well on us is because we were evolved to respond that way. …We have the ability to think about something—an action, say—and then not do it. It is a de-coupling. This is something that evolutionary biologists say would not have happened if not for evolution. This de-coupling gives us an advantage. …When we think about places that really work, places that exhibit these characteristics, whether you want to talk about New Urbanism or Old Urbanism, the fact is that it connects to you subconsciously as a person and as a place. That's victory.

Francine Houben
People, Place, Purpose

Paul Rudolph Lecture

My firm [is my] symphony orchestra: I really need to have architecture, restoration, interiors, landscape, model-building, movie-making, and graphics all in a coherent way. So I can take the people I need to make good music.

It may be strange for you that my architecture is not form-based, because that is often what is taught in schools. But for me that doesn't make sense.

So what I made in my book are ten statements that I think are absolutely essential to architecture. Our buildings are not so much form-based, but they make for beautiful things. …Given all of the different periods of the city's history, it is almost like the history of art and architecture in Birmingham. [When we started the library project], it was more important for our building to bring coherence to the city. I had a dream that I want to bring all of these people along the way into our library—I want to have a journey. I was dreaming of a sequence of tall masses, connected by escalators. And I looked to the materials of the city, [I find they] went through all these periods of history. You could see the craftsmanship of the industrial city: red bricks, blue bricks, steel, and of course they also had a period of international city building. Birmingham is also famous for jewelry, which is still active in the jewelry district nearby. More inspiration came from the cathedral windows nearby, which cast beautiful shadows on the floor. So I was trying to decide how a building could fit into the architectural rhythm of the city. [So] we started to sketch.

Intermediate Planning and Development

Urbanism & Landscape

Alexander Garvin

This seminar examines the interaction of property development and planning with local market conditions, financing alternatives, government policy, and the political context at the community level. During the first part of the term, students learn how to analyze a specific neighborhood in New York City by using fundamental planning techniques and examining national trends within that neighborhood. Topics include housing, retail, and office development, zoning, historic preservation, transportation, business improvement districts, and building reuse and rehabilitation. In the second part of the term, students prepare recommendations for the neighborhood that will meet the conflicting interests of financial institutions, real estate developers, civic organizations, community groups, public officials, and a wide variety of participants in the planning and development process.

Introduction to Urban Design

Urbanism & Landscape

Elihu Rubin

This course is an introduction to the history, analysis, and design of the urban landscape. Emphasis is placed on understanding the principles, processes, and contemporary theories of urban design, and the relations between individual buildings, groups of buildings, and the larger physical and cultural contexts.

Eugene Kohn
Working on Multiple Levels: The Opportunities and Challenges of Mixed-Use Housing

Gordon H. Smith Lecture

I have a connection to Yale. I've never lectured here, or taught, but one of my very first professors was Paul Rudolph, who played a role, obviously, in this building and at Yale. I was one of his first students in his first year of teaching at Penn. And later on I had Louis Kahn, who came to Yale as well. So I feel a strong connection between Kahn and Rudolph and Yale.

I'm going to talk about two things primarily: a little bit about the firm, how we got started, and maybe by showing you some of our work, and more importantly how we are organized and how we do our architecture may be of interest to the students in the room, as well as other architects. And finally the portion on the mixed-use building type, in particular the mixed-use tower, which has become a very important one in cities around the world. …

What I've been showing is that we work in some forty-one countries across the globe, in the six offices. It's been quite a challenge to manage a firm that works in so many different countries. I think what's been important for me is what we've been able to learn from doing every building type from the smallest 60,000 square foot buildings to five or ten million square foot airports, office buildings, hotels, schools, labs, hospitals, and museums. We have been able to [gain] a greater sensitivity to building types. Solving problems and being creative has exposed our staff to enormous opportunities for their own growth and future.

February 4, 2016

Hollander, Justin *Lecture*

March 31, 2016

Houben, Francine *Lecture*

January 21, 2016

Kohn, Eugene *Lecture*

Hans Kollhoff

Design & Visualization
Advanced Studio

with Kyle Dugdale

Kollhoff, Hans

133

The European skyscraper is not simply an extrusion of the site, driven by property value, but rather a vertical extension of the earth. The heroes of modern architecture—from Le Corbusier and Mies van der Rohe to Louis Kahn—understood architecture to be an extrusion of the earth rather than a constructed artifact to be dropped onto the ground plane. Architecture was consequently interpreted as a monolithic whole, even if assembled from parts. The highly ambiguous phenomenon of visual entities seen in relation to bodily existence, simultaneously nothing but a compilation of heterogeneous events, was called *Tektonik*. Without tectonic there is no architecture. Tectonic treatment is the articulation of mass by means of *lineamento* profiling, which accomplishes both the separation and the unification of the elements from which architecture is composed. Articulated mass as monolithic extrusion of the earth, articulated in relation to our visual sensibility, which is in fact bodily—that is what I call architecture. The studio tests the feasibility of the modified urban plan for Alexanderplatz, understanding this process as a case study with the potential for broader application elsewhere. The task is to design twelve multifunctional urban blocks with towers, each limited to a height of 150 meters.

Critics

Thomas Beeby (TB), Eve Blau (EB), Kent Bloomer (KB), Melissa delVecchio (MdV), Judy DiMaio (JD), Kyle Dugdale (KD), Frank Gehry (FG), Hans Kollhoff (HK), Barbara Littenberg (BL), Daniel Lobitz (DL), Michael Manfredi (MM), Helga Timmermann (HT), Anthony Vidler (AV)

Gina Cannistra (Feldman Nominee) 132

This new tower aims to create a sense of identity for its residents, contribute positively to the public realm, and maintain a relationship with the city regardless of one's position within the building. This project focuses on the architect's responsibility to the urban environment, the importance of tectonics, the current state of urban dwelling, and the future of the city of Berlin.

MM: *Part of this has to do with the discipline of drawing a building that close to you. You start to see it differently. You've drawn the project as if you could will it away. What's very strategic is that through the development of slots, each side might adjust itself. The project is extraordinarily sophisticated; it's almost Kahnian.* TB: *Instead of having everything perfect, you could have flawed perfection. What an idea.*

Aymar Mariño Maza 133, 134

The aim of the project became about how to create this interstitial semi-formal setting within the context of East Berlin while still abiding by the rigid parameters of the studio. The resulting architecture is an urban block that transitions from a solid street base to the residential tower pulling back from the street through the use of vertical slits that erode at the solidity and stoic nature of the Berlin block.

DL: *I want to say that this project is really interesting in a lot of different ways. I think it looks very residential, it has an intermediate scale, smaller scale, and bigger scale. I think that the entrance is read very clearly and the procession in and through the building is very nice.* TB: *I love the slots; I just wonder [if] anyone [would] pay for them.* MM: *I like the complexity of it. I like the breakdown of the tower from a kind of uniform and repetitive place to live, to a place that's more individualistic and has spatial variety.* JM: *It's got a complexity and certain playfulness that we have otherwise not seen here today and I commend you on that.* FG: *I'm surprised you like it. It's sort of Wrightian.*

Dov Feinmesser 135

This project is about fundamentals: their relationship to a past of popular culture mixed with a past of urban fabric. It raises questions of façade, the relationship of exterior articulation to interior space, and the significance of the tectonic in defining the gravitas of a base and its coalescence with a spire.

AV: *I suggest that one promenade is brought up. So, one says: "I enter the residential building, I do what I have to do in my residential lobby, I go up in the elevator, and I come out into another form of lobby which isn't just a kind of standard developer corridor, and I enter my apartment. And then I look out of the window." To me, that promenade which is completely architectonic, ought to be understood architecturally as a sequence.* EB: *One thing that Schinkel always did was to situate you—you walk into the building*

Kollhoff, Hans

134

and then you look out from the building to understand where you are. So there is an urban experience that is integrated into the architecture. There is a correspondence between the space of the city and the space of the building. It's a semi-public interstitial space you are going into.

Richard Green 136, 137
Against weightless, context-less glass towers which now proliferate, this tower celebrates its mass and materiality. Beginning with a series of superimpositions, from the large scale cruciform

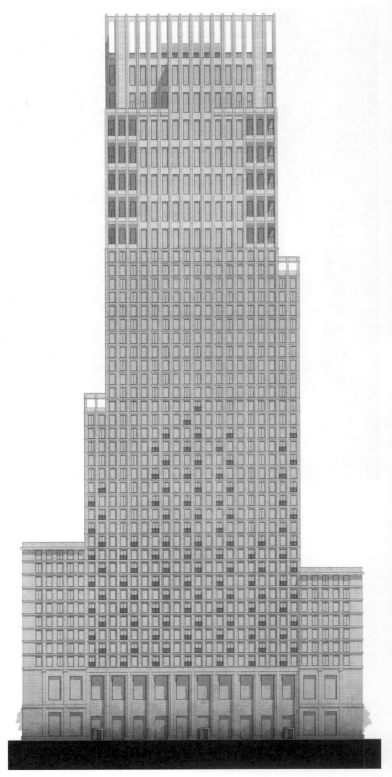

135

tower merged with a spiralling series of setbacks down to the language of its stone cladding, the tower's massing and façade articulation make it seem both stable yet upwardly dynamic. In a context where walls have been profoundly divisive, the wall of the tower is conceived as something connecting its inner world to the city; each apartment possesses inhabitable spaces within the wall, ranging from window seats to loggias and terraces.
MM: *It's a very clever sectional idea because it does solve the problem of privacy. At the same time, it brings more light into the balcony and in addition it creates an intermediate scale of the façade. I feel a little bit that the balcony got on the narrow side.*
KB: *It's a super proposition to use the Fibonacci sequence as a way of wrapping the building. It's not visually daunting.* HK: *We've talked about cornices endlessly and the students just dissipate because it's an anti-modern element. If you would make a cornice here on every second floor you'd solve every problem you have in construction. If you would make a cornice here, you'd find the relationship between block and tower in a much richer and a much more sophisticated way.*

Kollhoff, Hans

136

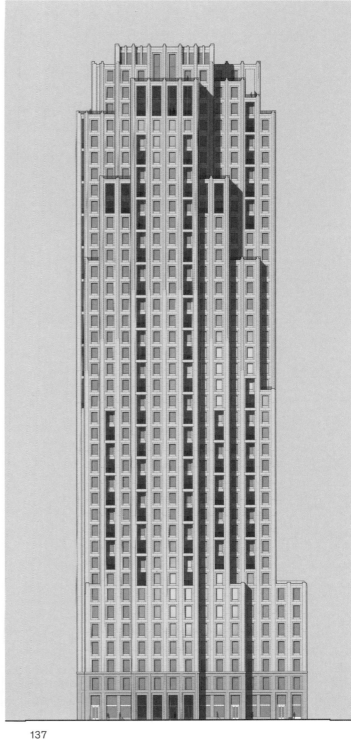

137

Launch: Architecture and Entrepreneurialism

History & Theory

Keller Easterling

This seminar studies the designer as entrepreneur. This seminar considers both historical and contemporary moments in architectural and urban design when architects conceived of buildings, building components, or formats as repeatable products—products that, in the aggregate, may have the power to create an alteration to a local or global environment.

Daphne Binder
The middle class vacation has by and large dominated the tourist economy since the end of World War II. While family travel is predicted to grow at a faster rate than all other forms of leisure travel, changing family structures, overbuilt infrastructure and untapped revenue streams beg [us] to rethink the car as the ideal vehicle of vacationing.

Elaina Berkowitz, Tess McNamara
Our product is spatial and ecological in nature. *Bee Line* starts by planting wild-flowers along the unused land on either side of these railroad tracks and highways. Then, with a team of beekeepers, we source bee hives and place them along the ribbons of infrastructure in the midst of our wildflower habitats. *Bee Line* is dedicated to improving the ecology of the Central Valley through pollinator interventions.

Jacqueline Hall, Kiana Hosseini, Alicia Pozniak
Current configurations of domestic labor in the home isolate those performing this work from their families and public life, namely women, who spend on average double the time men do on household activities. Our research reveals opportunities to reduce and collectivize these costs and tasks.

Charles Kane, Winny Tan
Better Cities Better Boxes, Inc. sees the potential power of leveraging the desires of both the town and these [global] companies in order to restore struggling areas. Many cities and towns suffer from vacancy, need additional services, and want increased street activity. With the right balance of parameters and incentives, BCBB can develop a mutually beneficial relationship to foster stronger communities.

Kollhoff, Hans

Learning/Doing/Thinking: Educating Architects in the 21st Century Symposium

Robert A.M. Stern
Pedagogy and Place: Celebrating 100 Years of Architecture at Yale

Symposium Opening Address

Rudolph left on June 30, 1965, and was succeeded by little-known West Coast architect Charles Moore, whose appointment coincided with rising student activism that resulted in a disciplinary shift from heroic form-making toward a historically and contextually referential approach that would come to be labeled Post-Modernism. Amid the tumult of the late 1960s Moore was, depending on whom you ask, either the best man for the job or the absolute worst. Certainly his was a very different sensibility from Rudolph's. Moore had little love for the Art & Architecture Building, which he deemed to be overbearing and a symbol of the architect as social oppressor. Moore permitted students to construct their own workspaces, transforming the architecture studio into a virtual favela, as seen in pictures by Roy Berkeley that sent shock waves through the profession when published in *Architectural Forum*. When asked why he allowed students to treat the building so poorly, Moore replied dryly,

"It has seemed to me for some time that an architecture school was a place where people were trying to be architects."

Yet Moore did more than just combat Rudolph's building. He also redirected the curriculum in recognition of a broader definition of architecture and the role of architects in society. He encouraged students to pursue experimental design, research, and construction methods and initiated several key programs that are still central to the school, including the MED program, which in its formative years was largely shaped by students like William Mitchell, who would help organize at Yale one of the first symposiums on the use of computers in architecture and would go on to become dean at MIT. Donald Watson, another key member of the first MED class, would later lead the program before becoming dean at Rensselaer Polytechnic Institute.

The late 1960s was tumultuous. Architecture students, who were particularly vocal in challenging authority, staged various protests in opposition to a lack of financial aid. Incendiary rhetoric tragically gave way to a literal fire on June 14, 1969. No one was hurt and the fire was quickly controlled, but the damage was significant. Because of the rebellious mood of the times, arson was suspected but never proven. The fire left the building with wounds that would take more than thirty years to heal. Until repairs could be made, students were spread out across the campus, a situation that chipped away at the school's cohesiveness.

Equal in significance to the socially responsive First-Year Building Project was the replacement of the "masterpiece" design theses of the Rudolph era with theme-based Advanced Studios. These can be attributed to the influence of Serge Chermayeff and to the succession of three studios led by Robert Venturi and Denise Scott Brown—most famously 1968's "Learning from Las Vegas," which challenged students to analyze the desert city as if it were Rome—an unorthodox assignment that offered students a way to see the world as it is, not as hero architects would wish to remake it. The unrest of the late 1960s initially pointed to a reexamination of the prevailing architecture pedagogy, but at Yale, as at most other radicalized architecture schools, these reforms were never fully implemented by the time the harsh political and economic realities of the 1970s dampened the radical exuberance of the previous decade. …

Today, as throughout its history, Yale seeks to balance core competence with artistic experimentation and the steadfast belief that the primary purpose of an architecture school should be training for leadership in the practice of the art of architecture. In many architecture schools theory is more prevalent than history, while hand-drawing and physical models have been abandoned in favor of digital methods that encourage, even demand, speculative investigations into radical forms that are divorced from tectonic authority. New ideas and technologies are exciting—and important to the future of the discipline. But in this new landscape it can be easy to lose sight of the fact that the principal purpose of an architecture school is to prepare students for the diverse disciplinary realities of architecture entailed in the art of building.

Dominant Models and Institutional Frameworks in Flux

Global Beaux-Arts,
Barry Bergdoll, Columbia University
Architecture, Science, and Technology:
The Polytechnic Model,
Antoine Picon, Harvard University
In Bauhaus We Trust,
Lara Schrijver, University of Antwerp

The polytechnic project, in the 19th century all over the world, entailed actually creating mediation between new cutting edge science and the variety

of concrete techniques. That mobilized a notion of application… The idea that what you teach at a polytechnic is the kind of intermediary knowledge between pure science and the diversity of what you do in practice.

Antoine Picon

Anthony Vidler
Architecture in an Expanded Field

Symposium Keynote Address

In 1979, the art historian, critic, and theorist Rosalind Krauss published a ground-breaking article in the journal *October*, entitled "Sculpture in the Expanded Field"; some years later, I opportunistically borrowed this title for an essay in *Artforum*, calling it "Architecture in an Expanded Field." This evening, however, I will not resume the arguments of these pieces, but simply note that both were pointed towards a phenomenon that has emerged recurrently in the modern period—from the Enlightenment on that is—to challenge the received limits of specific disciplines. In the case selected by Krauss, the nature of sculpture had been challenged from the outside by landscape, performance and installation art, and even, as with Dan Graham, architecture—or, in my case, the traditional boundaries of the architectural discipline—had been questioned by the new sciences and technologies of representation, environment, and urbanism.

Tonight, the "expanded field" I wish to consider is more defined, and in a sense less dramatically posed.

The question—raised in polemical fashion in the 1960s and I believe still pertinent—of the value, influence, and nature of historical and theoretical studies in architecture, or more bluntly, the role of history and theory in the teaching and development of design.

We have since the 1960s passed through a series of debates over this question; we have heard the arguments for autonomy or quasi-autonomy of the design discipline from Emil Kaufmann to Pier Vittorio Aureli, as well as those for its continuing need for history and theory in the digital age. Equally we have seen the expansion of scholarly historical studies in schools of architecture with the proliferation of PhD programs since the 1970s and beyond, the expansion of interests in these programs to topics and research that do not always seem entirely "architectural." At the same time we have seen the development of quasi-autonomous courses and studies in what is called "theory" and the expansion of these into topics that seem more naturally to fall into the philosophical and social science disciplines than the architectural.

The field that I wish to consider then, is composed of a series of sub-fields, many that might be called extra-, inter-, or intradisciplinary areas that are engaged in increasingly specialized research.

Here, I will return again to the '60s, and try to address the attempts of schools of architecture to address the very problems defined intellectually by Tafuri. I take as my two educational contexts the curricula of two schools that, under new management, so to speak, from the late 1950s and early 1960s, were responding to the professional inquiries in Britain (1959) and the United States

(1965), environments that I have experienced firsthand, and can now look back on as a historian.

First Cambridge. Leslie Martin came to Cambridge with a sense of the urgent need to re-invigorate architectural education on two fronts, and this in the very specific context of a university—a very different context from that of a free-standing school such as the Architectural Association for example, or say, the Cooper Union in New York.

The university demanded of architecture a professional activity, more than the apparatus demanded by the profession;

and from Martin's standpoint this was an excellent opportunity—a teachable moment—for the profession itself. (As an aside, having just gone through my tenth NAAB visit, this time my fourth at Cooper Union, I'm not sure that Martin's aims have yet been fully absorbed by the profession.)

Martin himself was a scholar—one of the few PhDs in the field having obtained his degree in the study of Spanish and Portuguese Baroque—and a convinced modernist before the war; he was also an educator having served as the head of school at the University of Hull. He came to Cambridge then with two apparently compatible, but ultimately incompatible aims: to establish the study of architecture as a humanistic discipline at a university research level, and at the same time to demonstrate its scientific credentials as design-research arm of the profession. I will deal with the idea of architecture as a humanistic discipline first.

To this first end Martin fabricated a curriculum at once centered on history and theory conceived as having close relations with design—this was helped by a faculty who, architects and critics, moved easily enough between the two. He himself, together with Colin St John Wilson, offered the lectures in theory; the history courses were also delivered by architects—Peter Bicknell (and once slightly improbably, Peter Eisenman) for the Gothic, Colin Rowe for the Renaissance and once for the Gothic too—all of whom took part in the studio culture. Here the distinctions Tafuri wanted to draw between operative and purely historical criticism were blithely ignored; everything was in the service of understanding, interpreting, and designing architecture. Everyone was, so to speak, their own Sigfried Giedion.

How did this play out in the studio? Well, in a paradoxical way, and with deep roots in the traditional teaching of design over the drawing board, the almost seamless absorption of history into design was accomplished through the reliance on what the nineteenth century Beaux-Arts system called "composition," and the complementary device called the "parti."

Indeed, throughout the nineteenth century, these devices, entirely "abstract" in nature, and largely un-theorized, had allowed for the continuance of a design practice that on the surface was differentiated by the eclectic play of the styles. It had been transmitted to the American and British schools through the Beaux-Arts experiences of their leaders, and in Britain established as the means by which modernism itself could be assimilated into largely Beaux-Arts institutions, from the AA to Liverpool. Most of the older generation had undergone the training, and the shift to modernism by the 1950s, and Colin Rowe, as we know, was no exception…

This is why, and precisely in a school in the university context, we have to engage in different levels of study, abstract and applied, and many levels in between; and why the structures of our curricula should enable and promote conversations among them, and also—and this after all is the importance of the university here—among fields that are ancillary to each of our own—with the goal at the end, and all along the way, of encouraging experimentation at the center of the discipline; its compositional practices understood in the broadest sense.

Innovative Platforms and Alternative Settings

Undoing the Master Class: Venturi and Scott Brown at Yale,
Martino Stierli, Museum of Modern Art
The IAUS: A Quasi-Institutional Group with Extra-Curricular Activities,
Kim Förster, Canadian Centre for Architecture
Knowledge Building
Nikolaus Hirsch, Frankfurt Städelschule

Venturi's pedagogical approach marked a decisive shift that reflects Charles Moore's old agenda as chair… Venturi seemed little inclined to follow what might be called the unwritten rules of the master class in which a singular outstanding figure introduces a group of carefully selected students into the art of designing the architectural masterpiece.

Martino Stierli

Paradigm Shifts

The Urban Turn: City as Frame, Substance, and Goal of Architectural Education,
Tom Avermaete, Delft University of Technology
Almost Politics: 'Environment' in Architectural Education, c. 1966,
Daniel Barber, University of Pennsylvania
Theory: It's Over—and Underdetermination
Mark Jarzombek, Massachusetts Institute of Technology

We are trapped in a mystic cultural and theoretical betwixt and between; it is highly unlikely that any of the assembled deans and chairmen here will propose to their faculty that we rename our institutions. But we could start by perhaps calling it the department of *jianzhu*. But to dismiss the problematic nature of even the word like architecture, which has of course proliferated in the globalization of English or assume that it's standard and universal without any kind of problem at all—and that we're off the hook simply because of the power of the English language in the international world—is to dismiss the opportunity to see the problem of abstraction in the global world.

Mark Jarzombek

Platforms

On the Ground: Site-Based Research,
Eve Blau, Harvard University
We Build with Wood,
Pekka Heikkinen, Aalto University
Built Ecologies
Anna Dyson, Rensselaer Polytechnic Institute

If the subject of the study is the condition of transition and its impact on architecture and urbanism, then the subject of the research shifts from urban form to urban practice, and to the dynamics of practice: issues of agency, intervention, authorship, and so on. We're using [practice] here to refer to architectural and urban practices, the authored production of material structures and very importantly, the production of formal knowledge that is particular to architecture.

Eve Blau

Teaching/Leading/Inspiring

Amale Andraos, Columbia University
Will Hunter, London School of Architecture
Monica Ponce de Leon, Princeton University
Jennifer Wolch, University of California, Berkeley

Closing remarks by Deborah Berke.

Greg Lynn

Design & Visualization
Advanced Studio

with Nathan Hume

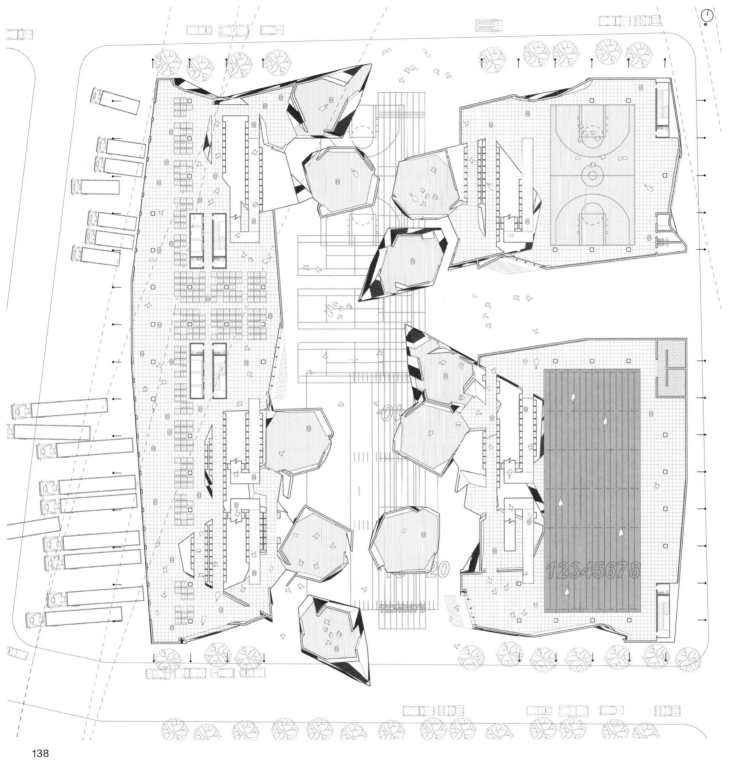

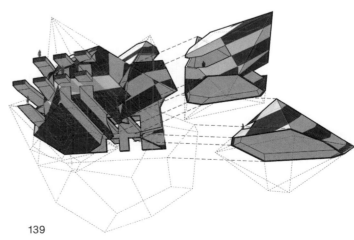

Lynn, Greg

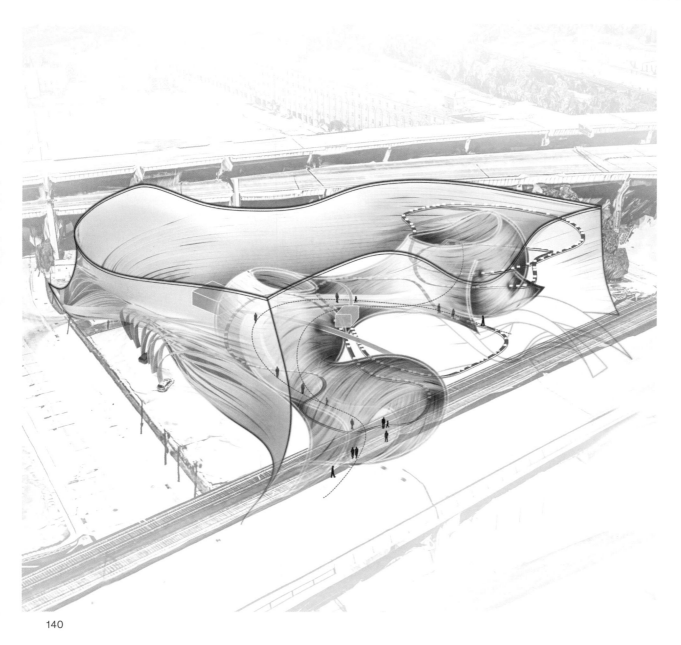

140

What typology could sound more promising for design than a fulfillment center? Yet architecturally and spatially, this typology couldn't be more banal. These environments are located at the nexus of regional transportation nodes, often in isolation and always in anonymity. Their interiors are organized at their core for swarms of robots shuffling shelving, to pickers and packers on their perimeter. They are a bottom-line economic and technologic tour de force that leaves cultural opportunity on the table unexploited. The studio introduces quality of life and cultural innovation into the infrastructure of goods distribution and in some cases production. Fulfillment include education, research, and recreation by combining the activities of a Google or Amazon campus with the distribution hubs. The synergy between production, distribution, storage, knowledge, and innovation will give each student a chance to develop a new spatial typology that intermingles people and machines; space and infrastructure. We work on how the architectural imagination can make these centers more fulfilling.

Critics

Michelle Addington (MA), Brennan Buck (BB), Hernán Díaz Alonso (HDA), Peter Eisenman (PE), Mark Foster Gage (MFG), Nathan Hume (NH), Jeffrey Kipnis (JK), Greg Lynn (GL), Wolf Prix (WP), Nina Rappaport (NR), Patrik Schumacher (PS), Robert A.M. Stern (RAMS), Anthony Vidler (AV)

Michael Harrison 138, 139

Adjacent to local professional sports facilities and regional distribution networks, this project takes the form of three buildings framing a reconfigurable yard. Large pods—enabled by autonomous movement systems—dock into crystalline figures on the building periphery. These pods shape the space of the yard for various small-scale athletic activities. The pods disperse themselves into the city for various sporting events, carrying products and displays—artifacts of the fulfillment process in the urban core. Inside the buildings, the crystalline docks are aggregates of dense product shelving and large figural rooms for the exchange of people and products. Long ramps puncture the crystals, allowing for retrieval of goods via 'pickers' and drones while allowing access to upper levels for spectators.

MG: *In your panning model shot you have the deliveries, shelving, and then you went to embedded figures. They went from programmatic description to formal dissection. It seems that the formal divide is where your problem is. You haven't told us why these giant figures are required for the fulfillment center to operate, which for me makes it seems like there is a fulfilment center program that is a rearrangeable recreational program which is even more interesting if it's plugging into a stadium, which is a lost opportunity you can elaborate on. But I don't understand what the required connection is between the two.* PS: *To me it's an interesting project—and it's an Eisenman project by the way, in terms of the early stages of faceted folding. It seems that you're interested in where the units of interaction of the parts are submerged into textured fields and conditions. The dazzle camouflage acts in the same way: it breaks up that unit and connects it back to the continuous splintered fields where figures and units of interaction crystalize and resolve concepts of space.*

Mengshi Sun 140

This project combines the program of a food market and the mobility of a fulfillment center. The conveyor belt system is no longer treated simply as a transportation tool, but a means to exhibit food and enhance consumers' shopping experience. Similar to the feature of a sushi-go-round restaurant, shopping

Lynn, Greg

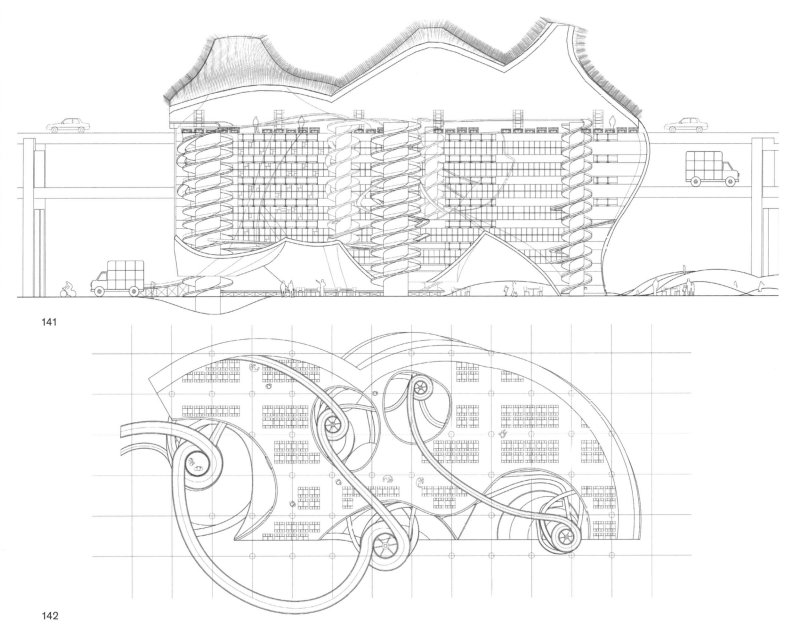

141

142

items are placed on conveyor belts that fly through the entire building. The architectural space is designed to enhance the dynamic and chaotic characteristics of conveyor belts, as items come into sight and disappear into the walls.
JK: *You've got the* Wayne's World *problem. "Wouldn't it be cool if I did this?" Then instead of working on that, you add another one. "... Wouldn't it be cool if I did this, and wouldn't it be cool if I did this?" The conveyor belt mechanism by itself is adequate to the entire project. To try and get them together is to just add ideas together that compromise one another. I can't see any place where the conveyor belt idea hybridized with the canyon idea to produce some design development.* PS: *I disagree. To some extent I don't care what the ingredients are, I'm looking at a unified building which has a certain logic and interesting variety and I think it's instrumental for this kind of retail experience.* JK: *Wouldn't you want to know what the support system for the conveyor belt mechanism would be before you turn your attention to the site? How does that thing behave?* PS: *I think you develop first an intentionality and then you can ask the question, "How am I actually going to realize this?"*

Dima Srouji 141, 142
The grain silo is an under-appreciated and overlooked typology in architecture, but its generic form is familiar and abundant universally. The silo, in this project, is renewed to adjust to today's dynamic fulfillment typology and further formally manipulated to encourage alternative spatial experiences that reimagine the Silo Cloud as a public viewing space and outdoor market. By collapsing the familiar form of a silo into itself and manipulating the figure, the compound figure creates a satisfyingly vague relationship between the original familiar form and the ambivalent larger whole. The two characters—the strange familiar form on the exterior,

and the technical machine character on the interior—work together to enhance the experience of the visitor making the machine an observational event for the city as the machine is working to feed it.
JK: *I love the project if it would just be—I'm going to say this as I'll never be back here again—de-Yale-ized, and more Greg Lynn-ized.*
GL: *I think these are beautiful studies in formal language. I would encourage you to burn your library and save your media. I think for your project to communicate, it needs to be a spectacle.*

Heather Bizon (Feldman Nominee) 143, 144
Making is at the core of communities. This proposal combines a dump/recycling/thrift market with assembly spaces for learning, machinery shops for construction, studio space, and exhibition space, proposing a civic place for making with a center for fulfillment. Junk is a cultural commodity. Within the pile and on the surrounding platforms, junk is everywhere, [randomly organized]. The pile becomes a mixing pot for robots, stuff, people, makers, shoppers, filtering through conveyors and stairs. Spaces are defined by movement paths between piles of stuff along the platforms. Market and exhibit on becomes mixed as one.
RAMS: *I think your project is highly picturesque and probably very arbitrary. It's a compelling drawing, but it's not even really an architectural drawing—it's a drawing with architectural elements.*
JK: *These are intended as visionary. These are not intended as actual architectural drawings. They are evocative. I think you should own and acknowledge what you're saying as exactly correct.*
MA: *I feel as though this is a drawing where every line is indicating a statistical probability of what that next moment might be. It is time-based—for me this is the animation. It's a different form of representation but that doesn't make it any less architectural.*

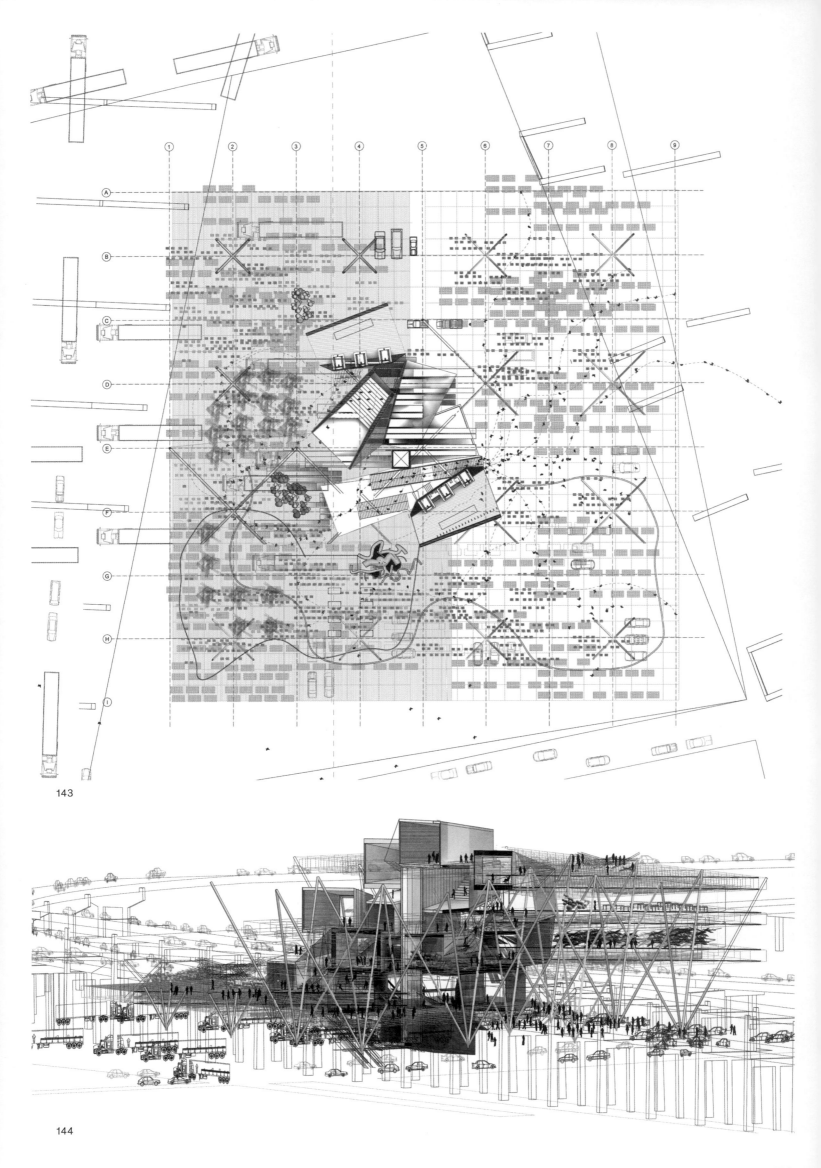

143

144

Lynn, Greg

M.E.D. Program

History & Theory
Masters of Environmental Design

Eeva-Liisa Pelkonen

M.E.D. Committee
Michelle Addington, Peggy Deamer, Keller Easterling, Karsten Harries, Alan Plattus, Elihu Rubin
First Year
Daphne Agosin, Gregory Cartelli
Second Year
Geneva Morris, Shivani Shedde, Preeti Talwai
True to the legacy of the M.E.D. program this year's students represents a wide range of backgrounds and interests. Even though they study the built environment through a variety of intellectual lenses, each class ends up sharing common ground. While studying a wide range of topics in different geographic and historical contexts, this year's graduating class shares an interest in the economic and social dimension of the built environment. Geneva Morris expresses hers by studying the notion of minimum dwelling; Shivani Shedde by exploring Indian gold mining during the colonial times; and Preeti Talwai by writing about the commercial use of digital screens. Ideas about identity and privacy loom equally large in each thesis. The first year students, likewise, share a curious intellectual affinity despite two seemingly different topics: both Daphne Agosin, who studies street theatre and Gregory Cartelli, with his interest in military training sites, share an interest in how space can be manipulated towards political goals with scenographic means.

Scaffolds for the City
Street Theater: Performance and the
Built Environment, 1968–1988
Daphne Agosin
Theater is etymologically a place before it is a performance; theater is a place for seeing. *Theatron* in Greek means a place for watching and it is specifically the place where in the theater of Ancient Greece the audience sat to view the performance in sight of the orchestra and *skene*. It is a type of architectural space that relies on the experience of the spectators. The collective engagement of the crowd in relation to what happens on stage can generate an identification between spectators if their presence is not omitted; this identification can produce a kind of public that witnesses itself. Certain typologies of theater spaces allow for this 'self-witnessing' to happen more than others: increasingly in Western history, theater spaces have minimized the presence of the public, turning it into an invisible audience by having little or no light in the auditorium. However, there are typologies of theaters that have not been enclosed in playhouses and have thus

maintained this active kind of public. A contemporary example is street theater.

Street theater as a cultural form draws inspiration from religious feasts, parades and carnival, but differs from all of these as a secular, contemporary theatrical form that delves with performativity. As an experimental art form as well as a means for political manifestation, street theater presented a possibility to break norms of behavior, blurring the relationship between everyday and performance space. As a political cultural form, it took part of post-war activism across the globe. However, among the differing rigidities of power representation in public space, it also offered an alternative to pure forms of contestation; a possibility to present discourse in a way that doesn't only present itself as breaching the peace, but rather constructs a different—either illusory, or only temporary—order and narrative of place.

Strategic Model Theatre:
The Subjunctive City
Gregory Cartelli
The Combined Arms Collective Training Facility (CACTF: pronounced /kak-tif/) is a model for construction of small installations that prepare soldiers for Military Operations on Urbanized Terrain (MOUT). While the training city has existed since the beginning of World War II in various guises, and its schema is rooted in the Greek and Roman war games and military camps, the CACTF design guide published in 2001 by the Army Corps of Engineers has served as a model for its 21st century iterations. Not simply a continuation of its precedents, the CACTF's techniques for structuring and enacting urban space represent a qualitative break from those that preceded it.

This thesis investigates how the CACTF operates as a training facility, a testing ground, and a model of urban space by tracing the historical precedents that have informed the CACTF. Since 1942, the physical layout and structure of urban training facilities, the visual tactics they employ, and the embodied experiences they facilitate have been continuously reinvented, redefined, and refined. These alterations reflect the imperatives of the contemporary wars to which they correspond, changing operations of military bureaucracy, and prevailing theories about how to realistically simulate embodied experience.

Beyond internal military history and theory, the CACTF speaks to broader cultural histories and theories of the model as prototype, reproduction, and performance. The deconstructions and constructions that are part of the life-cycle of the urban training area are also part of the lifecycle of the model. The CACTF is a "simulated theatre of operations" that replicates urban space to

produce a realistic experience of modern war. It is at once a stage set for theatrical performances, a cinematic backdrop, and a test bed for new technologies, one that, critically, is liberated by the potential of its genericism. What are the relationships between the virtual and the real in each of the iterations of the training facility? How does its unique position, being neither fully physical nor virtual, reflect ongoing contemplations of critical theory from Wittgenstein to Turner to Virilio that target the tenuous space that it occupies?

Life in One Room: Small Space Living
Typologies 1916–2016
Geneva Morris
Between 1940 and 1960, Chicago's black population grew from 278,000 to 813,000. This established the foundation of Chicago's African American industrial working class and substantially increased the need for housing in the city. More and more people moved to Chicago, many of whom were constrained in their choices by restrictive covenants and segregation. With such a large population influx, the government could no longer overlook the housing shortage—yet the newly constructed public housing could not even begin to house the growing African American population in the city. With waiting lists for public housing units full, newly arriving migrants to the city had to turn to the private market to secure housing.[1]

In this context, the kitchenette apartment emerged. Movement of middle class whites to the suburbs: [an] increasing black population and persistent racial housing restrictions created an incentive for landlords to purchase, convert and pack structures with black families who had no option out to pay higher rates. Building after building in Chicago's Black Belt was converted to kitchenette apartment units. The kitchenette apartment became the "new home between the margins of slavery and segregation [where] black consciousness surrendered to material actuality."[2]

The implementation of kitchenette apartments maximized profit for white landlords and almost completely neglected the human needs of Chicago's black community. In a 1944 study, the Illinois Inter-Racial Commission found that rents in black areas ranged from 15% to 50% higher than that paid by white residents for similar accommodations.[3] In his photo book *12 Million Black Voices*, Richard Wright wrote that the landlords, or the "bosses of the buildings," would often rent the units by week at the same price former white tenants paid for the month (about $50). The abundance of kitchenette apartments, and the lives within them, makes this typology an illuminating case study on a constricted community. Merely providing shelter to a growing population disregards the sociocultural and economic structures that are inherent to a community's identity.

1. Wright, Richard. "Death on the City Pavement." *12 Million Black Voices*, ed. Edwin Rosskam. Basic Books, 2002.

2. Schlabach, Elizabeth. *Along the Streets of Bronzeville: Black Chicago's Literary Landscape.* University of Illinois Press, 2013.

3. Weaver, Robert C. *The Negro Ghetto.* New York: Russell & Russell, 1967. The rent for a two room furnished apartment that shared a kitchen and toilet converted to black occupancy was $78 per month. Whereas, the rent for an apartment in Mayor Martin H. Kennelly's Gold Coast building, furnished by including an indoor bed, refrigerator, private bath, and kitchenette, was $74.50.

Zero
Shivani Shedde

Looking back at the Viceroy-General of India, the ambiguity of labor's role in this landscape was, and in many ways is, critical to the continuation of industry, even today. Curzon works under the assumption of the unifying ability of industrial space in creating forms of non-differentiated labor, working in tandem with the colonial pursuit of economic prowess and modern development. His assumptions, we can argue today, were far from accurate. As noted by most post-colonial scholarly work, imperial interventions in science and development were part of a larger entangled network of knowledge production and racialized moralizing missions that spanned larger global connections. Guided by powerful interests, the ability to portray certain representations of the industry is telling of the ways in which these interests shaped the physical landscape. The consequent reorganization of labor across time and space, and indeed crafting industrial landscapes to this end, was simply a means of prompting attention to the commitments of 'native improvement.'

Architectural rhetoric has long played lip service to continuing a status quo in today's global industry, and rarely acknowledges the unsaid, the unrecognized or the invisible processes behind the creation of the built environment. In light of excavating these three, this thesis examines the architectonic impulse behind both: the economy and politics in their quest for power. To begin to tell my story, I start at the beginning of the long history of the Kolar Gold Fields. My story sits squarely within its colonial history, in an attempt to make visible not just the invisible, but the forgotten. The behind-the-scenes processes at Kolar beginning in 1873, were a self-perpetuating cycle of policy and design, even if not by 'trained architects,' that were able to manipulate the built environment, its people and its natural surroundings in a bid to stimulate industrial production. Imbricated within processes of land acquisition, urban development and social reform, the landscape that emerged by the 1890s was one of silent violence. Spatial production went hand in hand with the control of workers' bodies. As the mines tunneled deeper and deeper into the ground, this control was increasingly hidden, both visually and discursively, within archives of government reports, company records and photographic imagery that laid emphasis on native improvement schemes and mine productivity.

Self, Space, Screen: Embodied Relationships in Hybrid Retail Environments
Preeti Talwai

The user interfaces that characterize digital wayfinding require a lexicon of minimalism and exclusivity to offset the comprehensiveness and overload of the virtual imaginary. Curated sensory input elevates service—as the vice president of eBay posits, digital wayfinding technology will "provide consumers with white glove shopping experiences."[1] In this paradigm, artificial attractions, congregation, and the universality of collective experience give way to navigation dictated not by the dynamics of spectacle, but by personal preferences. While Jon Jerde professed to "keep it elusive…to keep your perceptions off balance so they're always keyed up,"[2] Jibestream, a major wayfinding software developer, asks: "Why build an amusement park when you have experiential wayfinding?"[3] If the traditional mega-mall is marketed as comprehensive and universal, the hybrid mall is curated and temporally specific.

Thus, as the 'phygital' landscape turns the Gruen and Jerde transfer ideologies on their heads, it renders what cannot be seen as captivating as what can be. Appealing to the rhetoric of satisfaction, simplicity, and reduced stress, the allure of the digital is in its magical ability to parse complicated user inputs and reduce decision fatigue. In this way, the digital is not subversive, but coaxes consumers into happy complicity with their consumption. Companies developing this technology aim to generate revenue by encouraging shoppers to spend more time in stores, make more impulse purchases, and build more positive brand associations.[4] Furthermore, the sophisticated tracking capabilities built into these systems provide valuable data feedback by quantifying a previously anonymized mass of consumers.

From a preliminary reading, it might seem simply that the new experience of navigating the mall's interstitial spaces is built around looking down, keying into an almost instinctual behavior in our smartphone-centered culture. After all, consumers no longer need to look around to identify their cars, or look up to see cinema show times. They must decide between window-shopping and following a highlighted route. But consumer reviews of shopping environments reveal a more complicated situation. Across hundreds of global Yelp reviews for Westfield properties, consumers still seem to be attracted to the mall for its comprehensive retail options, which offer "everything for everyone." Other comments, both positive and negative, discuss cleanliness, atmosphere, crowding, and socializing. Such details evidence that the mall plays a role in the socio-spatial imaginary that is distinct from other retail channels.

1. "Simon and eBay Launch 'Connected Mall' at Stanford Shopping Center," press release, December 2, 2014, http://www.prnewswire.com/news-releases/simon-and-ebay-inc-launch-connected-mall-at-stanford-shopping-center-300003069.html.

2. Daniel Herman, "Jerde Transfer," *The Harvard Design School Guide to Shopping*, ed. Rem Koolhaas, et. al, (Koln: Taschen, 2002), 405.

3. "Why Build an Amusement Park When You Have Experimental Wayfinding?" Jibestream, December 19, 2014, http://www.jibestream.com/blog/why-build-an-amusement-park-when-you-have-experiential-wayfinding.

4. For one example of this type of rationale, see: "More on Mobile in Retail," *Two West*, 2011, http://clients.twowest.com/media/pdf/Two%20West%20Mobile%20In%20Retail.pdf.

Bimal Mendis

Design & Visualization
Second Year Studio

This fourth core studio, an introduction to the planning and architecture of cities, concerns two distinct scales of operation: that of the neighborhood and that of the residential, institutional, and commercial building types that typically constitute the neighborhood. Issues of community, group form, infrastructure, and the public realm, as well as the formation of public space, blocks, streets, and squares are emphasized. It postulates that new architecture can be made as a continuation and extension of normative urban structure and building typologies.

Critics
Kathleen Dorgan (KD), Keller Easterling (KE), Alexander Felson (AF), Deborah Gans (DG), Kian Goh (KG), Javier González-Campaña (JG), Andrei Harwell (AH), Denise Hoffman (DH), David Kooris (DK), Tim Love (TL), Bimal Mendis (BM), Alan Plattus (AP), Todd Reisz (TR), Joel Sanders (JS), Surry Schlabs (SS), Rosalyne Shieh (RS), David Waggonner (DW)

Wes Hiatt,
Benjamin Rubenstein 145, 147
Bridgeport needs tools to cast a different vision of itself. Rethinking how both residents and outsiders view the city is necessary to allow for the possibility of its betterment. We propose reading the city of today and yesterday through the eyes of circus magnate P.T. Barnum—Bridgeport's most famous resident—to create a fictional alternative to the present.

Through non-conventional and playful means such as animated shorts, toys, and a planned parade for the city, this project aims to ameliorate the very real issues the city faces by critically examining Bridgeport's history and deploying it as a new popular mythology.

DH: *I'm wondering how your use of irony would translate across many populations that you would have to communicate to with your apparatus?* SS: *It's not just fiction; it's an allegory of Bridgeport which is constructed out of the cultural-historical detritus of the city, imaginatively reconstructed and performed by the people of the city. I'm willing to accept the idea that this doesn't kick-start the development of a dozen national chains, or revitalize the entire economy, or socially restructure the city in one fell swoop, but that it celebrates Bridgeport as it is, as it was, and how it might be imagined by the people of Bridgeport. I don't think there's any irony or cynicism in this project as it is proposed.*

145

Ethan Fischer,
Nasim Rowshanabadi 146

In the theater of public life, Main Street is the main stage: the platform on which urban inhabitants act out competing values and desires. Subject to perpetual oscillation, Main Street is a mutating realm of urban possibility. Bridgeport's public mixing ground is not a verdant green watched by busts of its founders, but rather a city-owned parking lot adjacent to the Webster Bank Arena, a 10,000 person capacity event space. Built in 2001 on land formerly occupied by Main Street, the arena hosts a diverse range of events, from monster truck rallies to Catholic Masses. These events intensify and make literal the metaphor of urban theater, allowing inhabitants to reconstitute notions of public on a nightly basis. This project looks closely at the Arena and its immediate surroundings, utilizing dramatic structure as a means of speculating on the site's continued development as an essential public space.

147

SS: *We're all used to thinking of projects like this in terms of phase development, and what you guys insist upon is this notion that narrative matters and that this isn't about a phase development but rather a refiguring of urban experience in terms of a series of acts. I think that's a really powerful idea. So sure, you end up with an 'XYZ entertainment' developer proposal, but I do think it's more of a three-ring circus. I think this project is based on the assumption that the narrative that gets you there is important to the experience of the city over time. I think that's a really powerful idea.* TL: *Yes, but each of those interventions imply serious economic development money coming in. It's not little pop-up taco stands. This is industrial-strength phased entertainment.* SS: *So?*

146

Ornament

Design & Visualization

Kent Bloomer

This seminar begins by reviewing the major writings governing the identities of and distinctions between ornament and decoration in architecture: Owen, Jones, Riegl, Sullivan, Beeby, etc. Twentieth-century modernist actions against ornament are also examined. After individual student analysis of Victorian, Art Nouveau, and Art Deco production, the focus is on ornament in twenty-first century design.

148

149

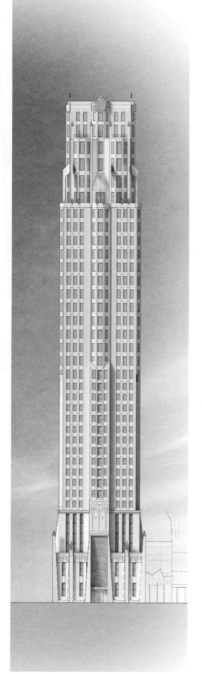

150

151

Parallel Moderns: The New Tradition

History & Theory

Robert A.M. Stern

This seminar puts forward the argument that what many have accepted as the mutually exclusive discourses of tradition and innovation in the modern architecture of the first half of the twentieth century—respectively identified as the "New Tradition" and the "New Pioneers"—in fact share common genealogy and are integral to an understanding of modern architecture as a whole. The seminar explores in depth key architects working in the "New Tradition" and goes on to explore its impact for postmodernism in the 1970s and 1980s.

Misha Semenov

In spite of, or perhaps even in part because of the fact that he has built comparatively little, Léon Krier stands out as one of the most influential thinkers in the fields of architecture and urbanism. A loud voice in architectural discourse beginning with his many publications and lectures in London in the 1980s, the polemical Krier has been persistent in his critique of modernism's technological fallacies, his documentation of functional zoning's disastrous conse-quences, and his advocacy of Classical architecture and its relevance to our time. …This exhibition attempts to tell the story of the development of Krier's beliefs and principles, culminating in a presentation of buildings and towns Krier has realized. The exposition is split into five themes that guide the visitor toward a more nuanced understanding of the architect; each section gathers related material—Krier's sketches, writing, designs, and teaching exercises from his years at Yale—together for a more complete picture. Writing back in 1984, Jaquelin Robertson asked: "is Krier really an architect if he does not build?" and concluded that, in fact, "that he may or may not practice (i.e. build) will not in his case make much difference; and in this, he is different from so many others."[1] Krier has now built, but today, it is just as relevant to ask whether it makes a difference. Ultimately, the exposition prods the viewer to decide whether Krier's crisp drawings and pointed polemics lose some of their power when they are realized within a real-world framework, or if, on the contrary, Krier's argument is only made stronger by the built realizations of his principles.

1. Jaquelin Robertson, "The Empire Strikes Back," *Architectural Design* 54 (July/August 1984): 18.

Patternism: Computation and Architectural Drawing

Design & Visualization

Brennan Buck

This seminar employs computational software to reexamine architectural drawing as traditionally understood: line-based representation that establishes spatial depth and tactility. The course begins by examining architectural drawing over the past forty years, particularly in relation to digital abstraction that stressed pattern rather than representation: coherent systems without physicality or character. Referencing the discourse of modern painting and sculpture, students are asked to formulate a thesis that responds to historical shifts they find between abstraction and physicality, between the flat graphic and the illusion of depth, and between distinct drawing types, such as perspectival and orthographic. After establishing a conceptual foundation, the seminar focuses on exploiting the full potential of algorithmic software and the production of large architectural drawings.

155

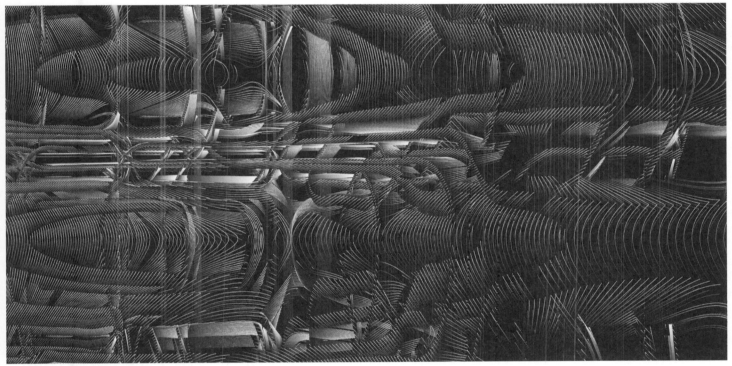

152

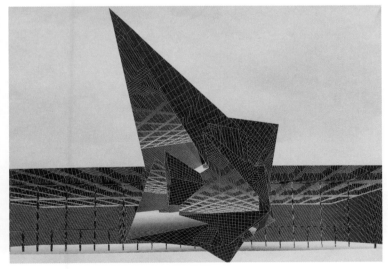

153

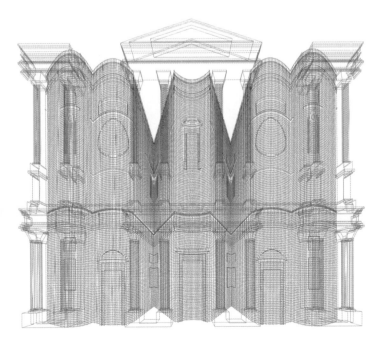

154

Ph.D. Program

In collaboration with PhD students in the Department of the History of Art at Yale, Forum allows for an exchange of inter-disciplinary topics, with invited speakers from across Yale's peer institutions. In parallel, the department hosts Dialogues, which gives current students and faculty an opportunity to share thoughts on developing work within an informal conversation format.

Forum

Should St. Paul's be in the Middle of a Roundabout? And other Planning Questions from 1940s London
David Lewis, Yale Center for British Art
The lecture will examine various approaches taken for the Royal Academy plan for rebuilding London after World War II. A number of leading architects were asked to act as city planners, and in the resulting collision of ideas about what modern architecture could be, proposals brought to light what would eventually be considered both problematic and visionary solutions from a range of designs. Among them included an incredibly prescient approach advocating a denser residential population in the city center, as opposed to encouraging residents to move to satellite suburbs. Likewise, more problematic schemes included a proposal to implement raised motorways winding their way through Piccadilly Circus. The presentation will elucidate relevant problems faced by urban architecture today, and will bring to light some surprising approaches that architects had applied to the problems consequent to the planning for the Royal Academy.

The New Brutal: Images, Mies and the Smithsons
Mark Linder, Syracuse University
What might architectural practice become if its primary means and ends were images? Imaging is a field of inquiry and possibility with fundamental challenges for architecture today. It is also a field with a history in architecture, and a clear beginning in the work and ideas of the New Brutalist architects affiliated with the Independent Group of 1950s in Britain, most famously theorized by Reyner Banham as topological 'image-making.' The New Brutal is increasingly pertinent in today's world of dense, instantaneous, superficial actualities which are as prevalent, and as necessary to grapple with, in architecture's production, reception and dissemination as in any other field.

Pilgrimage to Rhyolite: In Search of the American Ghost Town
Elihu Rubin, Yale School of Architecture
As an encounter with Western history, the ghost town is specific and generic at the same time. The characters and anecdotes change, but the story remains the same. The outlines of Rhyolite's trajectory could apply to hundreds of other places: a roguish, peripatetic prospector makes a strike. He promptly sells for a fraction of its future value and adjourns to the nearest saloon. Boomers rush to the site and file mining claims. Stock companies form to finance more intensive mining operations. A townsite company lays out a grid, divides the land, offers it for sale, and promotes the prospects of the emerging metropolis. Rival tent camps and settlements fade away. A successful mining company—the Montgomery Shoshone was the largest and most profitable in Rhyolite—establishes large-scale diggings and builds mills to process the ore. Railroad connections—Rhyolite had three—make or break the town.

The Phoenix Hall at Uji as an Architectural Audacity
Mimi Hall Yiengpruksawan, Yale University History of Art
There are few monuments in the history of Japanese timber architecture as celebrated and as studied as the Phoenix Hall in Uji, near Kyoto. Raised at the order of the statesman Fujiwara Yorimichi (992–1074), and dedicated in 1052—the year that marked the beginning of what Yorimichi and his contemporaries believed to be the Buddhist end times—the Phoenix Hall instilled wonder in those who stood before it. Unique enough in conception and construction as to prompt commentators, then and now, to liken it to a prime or a singularity, the Phoenix Hall is typically understood as encapsulating the genius of Japanese architectural and landscape design. But another way to think about the Phoenix Hall, and one that tests the limits of established exegesis, is revealed by the building itself and its siting.

Archaeologists' Palaces, Indigenous Villages, and Life at the Excavation
Zeynep Çelik, Rutgers University and New Jersey Institute of Technology

Dialogues

Breathing Architecture
Tim Altenhof,
guest Anthony Vidler
Just as fabrication and new technologies played an integral part in modern architecture, so did a new sense of the human body—namely an awareness of breathing—help to make a transition that ultimately came to privilege the essentially open form in architecture.

Alternative (Post)Modernism?: Urban Planning in Late Socialist Poland
Lidia Klein,
guest Alan Plattus
Focusing on Polish urban planning in the '70s and '80s, we will discuss how theories crucial for the postmodern turn in Western urbanism were interpreted and implemented under socialist conditions. Ideas interpreted as 'postmodern' became surprisingly useful tools for the state in its efforts to create a new image of a progressive and open socialist country. Tactics identified with the 'postmodern' such as collage or pastiche, as well as inclinations towards locality, historical allusions, and diversity were implemented using late modern indus-trialized technologies of concrete panel housing systems. Such hybrid design solutions require us to redefine notions of 'modern' and 'postmodern' and search for alternative methodologies beyond rigid polarities.

The Para-Modulor: Le Corbusier Has Never Been Modern
Skender Luarasi,
guest Anthony Vidler
In the RIBA debate on the 18th of June, 1957, proportion was voted out with 60 votes to 48. But what does it mean to vote out proportion from architecture? This presentation returns and attempts to breathe life to a well-known but seemingly 'antiquated' artifact, Le Corbusier's Le Modulor, by investigating its medium: geometry. It shifts emphasis from geom-etry as message to geometry as medium, from what this geometry is, to how it comes about.

The Promise of Pluralism: Varieties of Architectural Experience at Yale
Surry Schlabs,
guest Robert A.M. Stern
During his eighteen-year-long tenure at the Yale School of Architecture, Dean Stern has built his educational philosophy on a tradition of pedagogical pluralism, stretching back to the early 1950s and the chairmanship of George Howe. In "The Promise of Pluralism," Surry Schlabs considers this legacy in terms of William James's impassioned defense of pluralistic thinking, laid out most clearly in his seminal book on the topic, 1902's *Varieties of Religious Experience*. As an accredited school of architecture, Schlabs notes, one of our primary tasks here at Yale is the training of future architects for work in the profession. But as members of a broader intellectual community, the types of knowledge we pursue are many and varied. And the modern university, unlike the academies of old, is founded on the idea that knowledge is constructed not by appeal to authority—be that authority a person, a text, an established set of conventions, or any one esteemed faculty member—but through critical engage-ment with a multiplicity of viewpoints; that education is an active and ever-changing process of inquiry by which students aren't told what to think, but are shown how to think.

Wolf Prix

Design & Visualization
Advanced Studio

with Abigail Coover

155

156

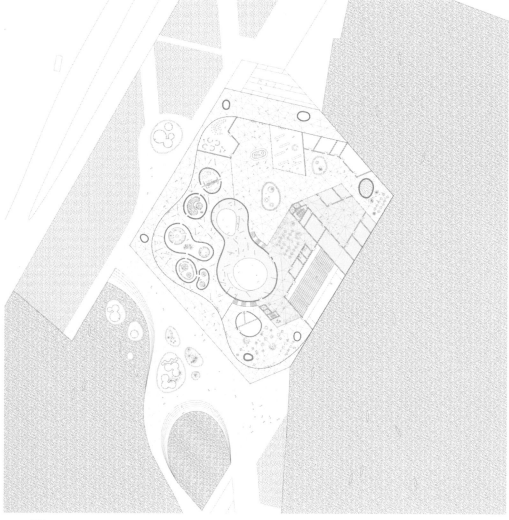

157

The theme of the work will be water: water as an upcoming important resource for mankind to survive but also water as a very dangerous power. Water is not only for drinking but also to generating energy and information about the medium of water. Around this we have to create a building which is definitively not a museum in the old sense but rather an information building. The site will be the island of Confluences in Lyon, France: a peninsula where the Rhône River and the Saône River come together. The program is to combine a large presentation space for a permanent show and seven exhibition and media spaces to show the aggregate state of water. The project does not consider itself as an exclusive temple for the intellectual bourgeoisie but as a public place providing access to the knowledge of our age.

Critics

Abigail Coover (AC), Hernán Díaz Alonso (HDA), Winka Dubbeldam (WD), Mark Foster Gage (MFG), Nathan Hume (NH), Lydia Kallipoliti (LK), Jeffrey Kipnis (JK), Greg Lynn (GL), Thom Mayne (TM), Rosalyne Shieh (RS), Peter Trummer (PT), Tom Wiscombe (TW)

Xinyi Wang 155

Water is the most political issue in the world, although the essence itself is neutral. The problem of the public comprehension of all the issues related to water is its pliable and formless character. The form of water is on various scales. It could be comprehended if only the observer is brought to different scales. The form of the pavilion follows the form of water in different scales. In the middle of the public level are embedded three apparatus of water transformation phenomena. The micro-scale scenery is hence recorded and projected to the three pavilions on top of the exhibition level. It's a water park. But as a wanderer you travel much afar.

TM: *It's very West Coast / SCI-Arc / '80s. I know you have a million ideas but you're not at the point yet where you can just coalesce them. I think it would help to have a big broad narrative to help figure out which of these ideas are essential and which are not.* GL: *I know this studio privileges the model, but I have to say that the drawings, especially the sketches, are just so great. It'd be nice if you had a modeling technique which worked like your sketches and drawings. I would say find a way to sketch the project longer, and use that intelligence further into the process. Also, the model is a little heavy-metal and serious, whereas in the sketches, there is a surrealism and history to them that the model in a certain way doesn't carry. What do you think, Wolf?* WP: *She will learn.* TW: *Yes, the hand drawings are whimsical and they just seem like you're exploding with mania. I thought at first the process would be damaging to you, but after* watching you work through some of these drawings, they are beautiful. JK: *It may not be coherent, but it's congruent in all of its elements. That makes it invulnerable to the fact that elements could be criticized or could be improved. It produces a project, meaning a projection. All the elements project something in relationship to all the other ones, which means I know how it would develop. Every drawing and every model continues to be active.*

Boris Morin-Defoy 156, 157
Developed in the context of Wolf Prix's studio, this project is an alternate proposal for his latest built work for the city of Lyon. The program challenges the accepted nature of the museum as it redefines the relationship of the architectural fabric with the subject of the exhibition. Considering the site's location at the conjuncture of the Rhône and the Saône, water becomes central to the theme of the 'exhibit.' In an effort to see art space as not a place for consumption of visual pieces, but a space for discourse and social catalyst, the main exhibition takes shape in a procession of public bath spaces. Re-embodiment and interaction are integral to the design direction. This project presents a clash of varying cultures of baths and visions of the body, creating a high contrast dialectic in architectural expression. It introduces a conversation between an aesthetic of purity, ethereality, order and minimalism and a voice that is organic, textural, warm and chaotic. The project takes shape in the act of dropping the organic elements of the baths into the normative layout which deformed and skewed the structure. This process resonates the ripples created by dropping solid objects into a body of water. TW: *It is not clear what your goal is. On the one hand the thing looks like its just been thrown onto the site and falls over the river—which I think is strong—but then you chop it to align with the street. So you do care how it's aligned. In the model it's just a flat plane if you look underneath, which I find very interesting as it just sits on the ground but in the section it connects to the ground, it merges with it. So it seems like you're torn. MG: It's the opposite of classicism, where you don't see any connection between the vertical member and the floor, and none between the vertical member and the ceiling. So it makes it really mysterious how this thing is being held up. It makes it kind of magical.*

Clarissa Luwia 158, 159
Two rivers meet in Lyon. This structure is a celebration of this confluence. An exclamation point for the previously unremarkable site, it is an icon and, consequently, an important public plaza for the city. Suggesting an edgeless, permeable shape, the form of a 'cloud' is adopted as a fitting proposition for the creation of civic place. It defines a space, yet no distinct boundary is formed

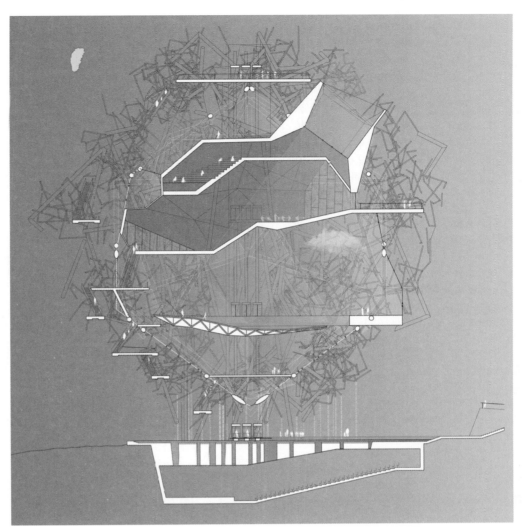

158

159

between the interior and the city. A cloud appears edgeless because it is an aggregation of particles and not a defined shape. Towards the edge of the cloud, the composition of water vapor decreases in density. This 'cloud' does the same. As water vapor is the component to a real cloud, the pipe form is the component to this building. The primary and secondary structure, the façade, the systems and any other parts belonging to the architecture adopts this form. And naturally, as a cloud precipitates, this 'cloud' rains onto the site. Water pipes pour water below— a fountain that completes the new gathering place of Lyon.

MG: *The thing that always disappointed me about the Blur Building is that it erased all architecture from the equation. This also translates the ambitions of clouds where you're fraying edges into a language of architecture that's not removing architecture completely. The strange thing is the spaces inside are so regularly architectural. I wonder if your architecture could have been an ultra-dense moment in your piping so that it wasn't so normative.* LK: *I was thinking of an image of the map of the world's internet connections. This is not one cloud. It's like the world defines the connections, aggregation, and personalization, and pathways become possible. It's really an image that defines the synapses of the brain. The project is not a cloud. It's a world [of] connections.*

161

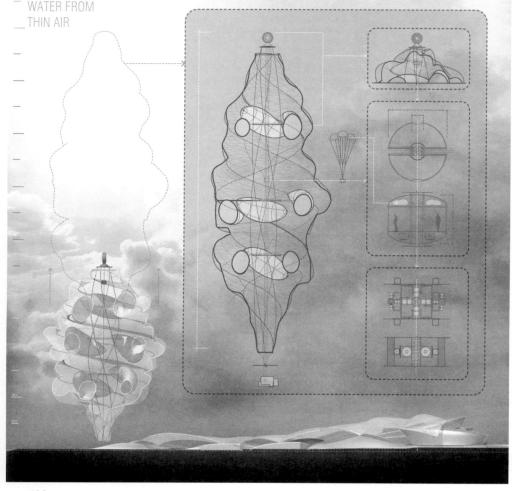

WATER FROM THIN AIR

160

Lila Jiang Chen (Feldman Nominee) 160–162

Rather than creating yet another architectural symbol to an arbitrary property of water, the project focuses on the most important issue about water—its scarcity. The Lyon Water Center is the world's foremost research and convention center. Spread across the site are exhibition pavilions encrusted into the landscape, explaining the challenges and latest efforts to mitigate them. Visitors meander through this sloping park site, in between the exhibitions and the water-collecting canopy. Culminating at the lowest point is the pavilion that delivers visitors up into the Cloud Catcher. This floating structure harvests fresh water from air humidity by using the natural temperature differential of increasing heights. Its changing altitude reflects the weather conditions suitable for water harvesting. This mobile structure could be employed around the world to target scarcity crises in our future cities.

JK: *My only recommendation is: don't use helium. Use hydrogen. And I know everyone is worried about the zeppelin but we've solved the static electricity problem. Helium is a scarce resource, we actually need it for other areas. Hydrogen is bountiful, easy to produce, [and] comes from water. So helium turns out to be a problem because we need all we can get for bombs and welding.*

162

Wolf Prix
The Himmelb(l)au Project

I could start with a short introduction about what I mean when I'm talking about architecture. I learned a term in Los Angeles a long time ago which was very astonishing for me as a Viennese. I learned the term "double decaf espresso," which is the most perverse thing you can imagine. Double espresso means a very strong espresso, but decaf takes away all the strength. So I found this is a good explanation for some architecture.

I've found out that there is architecture which is decaf architecture because it looks like architecture, it smells like architecture, but it has no strength. …So, the first part is about architecture, and what is architecture? And my answer is… Yes.

But the architect acts like a bumblebee. You know, the bumblebee is scientifically not supposed to be able to fly. But the bumblebee doesn't know. Like the architect. Architecture 2,500 years ago looked like that, now architecture looks like that, but this is not only

because of the difference of the *gestalt* but it's also that we have a lot of possibilities, technical possibilities, and I think we should use them. …This brings me to the idea that we are living in fear from someone. Are we afraid of our neighbors? Are we afraid of our cities? Why are we building medieval castles again? And why does this fear bring us to small, banal buildings? I am missing buildings [that are] very generous, bigger-than-life buildings. So how can we get back to these bigger-than-life buildings without expanding the budget too much?

This is the Himmelb(l)au meter. It expands the meter by five centimeters.

… If we are playing around with all the tools we have, it's ok. But someone has to say where the shapes and forms are coming from. And not by chance we have all this discussion about the small, energy-saving windows, the defense towers of castles. So there is a connection between the visible part of the architecture and the invisible part. I'm coming from Vienna, the city of Freud. I know what I'm talking about if I say this subconscious is influencing all our activities. If the architect is a constrained guy, only constrained architecture will come out. And now I have the feeling that we are fixed on architecture again, only architecture, talking about Vitruvius and Palladio—very bad architects. I have to say. Forgive me—it's like talking about stupid Greek architecture.

Religion and Modern Architecture

History & Theory

Karla Britton

This seminar offers a fresh theoretical reading of the history of modern architecture through the lens of realized religious buildings and sites. Intended to address how expressions of the ineffable are implemented materially and conceptually in a variety of cultural and urban contexts, the course is structured around a close comparative examination of pairs of iconic religious projects from 1921 to the present—temples, memorials, cemeteries, synagogues, monasteries, mosques, and churches. The comparisons probe issues of building type, spatial organization and circulation, material and structure, detailing and ornamentation, as well as philosophical, sociological, and cultural contexts.

Pop-up Places of Worship
Lucas Boyd, Chad Greenlee
Religious expression through architectural means has long been at the forefront of the discipline. The power that space has to both communicate and evoke has undoubtedly written it into the pages of many religious traditions' histories. At certain periods it seems that the development of a cultural architectural language has been synonymous with that of their religious identity. However, as is the case with any large scale, cultural shifts, much of the story has become muddied in the pages of history—an inevitable combination of dilution, exaggeration and misinterpretation that is undoubtedly present in all such complex cultural relationships. It is for this reason that we sought a means of reduction in order to refresh and declutter our understanding of religious architecture. In this pursuit we immediately were forced to address the largest and most profound questions pertaining the nature of architecture and its role in religious practice and identity: how does one reduce something that is inherently [an] excess? Does architecture's role in religious architecture even extend beyond symbols and cultural identifiers? If so, what is more important? This project explores the basic notions of iconicity, urbanism, and pluralism in regards to the three Abrahamic faiths through the development of corresponding 'pop-up' places of worship. The proposals act as both deliverables and as the vehicles for research. More specifically, the structures were used to interrogate the nature of the relationship between the said cultures and the spaces that they sanctify.

What does a synagogue/chapel/mosque look like? What are the critical formal pieces that help to connect a religious structure to a particular faith, and which of these elements could hypothetically be removed and still maintain its reading? While the project folds in many ideas of urbanism and our own ideas of sacred space, the icon remains the primary actor. Now, it is very important to distinguish between architectural/formal icons and liturgical/doctrinal symbolism. For example, we were much more interested in developing a sectional characteristic that represents Islam rather than simply deploying a crescent moon figure. What is the iconical synagogue/chapel/mosque type, and how is it viewed by the outside world? We found very early on that given the prominence of the global religions, the process of identifying each one architecturally certainly involves a level of comparison, or distinguishing.

Procession, Relic, and Destination—The Architecture of Memorial
Cecilia Hui, Andrew Padron
Following a relatively more traditional approach to the memorial, Yad Vashem and the Steilneset Memorial function relatively similarly in regard to the components identified for memorialization despite their difference in scale. Peter Eisenman's Holocaust memorial serves as a counterpoint to the previously mentioned projects through an active disassociation of memorialization to create a discomforting setting. These devices are employed through all the typical architectural idioms. Siting for Safdie and Zumthor's projects necessitate an extension of the procession through their relative remoteness. The places fundamentally become destinations due to their location, and procession to the space begins before it is even seen. Procession continues as visitors navigate its length and are indoctrinated to the tragedy through the placement of relics regarding the victims and the manners of persecution. Procession terminates at the destination, a space for introspective reflection on the victims and tragedy, whether it be Safdie's monumental explosion and framing of the landscape or Zumthor's isolation among the fire on the actual site of execution. These two projects are reserved as modern interpretations of traditional memorialization, and their contrast with the Memorial for the Murdered Jews of Europe show the flexibility in identifying and conveying an appropriateness for memorializing. Eisenman's project differs in nearly every facet: it is an urban site that strives on anonymity, strengthened through the disorientation of its abstraction. Safdie and Zumthor's projects rely on the visitor's interaction with relics for abstraction, while Eisenman's totally abstracts the notions of memorialization where it is

most appropriate. Eisenman's memorial does not necessarily commemorate the individual victim, but instead the scale of tragedy. The regularized grid of stelae impose an abrupt change on the city fabric, as visitors to the site experience an immediacy to the memorial opposed to the typical processional qualities associated with other memorials. The anonymity and scale of the gridded site causes visitors to become lost and through this abstraction, the scale and ordered nature of the Holocaust is conveyed. The three memorials, through both their variety in cultural and geographic context, as well as manipulation of the identified tools of memorialization, serve as case studies for developing a language of sacredness that extends beyond religion, but instead to a commonality in human remembrance.

Aniket Shahane

Design & Visualization
Second Year Studio

This fourth core studio, an introduction to the planning and architecture of cities, concerns two distinct scales of operation: that of the neighborhood and that of the residential, institutional, and commercial building types that typically constitute the neighborhood. Issues of community, group form, infrastructure, and the public realm, as well as the formation of public space, blocks, streets, and squares are emphasized. The studio is organized to follow a distinct design methodology, which begins with the study of context and precedents. It postulates that new architecture can be made as a continuation and extension of normative urban structure and building typologies.

Critics
Emily Abruzzo, (AB), Naomi Darling, (ND), Keller Easterling (KE), Rosetta Elkin (RE), Andrei Harwell (AH), Jesse LeCavalier (JL), Tim Love (TL), Bimal Mendis (BM), Alan Plattus (AP), Alexander Purves (APu), Elihu Rubin (ER), Aniket Shahane (AS), Rosalyne Shieh (RS), Jonathan Sun (JS), David Waggonner (DW)

Garrett Hardee, Michael Loya 163
The project identifies a unique opportunity to bring home Bridgeport's most famous citizens and steer the city towards an exceptional future. In January 2016, Ringling Brothers, Barnum & Bailey announced that they would be retiring all of their Asian elephant performers. By consulting with the Association of Zoos and Aquariums and the Hohenwald Elephant Sanctuary, we have capitalized on the benefits of the of the new Harding High School and designed a carefully coordinated experience that would not only stimulate these cerebral creatures but

also cultivate a new image for Bridgeport.
AP: *I think as soon as you invoke certain zoo diagrams showing scale and how they function—if you think about it, the condensation of the whole world of biology in one bounded piece of property—it is far more bizarre than taking one species that has a historical association to the city and giving them a designed environment.*

Anny Chang, Brittany Olivari 164, 165
This project anticipates the opening of the Warren High School along Seaview Avenue in the near future and capitalizes on the potential opportunities associated. Seaview Avenue contains a collection of vacant buildings that can be reused to support this new educational model and is also composed of a series of brownfields that are opportune for remediation and reuse. This design takes on the challenge of a new curriculum that is spread along the corridor and located on water-adjacent brownfields as a way of triggering new development in an effort to create a new kind of school and city altogether.
AP: *Whether the high school is just a stand in for what I would describe as a more general notion of industrial ecology, functions are related to each other along a food chain, a chain of production, or a cycle of consumption and waste. All of those sorts of things should be part of the thinking along a corridor like this. Aside from superficial ideas of having a walkway along the river it is really disappointing how little waterfront cities like New Haven or Bridgeport engage with possibilities of more serious and productive relationships. I think the high school becomes a kind of metaphor for an intention to have a larger productive narrative about water, about new industry. and along those lines it's a potentially fabulous thing. I think there is a bigger urban question about the extent to which this level of public and potentially private investment shift the centers of neighborhoods and communities.*

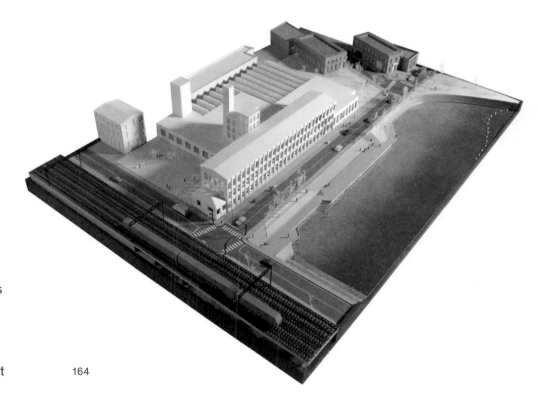

164

165

163

Shahane, Aniket

Rosalyne Shieh

Design & Visualization
Second Year Studio

This fourth core studio, an introduction to the planning and architecture of cities, concerns two distinct scales of operation: that of the neighborhood and that of the residential, institutional, and commercial building types that typically constitute the neighborhood. Issues of community, group form, infrastructure, and the public realm, as well as the formation of public space, blocks, streets, and squares are emphasized. The studio is organized to follow a distinct design methodology, which begins with the study of context and precedents. It postulates that new architecture can be made as a continuation and extension of normative urban structure and building typologies.

Critics
Kathleen Dorgan (KD), Keller Easterling (KE), Alexander Felson (AF), Deborah Gans (DG), Kian Goh (KG), Javier González-Campaña (JG), Andrei Harwell (AH), Denise Hoffman (DH), David Kooris (DK), Tim Love (TL), Bimal Mendis (BM), Alan Plattus (AP), Todd Reisz (TR), Joel Sanders (JS), Surry Schlabs (SS), Rosalyne Shieh (RS), David Waggonner (DW)

Robert Hon, Ilana Simhon 166, 167
Bridgeport is reinvented as a city for the self-driving car. A new network of blocks reorganizes an old system of houses. Cul-de-sacs, islands, squares, boulevards, and U-blocks replace the rigid grid system to open up the road space and transform it into a shared commons for the car and pedestrian. A pixelated ground plane acts as a conduit to communicate proximity, directionality, and velocity.
AP: *I think that there's more going on than you're telling us. Not really a fully achieved superblock, it is instead a reference to a superblock. It's like* SimCity*: you want to put Godzilla in here to disrupt the* Happy Land *aspect of it.* SS: *Like any good science fiction project this is less about a projective future than it is about the present. Alan's point about the fiction that the section suggests—that there is this frictionless path from mini-block to mini-block within the context of the superblock—a lament for the loss of urban community. At the same time it's couched in the technologically advantageous present where the driverless car—the pinnacle of Internet Era individualism—is heralded as the savior of community as opposed to its ultimate downfall.*

Cathryn Garcia-Menocal,
Tess McNamara 168–170
We seek to re-stage the vibrant interior life alive behind the blank façades of East Main Street. We design for current residents, levying an alternative to roll-out neoliberal urban development that seeks to attract new consumers to engineer profit. Bridgeport Inside Out identifies eight sites among the vacant lots and abandoned warehouses of East Main Street, ripe for intervention. We deploy light-weight structures on top of these lots and buildings, forming a variety of programmed spaces from an off-the-shelf kit of parts. Through specific, community-sourced programming, we harness the entrepreneurial spirit of the neighborhood to fill in the spatial and social gaps on the East Side.
DW: *Your definition of the word connected I think is too small. Your proposition is about connecting the social order of the street. Where is the landscape aspects that connects those things? How does the day connect to the night? Where does the lighting tie into the connective tissue of the street?*

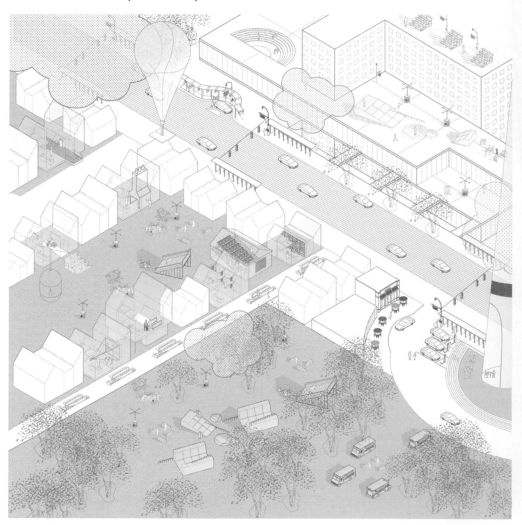

166

167

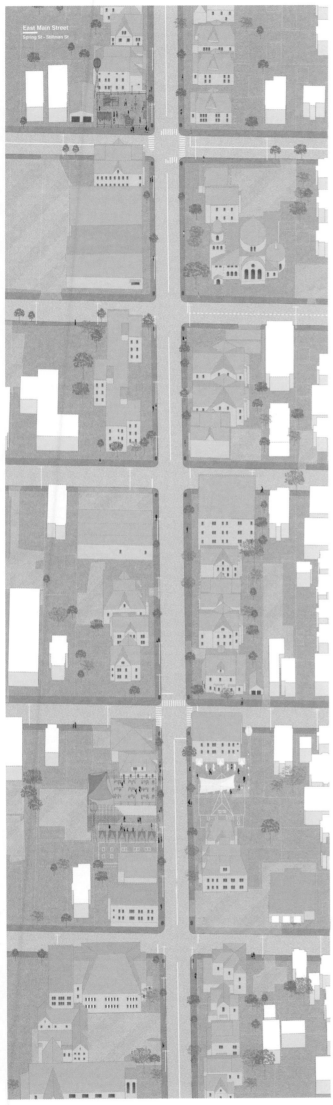

168

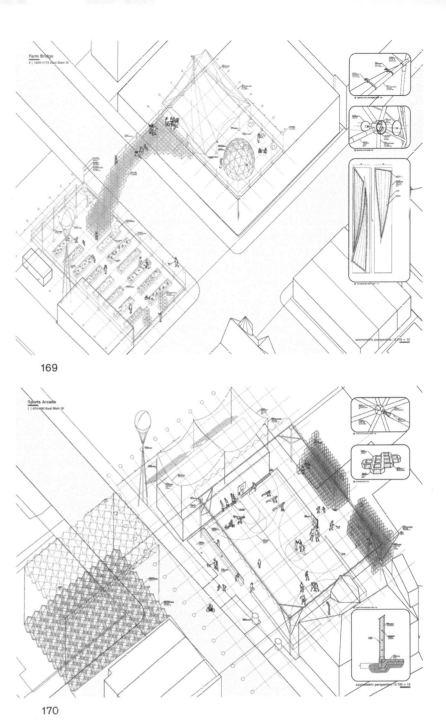

169

170

Sites + Building

Design & Visualization

Steven Harris

This seminar investigates buildings and their sites. Conceived as a vehicle for understanding the relationship between site and building through critical analysis, the course examines ancient, historic, and contemporary works of architecture and landscape architecture. Material includes works by Hadrian, Diocletian, Michelangelo, Raphael, Palladio, Durand, Schinkel, Lutyens, Asplund, Aalto, Wright, Mies, Kahn, Neutra, Saarinen, Scarpa, Bawa, Krier, Eisenman, Ando, and Gehry. The seminar focuses on site organization strategies and philosophies of site manipulation in terms of topography, urban, suburban, and rural context, ecology, typology, spectacle, and other form-giving imperatives. Methods of site plan representation are also scrutinized.

Shieh, Rosalyne

Robert A.M. Stern Interview

Questions posed by YSoA students to Dean Stern,
excerpted from *Paprika!* Fold XXIV.

YSoA students:
Your most traumatic experience with another architect?
Robert A.M. Stern:
[*bursts into laughter*] Well, there was a time when I had to peel Denise Scott Brown away from fighting with Paul Rudolph in my apartment over the subject of the way Denise and Bob Venturi had treated Rudolph's Crawford Manor. This was at a little party I gave after the opening of the Venturi show at the Whitney in 1969. It was a small show, very interesting. So that was rather traumatic. And I remember that Ulrich Franzen, the architect, came up to me at the party and said, "Bob you better go into the library, Denise is about to kill Paul Rudolph." That was pretty scary. There are probably some other moments.

YSoA:
[Would you agree] that your early work is more original?
RAMS:

I don't want to be original. I want to be good. That's what Mies van der Rohe said. I think that originality is the luxury of youth. You have to make filthy little spots to put yourself on the map. But it is often not the most important thing about architecture.

Quality of the physical thing, appropriateness of the thing in its setting, and in relationship to the activities that it houses, are things I value very much. Dada screams, "Very original but not very interesting." Is it more interesting to look at a painting by Jackson Pollock—very original, but very hard to understand, and maybe there is nothing to understand at all—or to look at a painting by his more or less contemporary Edward Hopper. There you go. They are both great artists.

YSoA:
Which has been more rewarding, practice or pedagogy?
RAMS:
I can't imagine my life of one without the other. This coming year when I will be on leave will be a heavy trauma. I will probably wake up at 4:45 am as I did this morning with no reason of getting up at 4:45 am. And I will probably run to Grand Central Station and sniff the train and then go back home. They are both rewarding. In my early days of teaching in the 1970s and early 1980s, when I was advocating what was called postmodernism but I was advocating its maturation to something that I came to call New Traditionalism, I found teaching very, very interesting, because I did win over—maybe intentionally, maybe just by the fact that they were truly interested in what I was saying—a whole group of young architects—this was when I was teaching at Columbia, although I did teach at Yale when Cesar Pelli was the dean. So that was very interesting. By the time I stopped teaching at Columbia, because I came to Yale as dean, I must say, I got a little tired of pushing the great big ball of architecture up the hill and it was always rolling down and deconstructing around me. But I take the long view. So I don't know. I love to be in an office. I love the experience of designing buildings with others. I'm not so big on going to the field. I don't stand in the field and give instructions. I'm bad at it. I have a shorter patience, as you may have noticed. A hard hat doesn't go with my look. When I want to walk through a project, especially in recent years when the Federal Government has made onsite inspection so much more subject of rules and regulations—you have to wear a hard hat, you have to wear special shoes, I can't wear my Gucci loafers—it's really a problem! But I think that if you have the pretense of being a master, you need to combine both, because the master needs to teach the young, bring them along, and the master needs to lead the people with whom she or he works as well, and show a certain mastery to build confidence. What does it mean in an office, if you're the head of the office, and nobody has any confidence in what you're saying? You're not a master. You're just the boss. I don't want to be thought of as just the boss.

YSoA:
Would you change anything about the course of your career?
RAMS:

Oh my, I don't know. I've done pretty well for myself. I don't want to sound smug. Maybe I am a little. You know. I have good days and bad days, as anybody else. But no, it's fine. I think I've been lucky.

YSoA:
How do you think that your career would have differed if you were to graduate in 2016?
RAMS:
I can't imagine at all. I suppose, I would have learned how to use a computer. My nine-year-old grandson can use a computer. My seven-year-old granddaughter can use a computer. I cannot. Now you might say, "Why can't you?" Because I didn't want to learn. I didn't want to become in its thrall, and because I do believe computing, while very useful for hundreds of things in an office or in practice, useful to make quick representations of design and intentions, in fact I think it's the worst way to go about designing: it homogenizes practice. And I could not achieve what I wanted to do by doing it on a computer. So to this day in our office, I make a little sketch, and then another, a plan, a sketch of an elevation, of a section like in the Beaux-Arts days and then we make a little clay model, and I usually don't hack at it because everybody is terrified when I lift a mat knife that I might not only kill myself but them, [*laughter*] but we model in physical terms. I think architecture is physical. It's not digital. Digital means is a way of drawing maybe at a certain point but I don't think it's about the physical. My feelings are no secret. I think everybody knows [what] I think about the computer at this point.

YSoA:
What architecture firm would you work for if you were to start your career over?
RAMS:
Well, you know I have been telling everybody that they have to get a job when they come out of school, preferably in a well-established, well-run office. Paul Rudolph said you have to get a job in an office, though not necessarily the one you thought was exactly what you wanted to do as an architect—because that would change in time anyhow—but one that had excellent habits of behavior, shall we say, high professionalism, knew how to work with clients, and deal with governmental agencies and give you agency to move a project along, so that when you finally went out on your own you would know what to do. So I would pick an office like that. The truth of the matter is I hardly ever worked for an architect. I once said to Philip Johnson when he wanted me to do something (which he got me to do), I said, "But Philip, don't you think I should go work for an architect?" He said, "What do you want

to do that for? I never worked for an architect." In some ways, what he asked me to do was incredibly beneficial and interesting, but as a consequence, in the early years of practice, I lacked a certain experience. I'm amazed how quickly I learned what I missed. And I think it can be said of my professional office, which is quite large, that it is extremely well-run and that when we make a design we know how to get the design into drawn form, work with collaborators, and actually get it built. So a drawer full of unrealized projects—you know Peter Eisenman may say that the drawing and the book are more important than the building—maybe for Peter, not for me. I like to kick the tires.

YSoA:

Would you endorse robotics in building construction?

RAMS:

I don't think endorsing them is my privilege. It is probably inevitable we will have more robotics, but they raise interesting issues. We're in a time where many people are unable to find work, because the kind of manual labor in the field and on the factory line that existed a hundred years ago is disappearing. So we have a social problem that is also an economic problem. Robotics are probably inevitable. But I have yet to see a robot that can lay a brick on another brick with an artistry of craft. So I still think hand construction is pretty nice. I get a kick out of brick walls.

YSoA:

Do you prefer drawing or writing?

RAMS:

I actually hate to write. I know that sounds like a complete "What is he saying?" Getting me to sit down to write even an e-mail is sometimes an agony. And I don't draw, like our students go to Rome and do those beautiful drawings. I would never make it through that class. Never, never, never. But I do draw well enough to communicate, and that's how I see drawing.

YSoA:

How has research and writing affected your practice as an architect?

RAMS:

Well, I tended to compartmentalize these different things. The research, say the books on New York, is an elaborate and rather expensive hobby. But of course there are times when in contemplating a design and working on a design and talking to clients or government agencies, I can call up in the conversation information that maybe many other architects don't have. So it's nice and useful. But that's not why I do it. I do it because I feel that's just a great interest. Because I enjoy it. Some architects play golf—I'd rather design the clubhouse and also write a book.

YSoA:

Why do you think architecture is important, and who do you think it serves, other than the golf players? [laughter]

RAMS:

Architecture is everything about the man-made environment. Some of it achieves the level of high art, some of it is good solid meat and potatoes, which is very important after all. You don't want to sit down to a dinner of foie gras every day in the week. Sometimes you want to have bangers and mash. So I think architecture is very important, but it is also something I want to do. It's important to me. If I were a musician it would be important to me. Maybe nobody cares to go to a concert. I'm not a concert-goer, but I think it's wonderful if you would say to me, "I'm about to go to a music school," I would say, "Wow, that's great! Good, you have to fulfill your own inner genius." I don't like your question. It's kind of a silly question. Not worthy. Architecture is an art—high and low.

YSoA:

Are you optimistic?

RAMS:

I think as an architect you have to be an optimist. You have to believe that what you're making is going to be good and that people will value it, they will appreciate it, not necessarily as great art—but that's not so bad—but as something that makes them smile, that makes them feel their lives are better, that they can do what they want to do in their lives in a better way. Those are all things architects can enable. In architecture school, and I was just as guilty of this as any student here in this school now, when I was a student I had no use for architects like me, who build all those buildings. Much later on, some Yale student complained about Cesar Pelli when he was the dean—he was a brilliant dean—they didn't approve of him because he does commercial architecture as though he was sending people to the electric chair or something. Fortunately most students need to get over this view of the world very soon.

YSoA:

What makes you hopeful for the younger generation of architects?

RAMS:

What makes you sure that I am hopeful for the younger generation? [laughs] Of course I believe there is always something new, something fresh. I think maybe I'm a little nervous. I know I'm harping on the same thing over and over again, but I think the divorce from the actual physical thing of architecture—the drawing, the model making, the building as construct rather than assembly—we fight it here at Yale, and I think so far reasonably successfully. But if you look at schools as a whole, or as the recent graduates who come out of those schools and apply for jobs in my office, they have no expression, no way to show what they have done at school except computer drawings, which I assure you look exactly like the ones you do at Yale—except if you're [in the] FAT studio or something like that. So I'm a little worried about that. Maybe you say, "He's an old guy." Well that's true, but I have a certain experience that also comes with being older. It's a concern. That's all. That's all I can say. I've said this so many times, how can I not say it again. Go ahead and ask me about something else. I like it better when we talk about my socks.

Structures II
Technology & Practice

Kyoung Sun Moon

The course introduces materials and design methods of timber, steel, and reinforced concrete. Structural behavior, ductility concepts, movement, and failure modes are emphasized. Geometric properties of structural shapes, resistances to stresses, serviceability, column analysis, stability, seismic, wind load, and lateral force resisting systems are presented.

Systems Integration
Technology & Practice

Victoria Arbitrio
Anibal Bellomio
Martin Finio
Kenneth Gibble
Rebecca Gromet
Erleen Hatfield
Robert Haughney
Kristin Hawkins
John Jacobson
Laurence Jones
Miriam Peterson
Laura Pirie
Victoria Ponce de Leon
Craig Razza
Peirce Reynoldson
Edward Stanley
Philip Steiner
Adam Trojanowski

This course is an integrated workshop and lecture series in which students develop the technical systems of preliminary design proposals from earlier studio work. The careful advancement of structural form and detail, environmental systems, and envelope design, as well as an understanding of the constructive processes from which a building emerges, are all approached systematically, as elements of design used not only to achieve technical and performance goals but also to reinforce and re-inform the conceptual origins of the work. The workshop is complemented by a series of lectures from leading structural, environmental, and envelope consultants.

Urban Design Workshop

Alan Plattus

The Yale Urban Design Workshop (YUDW) is a community design center based at the Yale University School of Architecture. Since its founding in 1992 by Alan Plattus, the YUDW has worked with communities across the state of Connecticut and around the world, providing planning and design assistance on projects ranging from comprehensive plans, economic develop-ment strategies and community visions to the design of public spaces, streetscapes and individual community facilities.

In all its work, the YUDW is committed to an inclusive, community-based process, grounded in broad citizen participation and a vision of the design process as a tool for community organizing, empowerment, and capacity-building. A typical YUDW project may include design charrettes, focus groups and town meetings, as well as more conventional means of program and project development. Workshop projects are staffed mainly by graduate-level professional students at the Yale School of Architecture supervised by faculty of the School, but often also include Yale College undergraduates, recent graduates of the School as full-time staff, faculty and students from Yale's other professional schools (including the Law School, the School of Forestry and Environmental Science, the School of Management, the School of Public Health and the School of Art), as well as outside consultants and other local professionals.

Visualization III: Fabrication and Assembly
Design & Visualization

Brennan Buck
John Eberhart

This course provides an introduction to the key relationships that exist among methods of drawing, physical materials, technologies of construction, and three-dimensional form making. The material and formal sensibilities developed in Visualization II are mined to explore drawing as a tool leading to full-scale fabrication. The gen-eration of form through both manual and digital methods is tested through materials and technologies of fabrication. Additive and subtractive processes, repetition and

mass production, and building information modeling (BIM) are introduced as tools for assembly. 'Assembly' is framed as both full-scale object and three-dimensional analog. Exercises and workshops provide students the opportunity to work physically with a wide variety of tools and materials as well as digitally with emerging computer-driven technologies.

Guillermo Castello, John Holden, David Langdon, Jack Lipson, Danielle Schwartz 171

Timon Covelli, Hunter Hughes, Robert Smith Waters, Alexandra Thompson, Samuels Zeif 172

Daniel Fetcho, Kevin Huang, Hyeree Kwak, Jeongyoon Song, Pierre Thach 173

171

172

173

Writing on Architecture

History & Theory

Carter Wiseman

The goal of this course is to train students in the principles and techniques of non-fiction writing as it applies to architecture. The course includes readings from the work of prominent architects, critics, and literary figures, as well as reviews of books and exhibitions, opinion pieces, and formal presentations of buildings and projects. Class writing includes the development of an architectural firm's mission statement, drafting proposals for design commissions, web texts, and other forms of professional communication. The main focus of the course is an extended paper on a building selected from a variety of types and historical periods, such as skyscrapers, private houses, industrial plants, gated communities, malls, institutional buildings, and athletic facilities.

Ecology and Adaptability Hold San Diego's Geisel Library Aloft
Caroline Acheatel

Pereira's willingness to leave his building unfinished and open to further modification shows at once a sense of prescience and modesty. By sacrificing the purity of his design intention to a demand for flexibility, Pereira shows his tendency to put his clients' needs first, before any own personal need for recognition. In this case, instead of detracting from the building's

distinctive design, the needs of the client and the program augmented the building's aesthetic, and proved it is possible to be both formally driven and empathetic.

As with the example of the Geisel Library, Pereira carried out the completion of his clients' briefs with grace and efficiency. Because of this, his firm was wildly prolific on the West Coast for multiple decades, yet today he is largely ignored and barely studied. There has been only one major monograph about his work to date, and one museum retrospective, put on by the Nevada Museum of Art in 2013. Overall, Pereira has been excluded from the genealogy of American architectural modernism, his designs seen by the East Coast intelligentsia as overly populist and accessible, pandering to the aesthetic impulses of the corporations who hired him.

This disdain, especially when juxtaposed with the inarguably iconic presence of many of Pereira's buildings and his awareness of site concerns, creates a complicated retrospective. Although Pereira did seek to give his clients exactly what they wanted at all costs, a probing of his legacy yields a portrait of not of a service professional, but of a judicious visionary. He was someone whose innovative approach to engineered structures, landscape design, and organic urban planning principles "convinced many clients and colleagues alike that he was a man ahead of his time." Furthermore, his dexterity and generalism was not a burden, but rather an asset, moving him beyond the realm of mere corporate architecture

to conceive both avant-garde solutions for both small infill projects and large urban planning initiatives, merging academic and public worlds. Yet perhaps ultimately it was Pereira's own "repression of a *Fountainhead* Roarkian ego"[1] and his characteristic modesty that had long term effects on his legacy. His willingness to compromise and his lack of intellectual theorizing has left him largely underappreciated. Today he wrongly is seen by most as just deft and competent, instead of an ambitious and radical artist with powerful convictions about architectural form.

1. Steele, James, and Julius Shulman. *William Pereira*. Los Angeles: Architectural Guild Press, 2002. Print.

The Wexner Center: Museum and Function
Dimitri Brand

The public, and the architecture community at large, still maintains, with defensible reason, utilitarian notions of what defines a successful building and art space. It was said by Kay Bea Jones that the Wexner Center, if it does not perform as an arts center, would be *"merely a monument to modernism which says that 'nothing is sacred.' [Only] through thoughtful answers to those questions will the Wexner Center be revealed as the emperor's new museum."*[1] The implication here being that the Wexner Center is all thought and no content, only accepted by the architectural and artistic establishment by belief in a collective lie.

In a conversation with Léon Krier in *Architectural Design*,[2] Eisenman discusses the presence (read: power of) buildings.

Unlike Krier, whose New Urbanist philosophy proselytizes imitation of historic precedents as a method for creating continual presence, Eisenman believes presence is based on cultural applicability. For Eisenman, presence is difficult to achieve for even the best buildings and is almost always short lived. The Wexner Center is certainly an indicator of a cultural moment, but it is difficult to discern what portion of its presence comes from its actual characteristics and what portion comes from the mythology surrounding it.

'But that is architecture.' Even today, Eisenman continues to mesmerize all corners with that passionate trope—so effective because it forecloses debate even as it claims to deepen discussion. —Jeffrey Kipnis[3]

It is this attitude that defends Eisenman's work from utilitarian criticisms, it is hard to criticize when the intention was never present. Eisenman and other architects with similar personal and professional mythologies are uniquely able to deflect such concerns with the power of their vision. The Wexner Center then is perhaps a cautionary tale for other institutions. The building is undoubtedly important—the internal discourse of the architectural community is stronger for its presence—but clients should be aware that with a willing patron the architect will often end up building a delightfully anti-utilitarian space.

1. Jones, Kay Bea. 1990. "The Wexner Fragments for the Visual Arts." *Journal of Architectural Education* (1984–) 43 (3). [Taylor & Francis, Ltd., Association of Collegiate Schools of Architecture, Inc.]: 34–38. doi:10.2307/1425071.
2. Eisenman, Peter, and Léon Krier. "Reconstruction Deconstruction: Peter Eisenman and Léon Krier–'My Ideology is Better Than Yours,'" *Architectural Design*, April 1990.
3. Jeffrey Kipnis. "P-Tr's Progress" in C. Davidson (ed.) *Eleven Authors in Search of a Building,* The Monacelli Press, New York, 1996.

XS: "Micro" in Japanese Architecture and Urbanism

History & Theory

Sunil Bald

This seminar focuses on recent trends in Japanese architecture and design culture over the past twenty years that developed since the bursting of the bubble economy and the architectural excess it enabled. The course looks at architectural, urban, and aesthetic concepts that embrace the diminutive. Topics include the contemporary Japanese house, micro-urbanism, return to nature movements, and concepts of both the cute and the monstrous. These are explored through a series of lenses that engage tradition, pragmatism, sustainability, gender, and nationalism. The seminar requires readings and class discussion as well as an independent research project that culminates in a presentation and a paper.

The Micro-Spaces of the New Urban Economy
Dorian Booth

The urban residue that these interventions capitalize upon, while outwardly appearing to be harmless, structures a way of life and organizes social practices at an imperceptible scale. It is precisely this imperceptibility that is the cunning of their capitalistic exploitation. These shelters, repurposed telephone booths, and bikes contribute to an ever-expanding urban mediascape that enacts a series of procedures to organize the routine and ritual experiences of everyday life in the city. The micro becomes a valuable urban commodity, contributing to an existing ideological structure through interpellation. Interpellation, in the Althusserian sense, refers to the process by which individuals ultimately become subjects as a result of ideology; one's own autonomy is undermined as they are forced to respond to the call of the Ideological State Apparatuses (media, family, educational institutions, etc.)…[1]

1. Cindy Nguyen, "Interpellation," *The Chicago School of Media Theory.* The University of Chicago, 7 Apr. 2016. https://lucian.uchicago.edu/blogs/mediatheory/keywords/interpellation/.

Metabolism and the Unit
James Kehl

Metabolism—a radical postwar Japanese architectural movement which saw the future of the city as networked mega-structures and formations of renewable dwelling units—was explored through speculative proposals, pavilions, and new housing from 1956–1973 (coinciding with Japan's 'economic miracle').[1] Although numerous professionals contributed to the movement's emergence, the Metabolist Kiyonori Kikutake initially conceived the defining proposals of their manifesto, *Metabolism 1960,* and the foundational concept of the interchangeable unit through built works such as Sky House and Tonogaya Housing.[2]

The inception of this movement coincided with, and fueled the development of global counterparts—Group Form, the Habitat, and Structuralism. Brainstormed primarily Fumihiko Maki, Moshe Safdie, and members of Team X—these architects also employed the architectural unit as a massing strategy to produce similarly aggregated urban configurations, but on a more horizontal (rather than vertical) datum. Although these less unified movements were, like Metabolism, a response to the critical need for post-war reconstruction and housing, they were ultimately concerned with the internal and external spatial configurations these aggregations could produce, and the relationships between each unit—not the aggregation's overall composition or infrastructural provision.[3]

1. Kingston, Jeff. *Japan in Transformation, 1952–2000.* New York: Longman, 2001. Print. pg 36.
2. Koolhaas, Rem, Hans Ulrich. Obrist, Kayoko Ota, and James Westcott. *Project Japan: Metabolism Talks.* Köln: Taschen, GmbH, 2011. Print. pg 128–157, 206–221, 336–370.
3. Maki, Fumihiko. *Investigations in Collective Form.* St. Louis: School of Architecture, Washington University, 1964. Print. pg 6–13.

Post-Bubble Japan and the Hubris of Humility
Apoorva Khanolkar

Educated in the '70s and '80s, this generation had front-row seats to a Japan of wild optimism and limitless possibilities. Many of their beliefs had been formulated during a period where commercialism on steroids ruled the practice of architecture, where construction entailed entire cities, dreamt up as giant, futuristic organisms capable of a full reconfiguration of the urban realm. By the time they inherited the mantle, the dream had long died, leaving the group tasked with devising their own mechanisms of survival in a newfound climate of austerity. Faced with severely limited resources, the Bow-Wow generation turned to a more straightforward and restrained mode of design. In a time where the architect was pushed to the brink of redundancy, they focused on distilling the meaning of architecture as opposed to eliminating it.

Tokyo in Manga and Anime: Between Nostalgia and Anticipation
Jingwen Li

The Neo-Tokyo is rendered in a dystopian vision of the present through a very dark atmosphere. The collective memory seems to be replaced and renewed around the techno culture, as if all traces and the trauma of the war and nuclear explosion are thoroughly erased. However as the movie progresses, anxiety and trauma turns out to be repressed and shrouded, rather than being erased and replaced.[1] The most noticeable scene in the film is the fateful cycle between the deconstruction and reconstruction of the city. The sharp contrast between glamorous Neo-Tokyo and devastated Old Tokyo is frequently seen in the movie and the bridges are endowed with important meanings, since it symbolized the interface between Tokyo's anticipated future and its repressed traumatic past.

1. Deniz Balik, "Spatial Encounters of Fantasy and Punishment in the Deadman Wonderland Anime," online *Journal of Art and Design,* Vol 3. Issue 3, 2015.

A Constructed World Symposium

J. Irwin Miller Symposium

The world is constructed. It is the product of material realities, philosophical concepts, and imaginary ideals. No part of the world remains unaffected by the cumulative impact of human activity. Through complex processes of exploration, habitation, cultivation, transportation, consumption, and surveillance, the world has become increasingly interconnected. According to ongoing scientific research, the world appears to have crossed the threshold of a new geological epoch: the Anthropocene. Scientists, geologists, and environmentalists acknowledge that humans are transforming the world at an unprecedented scale. This assertion begs the questions: How is the world constructed? What is the role of design? The symposium will explore how the contemporary world is being constructed both physically and conceptually. Leading voices from diverse fields such as architecture, anthropology, economics, geography, planning, and philosophy will address how humans are playing an increasingly decisive role in shaping the world and interrogate the implications of these actions. Using terms of construction as a framework for discussion, panels ask what it means to survey, excavate, demolish, scaffold, frame, or assemble the world. This dialogue provides the opportunity to enrich our understanding of the world and establish common terms of engagement in relation to dramatically changing conditions. As crises and opportunities transcend both municipal and national borders, the need to operate at the scale of the world has never been more urgent.

Joyce Hsiang and Bimal Mendis
The City of 7 Billion

Symposium Opening Address

Joyce Hsiang

Another approach [to defining the urban] is the statistical definition of 'urban' by the UN. The author of that report confuses and mangles definitions by municipality, region, and nation. Is it one hundred people per square kilometer? Four hundred people per square kilometer? Contiguous built area greater than 5,000 people? Greater than 2,500 people? Places with essential services? Places, in certain cases, that are something very specific, as determined by the department of town planning and housing of ministry? Every district with a municipality? Some places like the Maldives even name Malé, the capital, and say that's an urban area. So it's interesting for us to think about these.

The scale and scope of urbanization has tested, transgressed, and ultimately dissolved all traditional boundaries.

Is not every peak, plane, or recess of the earth we inhabit urban, beholden in some way to cultivation, extraction, quantification, industrialization, surveillance, and contamination?

Bimal Mendis

Consider then not a fable, but rather an allegorical painting to be precise, that imagines the urban and rural divide that might be engrained in our collective conscience or memory. Ambrogio Lorenzetti's fresco, *The Allegory of Good and Bad Government*, was painted in the Palazzo Publico in Siena in the thirteenth century.

On first impression, the divide is quite literally a wall, and there seems to be little ambiguity between where the city ends and where the countryside begins, between what is considered urban and rural. Yet on closer inspection, the city and the country are inseparable. The virtues and vices that are contained within the walls of the city spill out onto the landscape that support it, as things flow seamlessly back and forth. Under good government the landscape is fertile and productive as far as the eye can see, nourishing the city and allowing it to thrive.

But under bad government, the city and countryside are both falling into ruin, the fields unplowed and ablaze with conflict.

Surveys

Coordinating the World: Graticule, Grid, and GPS
William Rankin, Yale University
Resilient by Design: The Role of Environmental Intelligence
Kathryn Sullivan, National Oceanic and
Atmospheric Administration
The Constructed World of Economics
Aleh Tsyvinski, Yale University

A century ago, President Roosevelt… reminded us, tried to caution us, that this… profound schism between man and nature is not the right framework to operate from on this planet. Our language today illustrates how entrenched this schism has become. 'Conservation' and 'development' are now fiercely opposing words in our political vocabulary.

Kathryn Sullivan

Demolition

Designs of Destruction
Lucia Allais, Princeton University
Deterritorialization: Postmodern Ecology and the Emergence of Urbanism after 1993
Pierre Bélanger, Harvard University
Fallen Cities
Adrian Lahoud, Royal College of Art

Once we begin to integrate land and landscapes, and integrate time scales as a territory of intervention, life becomes an important aspect. How [do you] work with plant life at a species level—with hydrologic systems—and devise representational methods? We spend all of our time drawing lines. I like the fact, though, that all of our data starts with points.
Pierre Bélanger

Excavation

Cities Considered as Trace Fossil Systems
Mark Williams, University of Leicester
Excavating the Future
Mark Wigley, Columbia University
City Everywhere: Kim Kardashian and the Dark Side of the Screen
Liam Young, Architect

We have instances in the recent geological record of exceptional preservation of human artifacts. We can think about how these structures might preserve by looking at the structures that have been left after a long period of time. Think about cities as a part of the unique geological impact of humans on planet Earth. This is part of an unfolding story, unfolding over at least 2.5 million years.
Mark Williams

Peter Sloterdijk
Architecture as Spatial Immune Systems: Towards a General Theory of Topo-Immunology

Symposium Keynote Address

To begin, I would like to introduce you into the old world of monospherical idealism with the interpretation of a famous mosaic that was found in 1897 on the occasion of an excavation of a villa near Naples. It was, at that time, a real sensation. The picture shows the assembly of seven wise men—sages—but they are depicted in a way that makes clear that the difference between scientists and sages is not yet fully established. The German Hellenist kaiser interpreted the picture as a representation of the Platonic Academy, which is probably not correct. But some traces of the picture seem to support this interpretation.

First of all, these seven men meet not in the city. In the background they have created a kind of distance between urban life—they have retired from the *polis* community. They gather in a kind of grove. You see the remnants of a temple with offerings. The tree indicates the presence of a holy wood. On the clock you see that the period of time measurement has already begun, so we live in a beginning of modernity. And the real sensation is that this is one of the first visual representations of what we in modern times call as 'world picture,' because on this small table in the middle you see the classical sphere. This is not a naïve representation of the round cosmos because this roundness of the cosmos has entered into the stage of geometrical representation.

You see that by the meridian, there are latitudes, parallel lines, and so forth. Geometry has already come into existence and is used as a tool to understand what important. You must not forget that what we see here—this tiny form—is a cosmic symbol. It is not the Earth. It is the cosmos in its totality. The problem of the picture is that these men seem to be able to withdraw from their own existence—they should be contained in that fire—totality is really total. People should be part of the holy sphere, but obviously, they are not contained; they have become observers.

This is one of the first pictures that shows the arrival of Theoretical Man. You see intellectuals not belonging to their fellow people.

This theoretical distance is a presupposition to what we call constructed worlds. The riddle of construction is withdrawal, and this withdrawal leads to geometry and chronometry.

The last word is addressed to those among us who still feel that urge not to immerse into totalities. That leads me back to my introductory remarks about modernity as a farewell to monospherical construction. It is, and so the collective memory had preserved intuitive insight that the promise of totalitarian insight grows in tandem with the foment of the immersions of incorporating units. Today it is obvious that the people living in the second half of the twentieth century no longer have any regard for empire building. You see that is obviously said from a European point of view. They seem to live according to the motto: "No more grand success stories." They prefer to assemble those elements from home improvement centers, or from do-it-yourself markets, which helps them build immunity against totalitarian forms of immersion. And to them, it seems immediately evident that they must weave the fabric for their happiness in smaller, private dimensions. And from this perspective,

the building supply centers or the do-it-yourself markets, are the assurance of democracy. They house the popular support of everyday anti-totalitarianism.

And the moral of the story is obvious. Literally it would go like this: dwell in your own place, and refuse the immersion in false connectivities. Do not dwell in racial totalities. Do not engage in super-collectivizations. Choose your furniture from your own suppliers. Take responsibility for the micro-totalitarianism of your dwelling circumstances and never forget in your homes, you are the infallible perpetrators of your own bad taste.

Scaffolding

…transbordering south-north movements are beginning to expand beyond cultural practices, people, or goods to include government and NGO approaches to dealing [with] poverty, exclusion, and violence.

Clara Irazábal

Framing

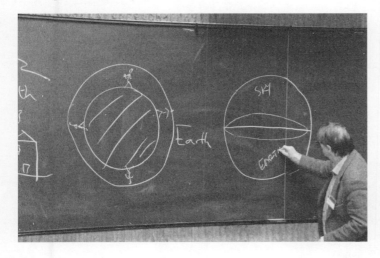

There are, then, two Earths. This is, on the one hand, the inhabited Earth, as Heidegger put it: "the earth on which man lives." The little 'e' earth. On the other hand there is the ex-habited earth, the globe as seen from space. The big 'E' Earth.

Tim Ingold

Assemblies

But unlike modern political states that may have exploded into being by the

breaching or establishment of specific symbolic centers, the constitution of violence of planetary computation platform sovereignties occurs at the surface of the entire city, in and on any object seemingly all at once. [It is] as ubiquitous and convergent as it is partial and partitional.

Benjamin Bratton

Hashim Sarkis
The World According to Architecture

Symposium Concluding Address

We cannot have an approach in architecture that is not constructionist. There is no other way. And this is my response to Sloterdijk's critique of constructionism. Architects construct new worlds and encourage new forms of inhabitation or habits in these worlds. This is not bad.

There is a welcome tension between the internal world that the architectural object represents and the world outside it.

From this constructionist approach one can also infer that these smaller worlds, through which architecture rehearses, are predicated on the fact that we inhabit these new contexts with new eyes, shaped partly by the architecture and habits of seeing. The new habits of living encourage new forms of representation as well, which in turn help in achieving another level of significance to architecture. But we have to constantly remind the world and ourselves that these habits are acquired rather than imposed, they are encouraged rather than dictated.

At one level the advent of globalization—the topic of our two-day event—brings with it attributes that seem to be scaring us: attributes such as sameness, repetition, placelessness, scalelessness, and homogeneity. The desire for wholeness and centrality may provide us with a possibility or a new language that takes us away from being scared and compelled obsessively to articulate and differentiate by architecture. These could be turned into a gold mine of qualities waiting to be explored. At another level, it is architecture that leads the way in constructing a world of new multiplicities rather than accepting inherited ones. New forms of architecture may not fully relate to forms of life that globalization has produced, but displacing them in order to make us aware of their artifice. [This] is where architecture's power lies. By virtue of its ability to work from internal to external worlds, from intention to extension, architecture maintains a certain level of operative distance rather than being drawn in fully to claim responsibilities that it may want to but cannot fulfill, no matter how urgent or global they are. But then, isn't this strategic withdrawal, this renewed negative capability, one of the more eloquent expressions of this global condition we are trying to understand? Do we really need to understand it fully?

Emily Abruzzo

Design & Visualization
Second Year Studio

This third core studio concentrates on a medium-scale institutional building, focusing on the integration of composition, site, program, mass, and form in relation to structure and methods of construction. Interior spaces are studied in detail. Large-scale models and drawings are developed to explore design issues.

Critics
Emily Abruzzo (EA), Daniel Barber (DB), Stella Betts (SB), Gerald Bodziak (GB), Carol Burns (CB), Peter de Bretteville (PdB), Martin Finio (MF), Louise Harpman (LH), Mimi Hoang (MH), Mariana Ibañez (MI), Everardo Jefferson (EJ), Tessa Kelly (TK), Gordon Kipping (GK), Amy Lelyveld (AL), Mary McLeod (MM), David Mohney (DM), Joeb Moore (JM), Joel Sanders (JS), Robert A.M. Stern (RAMS), Dimitra Tsachrelia (DT), Claire Weisz (CW), Laetitia Wolff (LW)

Paul Rasmussen 174, 175
In this building, students will dedicate a tremendous amount of energy to the pursuit of architecture. It is a structure that facilitates the worship, learning, and development of architecture. In this sense, the building is both the subject and object of adoration: architecture that worships architecture. A variety of extreme spatial conditions instill a hyper self-awareness of the body's position in space. The first floor continues the ground plane opening to an airy space housing public program with four bars rising above. Containing the studios and subsequent support spaces, each bar mediates the dynamism of individual and collective work environments.
DB: *I think these comments have really allowed me to see past the mystification that you've applied to the building, as the literal misting feels obfuscatory rather than revelatory, which is to say that I understand the project less because of the character of the images.*

Madison Sembler 176, 177
This school positions architecture as a continuum between people, ideas, and ultimately, space. By conducting the studios on one open floor plate and providing

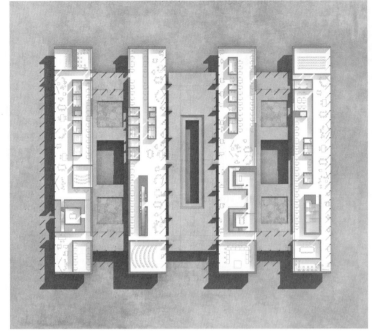

175

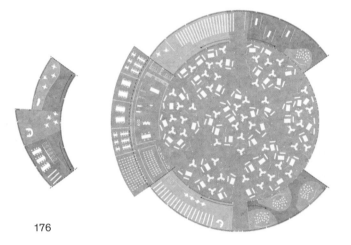

176

177

174

shared work surfaces, the school facilitates a collaborative learning and making process. A gentle ramp housing collective program encircles the studio floor, allowing for vertical displacement of people and spaces while dissolving hierarchy. The school is an infinite loop yielding a physical and social continuum.

DM: *Your central space is strong enough that it allows you to vary the external piece and not have to be bound up with it. You could start to deform it in a way.* PdB: *If you started to manipulate the perimeter more freely relative to the interior so as to connect back to the site, the perimeter begins to thicken and manifest itself into other forms that arrive at critical places.*

Matthew Zuckerman 178, 180

Michael Graves College embraces its visibility along Morris Avenue while cloistering a zone of protected retreat removed from the street. The college is conceived as a layered courtyard building in which individual studio spaces form a tightly-packed exterior and a looser stack of collective volumes wraps the interior void. Program is arranged on a gradient from individual to collective, where private studio desks give way to shared work surfaces, pin-up zones, gathering spaces and classrooms. From inside, Michael Graves College celebrates interdisciplinarity and collaboration. From outside, the college celebrates an indexical reading of individual studio production, a thick bounding wall in which every student is given representation.

DB: *The next excercise for you is to turn it inside out. The interior façades are very dynamic and are trying to express the different programs and circulation. I'm still kind of stuck on why the façade is so bland.* GK: *Or you can leave the interior and look at the exterior's solar orientation. That actually responds to the environment and gives the skin some character.*

Daniel Marty 179

Three characters walk into a bar…
Beginning as a relationship of three architectural characters, this proposal for an architectural school at Kean University creates an in-between space amongst three architectural bodies. This in-between space is a regularized field of studio space with three volumes inserted into the field. Each volume expresses a different tectonic character that relates to the program it holds: a stereotomic character holding all discrete volumes, a planar character holding pin-up spaces, and a weave character holding group work areas.

DT: *I like how you play with this stereotomy, surface, and weave as these archetypes but they also really connect with the problem. The walls for pinups seem to be working very well and your graphics are provocative. I like when you just said, "This is a view from here to there." It's not just an abstract representation.*

180

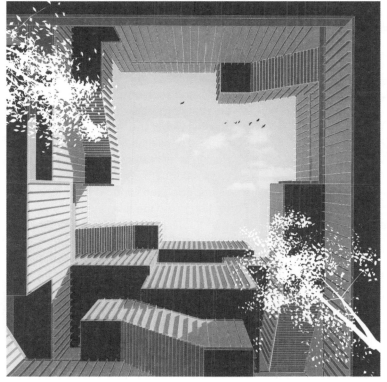

178

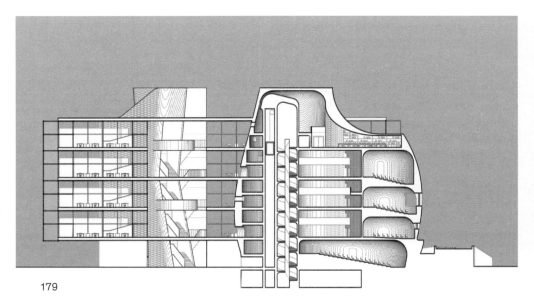

179

103
Abruzzo, Emily

Architectural Practice and Management

Technology & Practice

Phillip Bernstein with John Apicella

This course provides an understanding of the fundamentals of the structure and organization of the profession and the mechanisms and systems within which it works, as well as the organization, management, and execution of architectural projects. It explores the role and function of the architect, the legal environment, models of practice and office operations, fees and compensation, project delivery models and technology, and project management in the context of the evolution of architectural practice in the delivery of buildings.

Architectural Theory I: 1750–1968

History & Theory

Marta Caldeira

History of Western architectural theory engages the period between 1750 and 1968, through the close reading of primary texts. Topics include discussions of theories of origin and character, the picturesque, debates regarding style, historicism, and eclecticism, Gothic Revival, questions of ornament, architectural modernism, functionalism, and critiques of modernism.

Jacqueline Hall
Beginning during the Industrial Revolution, architectural theorists alongside political theorists and activists became increasingly concerned with the nature of labor and the changes to social structures catalyzed by an industrializing economy. One part of this conversation in the mid-nineteenth century addressed the relationship of laborers to architecture and city planning, and the question of whether or not architecture could cause changes in laborers' conditions or if it would be the result of changes achieved through other means. However, in these analyses, the sites of moral upheaval caused by labor conditions which are analyzed, critiqued, and prioritized (building construction and spaces of industrial production), are both predominately occupied by men. The site of labor

traditionally [occupied by] women, as well as a common need of all laborers throughout history [and] housing can be seen as the most universally relevant built form through which to debate the relationship of labor to architecture.

In John Ruskin's book, *The Stones of Venice* of 1853, [the] chapter, "The Nature of the Gothic," evaluates the value of Gothic architecture primarily by attempting to understand the quality of the experience of the laborers who built it. Although this analysis is speculative and seems to project certain religious and moral values onto historical conditions for which evidence is not clearly demonstrated, the intended message of the argument is unique. Ruskin does not analyze ornament based on ideals of beauty, nature, and harmony nor does he seek to establish rigid adherence to type. He focuses on the meaning of the act of creating architecture by a group of individuals. In defining what makes it possible to classify buildings under the title of Gothic architecture, Ruskin writes that "its elements are certain mental tendencies of the builders, legibly expressed in it; as fancifulness, love of variety, love of richness, and such others."[1] His analysis is very preoccupied with the individual laborer, his value, and the importance that he express himself in his work. Expression for Ruskin is intimately tied to the idea that humans are inherently imperfect and that these imperfections should be celebrated. Perfection in architecture suggests working conditions that strip builders of their humanity and their ability to take pleasure in their work. In the consistency, symmetry, and perfection of Greek and Roman ornament, Ruskin sees evidence of slavery, of men bent to execute the creative undertakings of others. In looking at the variety of sculpture on a cathedral front, he proclaims that "they are the signs of the life and liberty of every workman who struck the stone; a freedom of thought, and rank in scale of being, such as no laws, no charters, no charities can secure; but which it must be the first aim of all Europe at this day for regain for her children."[2]

1. John Ruskin and John D. Rosenberg, *The genius of John Ruskin: selections from his writings* (London: Allen & Unwin, 1964), 171.
2. Ruskin and Rosenburg, *The Genius of John Ruskin*, 179.

Daniel Marty
"Character's" transition to a noun begins to happen through its expression of meaning and symbolism; however, the two time periods approach symbolism in two different ways: the 18th century through signs, the 21st century through graphic logos. In 1749, Jacques-François Blondel wrote:

All the different kinds of production which belong to architecture should carry the imprint of the particular intention of each building, each should

posses a character which determines the general form and which declares the building for what it is.[1]

A building's character is explicitly understood as a relationship between a building's form and its function. Étienne-Louis Boullée and Jean-Jacques Lequeu use symbolism to clearly express the function by creating architectural objects that are instantly definable and recognizable. Creating such objects was pursued in two distinct approaches. Boullée through reduction; he reduces form to a primitive shape, arguing for clear platonic geometries due to their definability and recognizably, such as the Newton Memorial in the shape of a perfect sphere. Lequeu does this through an increase in formal complexity by imitating anthropomorphic forms and objects that are instantly recognizable. Anthony Vidler calls these "speaking monuments," due to their ability to make a "language of monuments visible to everyone."[2] For example, Lequeu's cow stable uses the shape of a cow to advertise with undeniable clarity that it is indeed a cow stable. This brash and almost cartoony version of symbolism is similar to that of billboard signage; character becomes a linguistic dialogue—albeit one way—between architectural objects and the human subjects that inhabit them.

1. Blondel, Jacques-François. *Cours d'architecture* vol. 2 (Paris: 1771–1777), 229.
2. Vidler, Anthony. "The Idea of Type: The Transformation of the Academic Ideal, 1750–1830." In *Oppositions 8*, (1977), 103.

Babel

History & Theory

Kyle Dugdale

Few buildings can claim a longer history of interdisciplinary influence than the Tower of Babel. This seminar studies the various arenas of Babel's appropriation—archaeological, art historical, theoretical, philosophical, theological, ideological, military, linguistic, and literary—with an eye to understanding the multivalence of architectural ideas as they circulate within culture. The course pays particular attention to Babel's dramatic reassertion under the conditions of modernity, as a marker both of aspiration and of doubt; it aims to speculate on the Tower's potential future.

Monuments, Image, and Identity in Post-WWII Warsaw
Cynthia Hsu
Is it by coincidence, then, that the tools and methods employed by architects run parallel with the military? In particular, the use of aerial photography for surveillance and the special attention paid to a city's

monuments of historic and cultural value are essential to both the military and to the urban planner. Architects are known to habitually shy away from social-political obligations or associations. However, in the planned annihilation of Warsaw during World War II, we observe a prime example of architecture and military occupation running not only parallel, but walking hand-in-hand in realizing a city's destruction.

The 1939 Pabst Plan was approved to replace the existing city of Warsaw in Nazi-occupied Poland and become a symbol of Germany's claim to the East. Complete with picturesque narrow streets and timber-framed houses, the *Neue deutsche Stadt Warschau* was designed to resemble a medieval German settlement, calling for the city of Warsaw to be razed to the ground, sparing only culturally significant monuments the Nazis deemed worth preserving and repurposing. The Pabst Plan may have been a perfect demonstration of the *schadenfreude* of architects and urban planners through the disruption of continuity in a city's urban development by means of erasing its existing historic and cultural heritage.

The Task Force for the Reconstruction of German Cities, led by Albert Speer, ordered a reconnaissance mission to document German territories using aerial photography. A collection of 110 negatives from the Luftwaffe's aerial survey of Warsaw in 1944 offers a valuable glimpse at a city now lost. The photos showed important districts and their historical monuments in the Polish capital, already bearing scars from battle, in their last days of existence.

The Construct of A Ruin: Aldo Rossi's Cataldo Cemetery
Aymar Mariño Maza
The concept of Babel is inherently paradoxical. At once a project under construction, perpetually unfinished, and—at the same time—a physical city or conceptual hope that has been destroyed. When God comes down and sees Babel, He doesn't tear down the walls or crumble the city. Instead, He attacks the conceptual foundation of Babel: the idea of universal understanding. In destroying Babel, the city, God makes Babel, the idea. Through its destruction, Babel becomes the purest manifestation of allusion: formally nonexistent, the idea of Babel exists as a reference to a formerly physical entity. The destruction of the constructed physical city becomes the construction of the destroyed hope for a completed construct. Babel (the concept, not the city) straddles two concepts, that of a ruin, but also that of something unearthed. Babel, as defined in this essay, is the mental construct of a ruin.

The ruin of this essay is the Cataldo Cemetery by Aldo Rossi. The project is in fact an attempt at the definition of a self-critical architecture. In becoming self-critical, Rossi's cemetery is a symbolic critique of the city, but doesn't actively critique the city. The forms Rossi constructs are references to the monuments of the city, but are not monuments themselves: the framed space is not framing the memory of a city, but the reference to that memory. It is this architecture's mimetic quality which might be its downfall.

Rossi, in framing his architecture within a context of death, assassinates it. Preemptively critiquing itself, it demands no further critique. And, seeing as this architecture's self-critique only goes as far as a Babel-like allusion, it might not be enough to give hope for a new positive after this negative. It is not surprising then that visitors find in the Cataldo cemetery such a hopeless space.

The Power of Absence
Laura Meade
Stories or ideas like the Tower of Babel suggest an entirely different category of architecture: the essentially unbuildable. Although completely autonomous from the architecture of material realization, the unbuilt is still an architecture that serves as a means to a constructed end and cultivates important criticism as a spatial construct. The unbuildable is an anticipatory architecture.

The Tower of Babel was constructed the moment humanity no longer thought it needed to respect a purpose greater than itself. The people had lost sight of their position in the cosmic hierarchy, and the moment they tried to cross the border between earth and sky, constructing a monument to their own hubris, the unbuildable concept literally came crashing to the ground. This monument still exists today and forever in its proper format: as an unbuildable work of architecture.

The forceful destruction of the tower by God was intended to produce a future for humanity. It did not mark the end of something, but rather the beginning. He destroyed this monument to human achievement in a cloud of dust that would have obscured its clarity, a physical manifestation of its absence, acting as the backdrop upon which humanity's new mission would be projected: to navigate through the rubble of its toppled ambitions. The mess would have been a space for imagination and memory of the tower to reside. After a while, there would be no need to reconstruct the tower, because the original structure would still haunt humanity through paintings and stories that keep it alive with a richness that the real structure itself might have lacked.

Construction of a monument like the Tower of Babel will never be repeated, but the idea continues to inspire utopian quests for the 'new.' It is the belief in human progress, which can never be totally achieved, but remains in anticipation. This quest will always be in the process of becoming. Time is suspended due to the perpetual state of construction and destruction, and in that purgatory between anticipation and realization exists a memory of the future—the allegory of Babel.

That Which Requires a Name
Alexander Stagge
The name of the World Trade Center can be viewed as symbolic of the project's Babelic nature. World Trade notes the aspiration of new global unity through trade; Center, on the other hand, is an admission of specific place. Its universal aspirations are cut short by its worldly constraint. A 1966 quote from Austin J. Tobin, the executive director of the Port Authority during the conception and design of the WTC, currently adorns a wall in the underground portion of the museum which now sits on the site:

> In spirit, the Trade Center is a United Nations of Commerce. In concept, the Trade Center is a marketplace for the Free World. In operation, the Trade Center will be a thriving city within a city, the dynamo of the port's trade with the world.

The aspirations of the World Trade Center project are clear in Tobin's words. Similar sentiments are echoed by Walter Gropius and Minoru Yamasaki, the two most seriously considered candidates for architect of the WTC. They both go a step further by discussing trade's ability as an agent for peace. "By its very nature trade is cosmopolitan and liberating to society," Gropius adds in his submission to the Port Authority. At the first meeting to unveil the project model, Yamasaki states his opinion on the possible power of the project to be the "physical evocation of the 'relationship between world trade and world peace,' and a 'living symbol of man's dedication to world peace.'" All of these comments build on a worldwide optimism for peace in the wake of the two world wars. In describing the Unisphere at the 1964 World's Fair, Rem Koolhaas writes, "It dramatizes the interrelation of the peoples in the world and their yearning for 'peace through understanding'…" The World Trade Center was built with the aspiration of a new Babel, as the latest iteration of "a recurrent human dream, a dream of humankind united, living together in peace and freedom."[1]

1. Robins, Anthony. *The World Trade Center.* Englewood, FL: Pineapple, 1987. Print. 10.

Sunil Bald

Design & Visualization
Advanced Studio

with Nicholas McDermott

181

This studio is an attempt to reclaim the experience of looking into the stars as a public endeavor. We examine the observatory as an object intertwined with landscape by day and as an architectural instrument that connects to the sky by night. As such, we have ceded the advantages of radio wave telescopes to the multinational institutional partnerships that operate them and embraced the technology of the enthusiast and the amateur. The 'amateur scientist' has an especially long tradition in England. Kielder Observatory, a modest structure commissioned following an international competition a decade ago, has embraced and supports this tradition. Sited in Northumberland's Kielder Forest, the observatory takes advantage of Northern Europe's largest sky plane unpolluted by light. This striking landscape is the UK's largest man-made forest and houses a provocative contemporary arts and architecture program with multiple site-specific interventions. These structures have been highly successful in drawing visitors from the curious to the obsessed to examine the sky.

Critics

Sunil Bald (SB), Anna Bokov (AB), Susannah Drake (SD), Kenneth Frampton (KF), Leslie Gill (LG), Joyce Hsiang (JH), David Lewis (DL), Michael Manfredi (MM), Nicholas McDermott (NM), Billie Tsien (BT), Anthony Vidler (AV), Michael Young (MY)

Benjamin Bourgoin 181

This project examines a crash landing as metaphor for perhaps the most violent method of unfolding. The crash site leaves shards embedded in the earth, each remnant a ghost of the whole as they trace in their arrangement the trajectory of impact and excavation leading to new inhabitation. The new program elements are distributed along the site perpendicular to the slope and accessed via a system of trenches that connect each building back up to the existing observatory.

MY: *Your project is best when it's hovering in that tension between the ancient and futuristic, which leads me to one question: Are those going to be double-hung windows? That's where it kind of becomes* Drop City. KF: *Is there a particular narrative between the buildings? I ask because I think of it as an atmospheric religious site with a narrative in the sense of what the different parts mean. In fact these images are a little scary. ...And who's that Martian?* [laughter]

Luke Anderson (Feldman Recipient) 182, 183

This project exploits the natural tendencies of an observatory: darkness and seclusion. Sited within the gridded trees of Keilder Forest, this observatory provides a quiet and discrete refuge for the amateur astronomer. Eight large rooms, each eleven meters in diameter, are clustered around a small interior court, protecting this space from the cold and wet climate. The entrance is from the northwest corner of the building and visitors descend first into an open room sunken into the slight slope of the hill. Galleries, warm rooms, and a café are accessed from this floor. In the northeast corner tower, the planetarium rests even further down into the landscape, allowing for a research space and observatory above. Allowing the interior court to slip down into the landscape below, the dormitories and resident astronomer's living quarters are raised above the landscape. There are no exterior windows flush to the outside façade; instead, light leaks into the interior between the overlap of the weathered wooden roof of the exterior and the cylindrical walls which wrap into the building. The moments of dislocation between the roof and interior wall also allow visitors

182

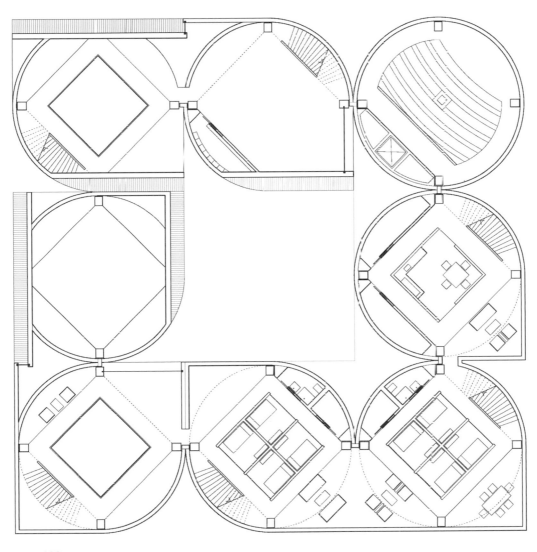

183

107
Bald, Sunil

184

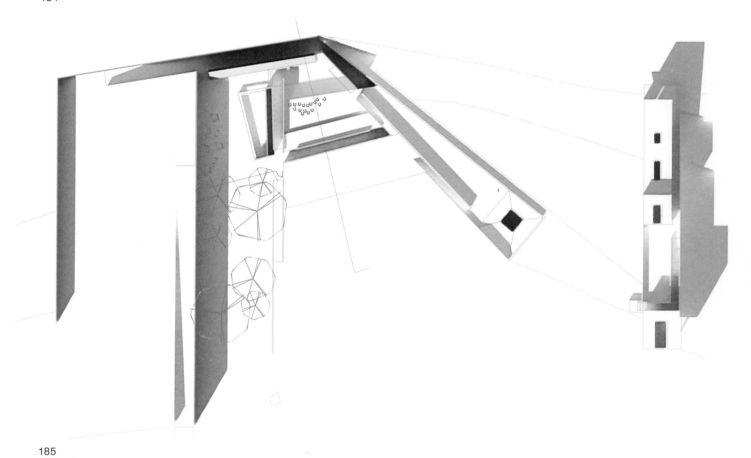

185

to move into, out of, and between the different volumes. At the peak of each roof is a skylight which allows direct light and moonlight to illuminate the upper space of the interior. The limited and controlled moments of light leaking into the interior provides the tenuous relationship between interior and exterior, light and dark, and astronomer and night sky.

BT: *It's interesting because it's kind of Kahn. I think it's also quite original, which is a hard thing to do.* KF: *I think it's very important, this dynamic between tradition and innovation in architecture which is built culture. It's not abstract art and your passage from something that's a heuristic device is alright if it produces something that can then feed an idea but not dominate it. With Kahn, what is it exactly that he is so clever at? Part of it, I think, is building tradition. There are piers, there are arches; the geometric scheme opens up to architectural elements that then transform the geometrical scheme. I think the architectonic doesn't penetrate the abstract idea to convert it into the architectonic idea.*

Elizabeth LeBlanc 184, 185

In order to clearly view the stars, our eyes need time to adjust to darkness. This design addresses three site conditions: white light, red light, and darkness. The design restricts white light to a small area and provides red light, fire light, for all areas of activity prior to observation. Where observation occurs there is only darkness. The architecture creates these three conditions to address a

fundamental part of viewing the night sky and the eye's ability to receive information.

KF: *Your drawing technique is very sophisticated. I can't resist reading it as an abstract painting. It's almost in conflict with the two-dimensional space. It's seductive in the sense that its own aesthetic takes over.* MY: *It's a little bit like a Moholy-Nagy photogram, and, maybe that makes sense if we're talking about light.*

Jingwen Li 186, 187

The proposed expansion of Kielder observatory is a disc sunken into the landscape that dissolves the building's distinctive form and objectivity. The purity of the proposal is manifested by the inherent simplicity and weightlessness of geometrical form. The disc itself incorporates distinct programs which are adjusted to the form. Inside the disc, a projected artificial sky inhabits a variety of astronomical activities. Standing underneath the disc, one reaches the highlight moment of the project where the building becomes the frame, and the horizon of the real nature dominates.

AV: *The diagram is beautiful and I love the relationship to [James] Turrell and the other observatory, but too much architecture. Too much stuff trying to get in the way of the experience of your beautiful visual. I need the architecture of nature to bring me in the dome.* MM: *That doesn't take away the responsibility of being a very focused architect.* AV: *No! No! You have to become more focused. More minimal. More intense.*

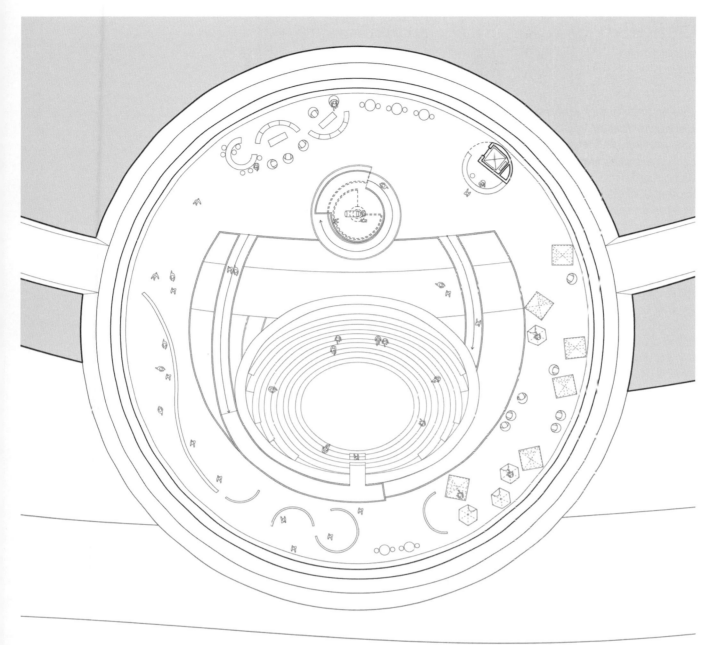

186

187

109
Bald, Sunil

Brennan Buck

Design & Visualization
First Year Studio

In an era of information architecture, where the idea of virtual space is increasingly prevalent, this studio examines and reasserts the role of physical spaces, sites and structure. Three distinct projects explore the architectural potential of alternate modes of learning in contemporary culture. The first project asks students to design a study, a volume that contains, hosts or organizes alternate modes of learning. The second project for the design of a seed vault as an exterior study shifts focus towards site as a subject of study, informing the design approach as well as the literal program for the project. The third project examines the urban public library as a type that historically functioned as a container of books, social center and monument for a neighborhood but is recast in light of questions of the role of the library in a digital age. This project asks students to reinvigorate the public library as a universal cultural institution.

Critics

Sunil Bald (SB), Annie Barrett (AB), Phillip Bernstein (PB), Brennan Buck (BB), Abigail Coover (AC), Trattie Davies (TD), Dana Getman (DG), Eugene Han (EH), Andrew Holder (AH), Joyce Hsiang (JH), Nahyun Hwang (NH), Kathleen John-Alder (KJA), Skender Luarasi (SL), Daniel Markiewicz (DM), Carrie McKnelly (CM), Shane Neufeld (SN), Ben Pell (BP), Julia Sedlock (JS), Rosalyne Shieh (RS), James Slade (JS), Michael Szivos (MS), Anthony Titus (AT)

James Coleman 188
AH: *It's sort of like a tisket, a tasket, a genius in your basket.* AT: *It's a very provocative project. What is crucial is the in-between.* AH: *I can't insist enough this is not a future utopian project; this is a nostalgic project.* JS: *I find it intriguing and ambiguous. On one hand it is fortress-like and on the other it's incredibly open on the interior.*

David Langdon 189
SB: *I really like this; there's a lot to like about it in terms of its vision. Architecturally speaking, the way it expresses itself on the landscape is a bit of a mess. It seems like you are collaging incidents rather than something that might be more singular.* SL: *There is a project in itself there in the shape of the outline and how the outline produces these weird but controlled spaces.*

Christian Golden 190
JS: *I think what's interesting is the ambiguity between figure and ground and how you're bringing the architecture into the landscape. There could be a way to push the program further—to have it rub up against the landscape.* SB: *It's great the way you characterize these artificial landscapes and took them on as a way of extending this*

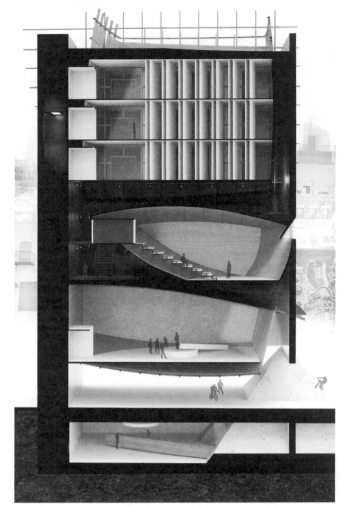

188

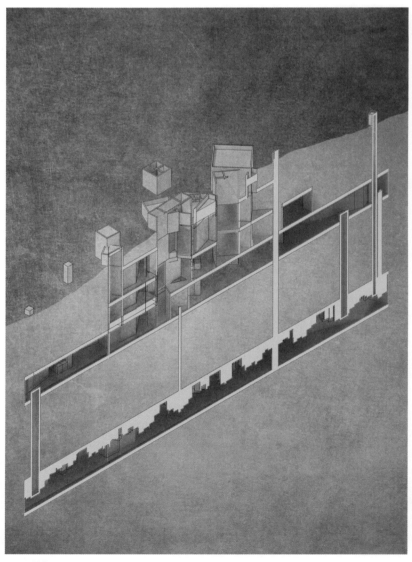

189

191

artificial collection of possibilities—but tectonically there is an issue of determining what is a wall and what is a bar.
Danielle Schwartz 191
AB: *Your project is formally complex and interesting but I take issue with the idea that there is something good about disorientation. I challenge the notion that some spaces are regular and some spaces are irregular. I think every space is f—ing crazy.*

Built Environments and the Politics of Place

Urbanism & Landscape

Dolores Hayden

Call it the built environment, the vernacular, everyday architecture, or the cultural landscape—the material world of built and natural places is intricately bound up with social and political life. This research seminar explores research methods and sources for writing the history of the built environment, such as maps, aerial and ground photographs, planning documents, landscape analysis, and GIS. The course includes readings from history, geography, anthropology, and architecture as well as readings on narrative and graphic strategies for representing spaces and places.

Elaina Berkowitz
St. Petersburg, Florida has a history of capitalizing on its ideal climate to define its identity. During its early growth, much of that identity was created by its vibrant pedestrian culture, which was epitomized with its unique and famous green benches. The benches were placed in the downtown commercial district, where they lined wide sidewalks, adjacent to parking spaces. At the height of their influence, green benches would be packed with tourists and residents alike; they were informal spaces for meeting, gossiping, making business deals, or just sitting in the Florida sunshine. While the green benches epitomized an active and unique social culture for one group of people, they became a symbol of exclusion for a group that was stigmatized at the time—the African American population. This social group was actively banned from participating in the downtown culture of white St. Petersburg citizens. However, the African American community in St. Petersburg found strength by developing their own unique social culture.

Why Does the Mosque Look Like a Church? The Confused Space, Rigid Structure, and Continuous Ritual of the Military Training City
Gregory Cartelli
The production of military training cities is an extensive but overlooked field that operates parallel to that of contemporary urban planning, architecture, and design. These constructions borrow techniques from landscape planning, community development, and vernacular architecture to create representations of alternative realities and possible futures that exist alongside our own, in a different sector. They are condensations of the operational aspects of the global urban into navigable, enclavic spaces that act as models of potentialities more than duplications of realities.

Farming Katrina: Crisis-Motivated Change in the New Orleans Food System
Tess McNamara
Across New Orleans, and particularly in the neighborhoods of Village de L'Est and Hollygrove, communities responded to issues of food access after Katrina by farming the land that was flooded from beneath their feet. The community-led urban farm movement is a physical manifestation of residents' desire to take matters of survival into their own hands in the face of institutional impotence shown by all levels of government. The informal food systems that were farmed from Katrina, backed by new tightly knit community groups, will prove resilient in the face of the next environmental, political or economic disaster.

Madison Sembler
The successes and failures of the Yale School of Architecture First Year Building Project can be traced through issues of economic and social class divide between Yale architecture students and the participating communities. The divide between pedagogical agenda and community needs became particularly evident in the housing series after 1989, shifting from public buildings to private dwelling structures in New Haven. The initial intent of the Building Project, a socially engaged construction, has steered off-track with the relentless construction of an affordable house each year regardless of the market economy and the deterioration of former BP houses left vacant in neglected neighborhoods. This paper claims that the continual addition of houses to the working class neighborhoods of New Haven prove Building Project's agenda privileges willful designs prompting the advancement of an architecture rather than a people.

Sara Caples and Everardo Jefferson

Design & Visualization
Advanced Studio

with Jonathan Rose

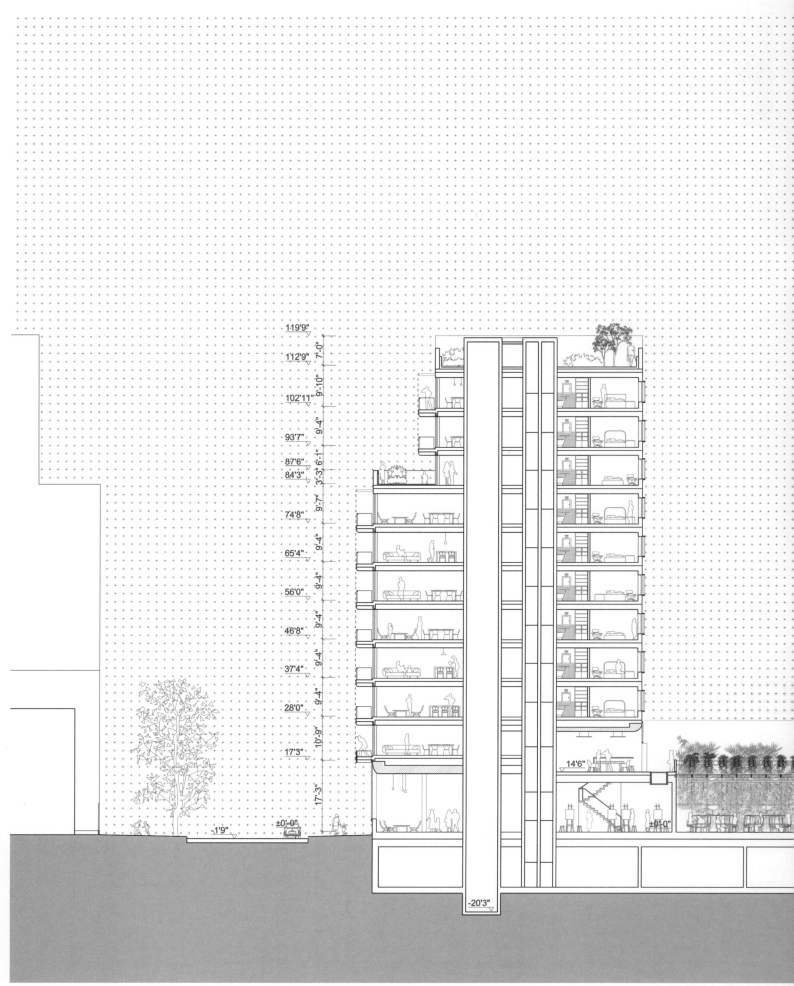

192

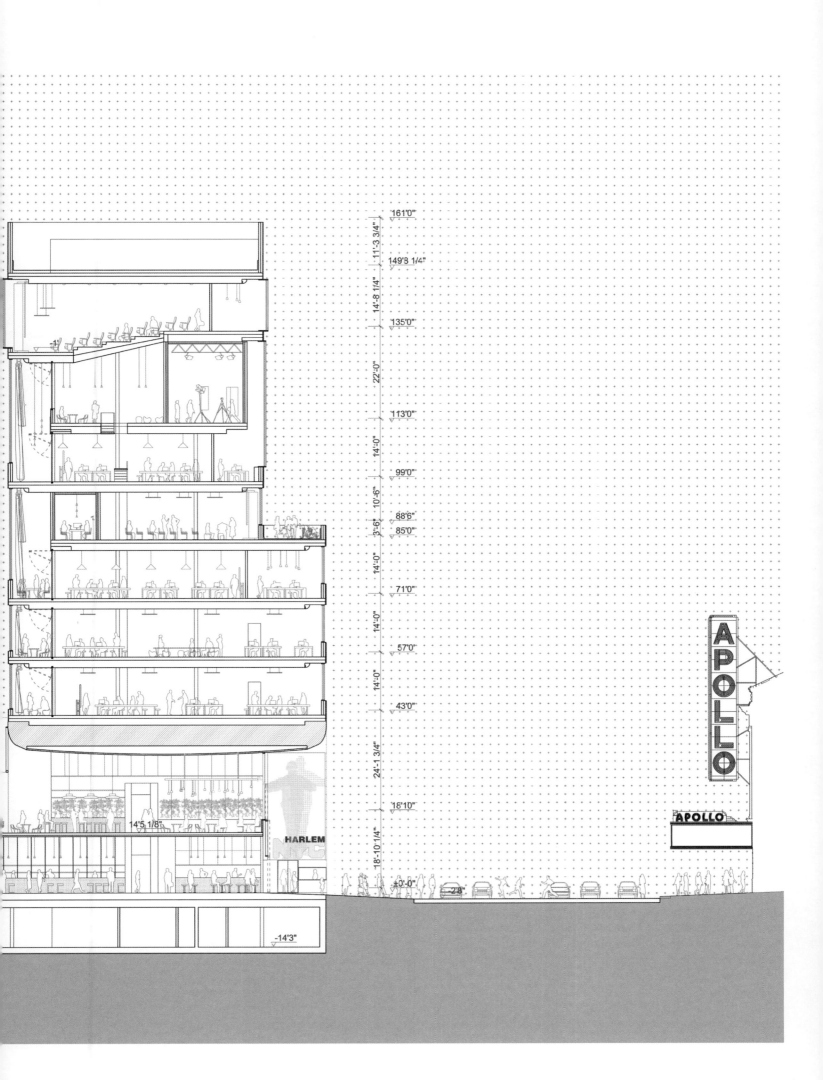

161'0"

11'-3 3/4"

149'8 1/4"

14'-8 1/4"

135'0"

22'-0"

113'0"

14'-0"

99'0"

10'-6"

88'6"

3'-6"

85'0"

14'-0"

71'0"

14'-0"

57'0"

14'-0"

43'0"

24'-1 3/4"

14'5 1/8"

16'10"

18'-10 1/4"

HARLEM
NYC

±0'-0"

-2'8"

-14'3"

APOLLO

APOLLO

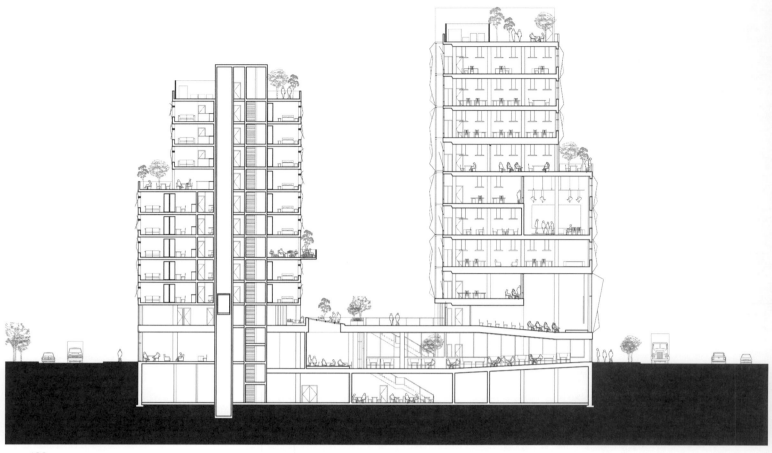

193

The studio questions issues of cultural representation versus the mutability of the site's ethnic anchorings. It requires the designer to consider each space from the user's perspective. And it demands high standards of sustainable design, headed towards net zero, that support a more satisfying occupant experience, with maximal use of controlled daylight and natural ventilation. Because innovation often comes from digging into areas that others perform perfunctorily, each project will be required to demonstrate deeper consideration in the following areas. Programming: going beyond defining spatial sizes and arrangements. Building construction: involving all major building systems and detailed sustainable envelope construction. Cultural issues: their possible impact on the physical construction, and upon the visitors' perception of the resulting fabric. Buildings: urban markers of history and culture, as creators of unique place within the city.

Critics

Sara Caples (SC), Vincent Chang (VC), Dale Cohen (DC), Alexander Garvin (AG), Lisa Gray (LG), Julie Iovine (JI), Everardo Jefferson (EJ), Kenneth Knuckles (KK), Steven Lewis (SL), Alan Organschi (AO), Terence Riley (TR), Verdery Roosevelt (VR), Jonathan Rose (JR), Madlen Simon (MS), Robert A.M. Stern (RAMS)

Xinyi Wang (Feldman Nominee) 192

TR: *Your building becomes the foyer for the Apollo Theatre and it proves the need to push back on some of these regulations.*
JR: *If I were to pick a project to fight for, I would fight for this one.*

Jeannette Penniman 193, 194

Both sides of the site are designed around spaces meant to promote socialization and cross-pollination of ideas: communal living rooms and a generous fitness center in the affordable housing, and a series of shared meeting and production spaces on the cultural side. The public sequence pulls individuals—whether residents, commercial tenants, or the general public—through the public layer and into a central elevated courtyard, using daylighting and a strong organizing diagonal. This central courtyard, along with the smaller communal spaces on both sides, is meant to foster social interactions between otherwise distinct groups, capitalizing on the striking demographic change playing out in Central Harlem.

MS: *This building is creating new ground. All of the waviness in plan and section is perhaps integrating these two levels together and also [making this a] real landscape that you're entering into.*

Katherine Stege 195, 196

Half affordable housing and half a digital arts mixed-use community building, Harlem MART 125 is a through-block urban infill project that deals both with the strict programmatic, economic, and urban demands of the developer, and the nuanced cultural context of contemporary Harlem. This proposal for the new Mart 125 interprets the building's role as a network of cultural production and display. This network ranges from the urban to the individual scale, and solidifies around ideas of identity, layers of control, and programmatic performance. Using specific formal and material choices related to the nature of the site, solar exposure, and climate, the two sides of the building create an inward-focused versus outward-facing scheme, woven together through a transitional middle. Varied, diverse spaces, especially at the urban level, are flexible to allow for continuous occupation with distinct visual and physical connections to one another.

VC: *I'm thrilled! I think it's a beautiful project. The coherence here, the narrative is exquisite. My sense is the diagram looks almost like a sequencing of DNA. When you then look at the individual strands and programs and allow them to infect one another, there's even more joy to be had in that.*

James Kehl 197

This design negotiates and engages with the unique characters of 125th and 124th Streets through 'urban layers' at the building's street-wall and ground level. These layers are programmed on 125th as collaborative office-areas, made divisible by curtains that can be digitally projected on. Media content generated by artists or the building's tenants illuminate the north façade at night, contributing to the street's vibrant public life. In contrast, the south side becomes a vertical garden—a layer of sunrooms covered with planting—creating an oasis and porch space in an otherwise dead street. These vertical layers are connected through a specially programmed, continuous ground level.

VC: *The plans are beautifully resolved on the commercial building, reductive and exquisite.*

194

197

195

196

Caples Jefferson
This Particular Time and Place

We have a lot of people and a lot of firms right now who want to do public and community work. They try very hard to do beautiful buildings. I think one of the things that helped us, especially in the young part of our careers, [was that] Everardo and I were very often working in conditions of adversity. People were not necessarily taking us very seriously. In a way, that was great preparation for public work. Very often the conditions for both public and private work will have horrible contractors and horrible disputes and incompetent this and failed that. That's the condition that a lot of this work has to be done under, and if you don't have this crazy persistence and the ability to spring back against these forces of resistance, you cannot build the work that you intend. In a funny

way, that was a great preparation to make it possible.

I think that is one of the things that is very interesting about the rising generation now is that there is much more of an interest in entrepreneurial contact. Young architects are much more proactive in that sense and much less afraid in a way of accepting whatever is there as a given. So there is a boldness that maybe we didn't have. Typically people would find us or we would find somebody. I hope you understand that it is very important for our work to find clients who have commitment to this crazy long process. They might not be trained artistically. Some of them are very sophisticated and some of them are not. But they have a determination to build something extraordinary for their place. That commitment is very important to us, and sometimes

those people find us. [For] a lot of this public work, we compete. For the Louis Armstrong museum there were forty-four other firms that wanted this project. It's very competitive. But when you get it, what you make of it is also very challenging.

Case Studies in Architectural Criticism

History & Theory

Carter Wiseman

This seminar concentrates on issues that influence the way modern buildings and their architects are perceived by critics, scholars, and the public. The careers of architects such as Frank Lloyd Wright, Eero Saarinen, Louis Kahn, Philip Johnson, Robert Venturi, and Frank Gehry provide a framework for the examination of how patronage, fashion, social change, theory, finance, and politics affect the place of prominent designers and their work in the historical record.

A Critique of Silliman College
David Langdon

Working in an era long before Venturi and Moore made pastiche eclecticism the hot new thing, the architects of Silliman College freely took from the grab bag of historical quotations with reckless abandon. Over the monumental College Street entrance, whose pointed arch is presumably of collegiate gothic pedigree, stand the abruptly truncated bartizans of a medieval fortress formerly known as Vanderbilt Hall. Jarring casement windows are clumsily scattered across the surrounding façade, thwarting any possibility of authenticity or convincing historicism. This bizarre gatehouse is sandwiched on either side by buildings obviously not original to the college, which would not in itself be a bad thing were it not for the shoddy effort at visual transition and harmony made (and not made) by the architects. Around the corner on Grove Street, where the Old Yale dormitories begin in full, the progression from Gothic to stylized Neoclassical to dressed-down New England vernacular reaches the apex of its discomfort.

The odd assemblage of volumes, styles, and themes that surround the courtyard never really achieve meaningful integration beyond a superficially unifying theme of excess and faux monumentality. But even at a smaller scale, at the level of the discrete building units themselves, Silliman lacks the attentive detailing and character that is more typical of the New Haven streetscape. The bland limestone of Vanderbilt Hall forgoes texture, rustication, ornament, or any other kind of attentive architectural caress that might have prevented it from dissolving into a dreary monolith. The Georgian section along Grove Street has the pretentious look of a French Château, porte-cochère and all, only with clumsier massing and none of the intimate alcoves and nooks that one

might enjoy in an original. Statuary niches go unoccupied, as if the building had been thrown up in a rush with the intent to add finishing touches at an unknown later date. If Silliman has a finest moment, it would be the large cutaway on the back façade that allows it to visually appropriate Timothy Dwight's bell tower and subsume a better work of architecture wholesale into its folds.

Rudolph Hall: A Building I Dislike
Andrew Sternad

Our building is made for training architects, and it succeeds in teaching us what not to do. Fortress-like, the building elicits curiosity from passersby, but few are brave enough to pass the gauntlet of its entryway. It is glaringly different in scale, orientation, and material from its immediate context, and is a sorry contributor to the energetic street life of York and Chapel Streets. Students are sequestered in the building, perpetuating stereotypes that architects are egoistic navel gazers who can't relate to the city or the public they ostensibly serve. To add insult to injury, the building will injure anyone who accidentally brush against its sharp, bush-hammered walls. The building literally bites.

Rudolph Hall: A Building I Like
Andrew Sternad

Our building is made for training architects, and it is a good teacher. It literally trains: dimensions and artifacts embedded in the concrete are a constant reference point. And it subtly trains: spaces are inwardly focused, but always maintain an awareness of the city outside. Continuous studio spaces flow from floor to floor, providing novel vantage points and new perspectives on the work being produced within. I find ways to constantly rediscover the building and make it my own. Every surface and nook in the building seems well intentioned for some specific use. Nothing is guarded or off-limits, and it is easy to step away for a break to refresh. This openness inspires a spirit of camaraderie and sharing ideas in the building—a sensation directly resultant from the design of space. I especially like the many outdoor terraces, most of all the roof. The Parthenon derives its power from an innate human desire to be elevated toward the heavens, closer to sky than to earth. We can get a hint of that feeling from a good rooftop terrace.

Composition

Design & Visualization

Peter de Bretteville

This seminar addresses issues of architectural composition and form. Leaving aside demands of program and site in order to concentrate on formal relationships at multiple scales, these exercises are intended to

establish proficiency with "the language of architecture" as well encourage confidence in personal, formal proclivities.

198

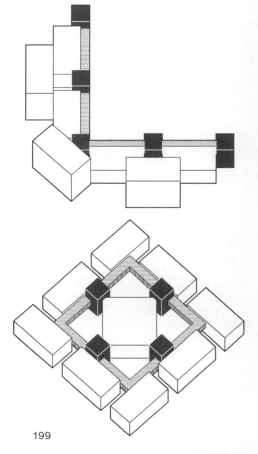

199

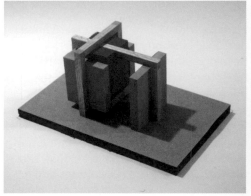

200

201

Computation
Analysis
Fabrication

Design & Visualization

John Eberhart
and Amir Shahrokhi

This course investigates and applies
emerging computational theories and
technologies through the design and
fabrication of a full-scale building component and/or assembly. This investigation
includes various static, parametric,
and scripted modeling paradigms,
computational-based structural and
sustainability analysis, and digital fabrication technologies.

Pauline Caubel, Aymar Mariño Maza 202
Gina Cannistra, Andreas De Camps,
Jennifer Fontenot 203
Patrick Kondziola, Jeremy Leonard,
Shreya Shah 204
Gina Cannistra, Richard Green 205

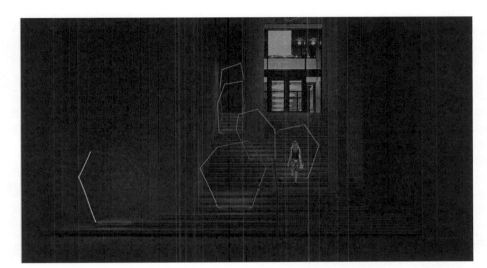

203

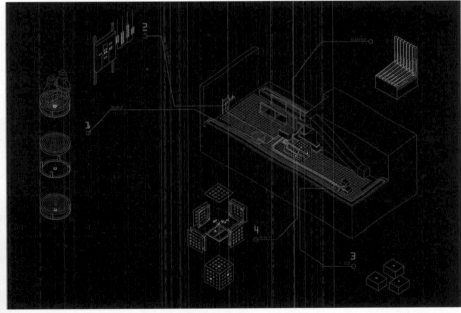

204

202

205

Custom Crafted Components

Design & Visualization

Kevin Rotheroe

This seminar requires individual aesthetic expression through the crafting of tangible, original, intimately scaled architectural elements. Exploration and experimentation with unusual combinations and sequences of analog and digital representation are encouraged by way of challenging pre-conception and expanding the spectrum of aesthetic expression. Selected iterations are developed into designs for specific building components and contexts. Relationships among creative liberty, craft, and manufacturing are explored through prototyping custom components using materials, means, and methods that are reasonable in contemporary professional practice.

Jason Kurzweil 206
Graham Brindle 207
Ilana Simhon 208
Robert Yoos 209

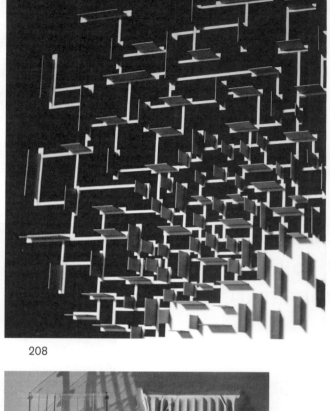

208

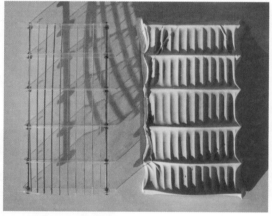

209

206

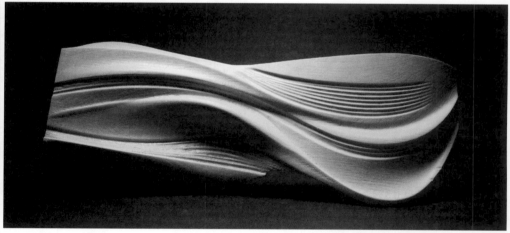

207

Elizabeth Danze Lecture
Space and Psyche

David W. Roth and Robert H. Symonds Memorial Lecture

Psychoanalysts in large part strive for the same thing, working on a one-on-one scale with patients to foster self-reflection to create freer, happier, healthier restorative relationships. One common aspect with each of these is self-reflection. Psychoanalysts promote mindfulness in their patients while architects enhance awareness of the self in the physical world.

Buildings are, in fact, inert objects, but our experience of them transcends the physical realm and extends into our deepest consciousness. Our psychic reality is defined as the subjective experience that results from the interplay and integration of sensory perceptions of an objective, incompletely knowable external or material reality.

Architecture works with the tangible, the physical, the factual, but it has the potential to address the intangible. Architecture, in particular, which moves beyond mere building, strives to enhance the human condition and promote emotional well-being through the manipulation of space, light, material, and form.

Trattie Davies

Design & Visualization
First Year Studio

In an era of information architecture, where the idea of virtual space is increasingly prevalent, this studio examines and reasserts the role of physical spaces, sites and structure. Three distinct projects explore the architectural potential of alternate modes of learning in contemporary culture. The first project asks students to design a study, a volume that contains, hosts or organizes alternate modes of learning. The second project for the design of a seed vault as an exterior study shifts focus towards site as a subject of study, informing the design approach as well as the literal program for the project. The third project examines the urban public library as a type that historically functioned as a container of books, social center and monument for a neighborhood but is recast in light of questions of the role of the library in a digital age. This project asks students to reinvigorate the public library as a universal cultural institution.

211

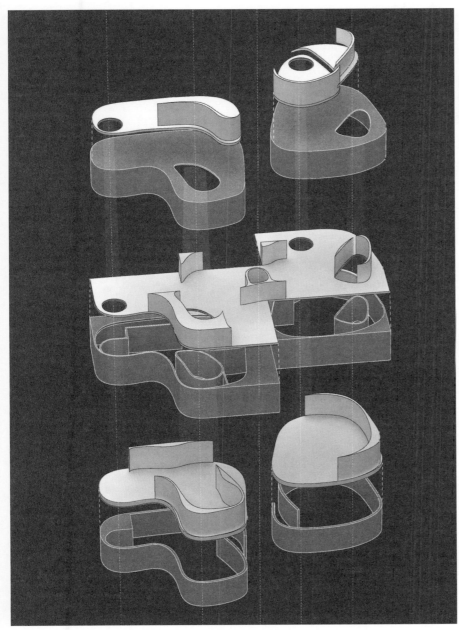

210

Critics
Anna Bokov (AB), Julian Bonder (JB), Miroslava Brooks (MB), Brennan Buck (BB), Marta Caldeira (MC), Trattie Davies (TD), Rosetta Elkin (RE), Dana Getman (DG), Lizzie Hodges (LH), Joyce Hsiang (JH), Max Kuo (MK), James Lowder (JL), Nicholas McDermott (NM), Kyle Miller (KM), Alan Organschi (AO), Alexander Purves (AP), Rosalyne Shieh (RS), Robert A.M. Stern (RAMS), Michael Szivos (MS), Irina Verona (IV), Elia Zenghelis (EZ)

Margaret Marsh 210

AP: *You might be too fixated on the plan manipulation and not the section, because all of the vitality that is suggested by the plan is lost in the section, which is a sandwich. The promise of the building is really something quite extraordinary, but instead we have these pancake moments.*

Ron Ostezan 211

MK: *It's such a weird project; it's one of the most didactic projects that I've seen lately, and yet you present it in this extremely benign language. It's like a slight of hand: you're talking about it but your left hand is doing a completely different thing. It feels to me somehow punitive, to separate and make all of these very strong divisions.*

Ziyue Liu 213

EZ: *You are a very talented person, but you give yourself too many liberties. There's more to me than just spaces; if you don't want it to only be a library, you should think of the content. The whole formal composition looks like a slice out of a cake. You do things very well and beautifully, but it's not enough.*

Guillermo Castello 212

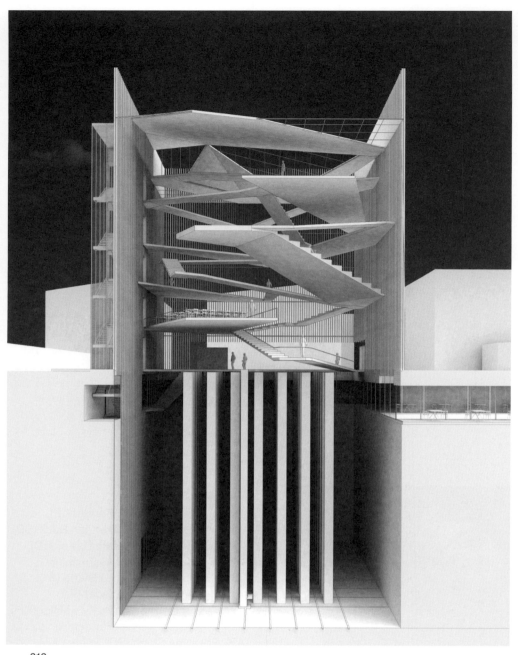

212

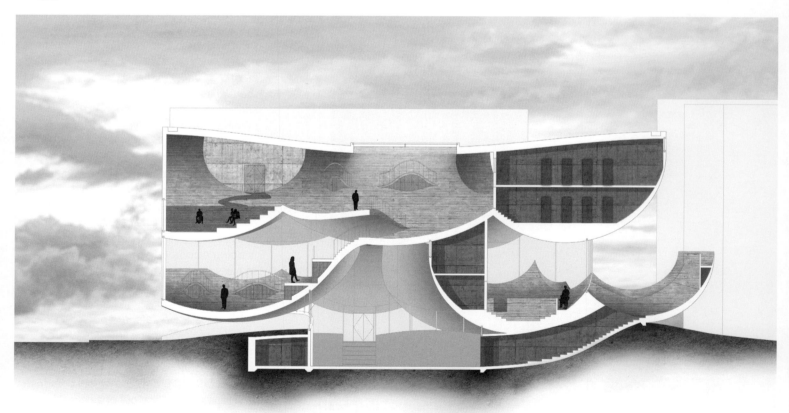

213

Fall
Davies, Trattie

Peter de Bretteville

Design & Visualization
Second Year Studio

This third core studio concentrates on a medium-scale institutional building, focusing on the integration of composition, site, program, mass, and form in relation to structure, and methods of construction. Interior spaces are studied in detail. Large-scale models and drawings are developed to explore design issues.

Critics
Emily Abruzzo (EA), Gerald Bodziak (GB), Carol Burns (CB), Peter de Bretteville (PdB), Martin Finio (MF), Louise Harpman (LH), Mimi Hoang (MH), Everardo Jefferson (EJ), Tessa Kelly (TK), Amy Lelyveld (AL), Mary McLeod (MM), David Mohney (DM), Joeb Moore (JM), Joel Sanders (JS), Robert A.M. Stern (RAMS), Dimitra Tsachrelia (DT), Claire Weisz (CW)

Rachel Gamble 214
This proposal is inspired by the tripartite diagram of the classical basilica—a central gathering space flanked by smaller, more personal aisles. The smooth, continuous grain running through the studio and office bar is interrupted, and the gap between student and professor thus bridged. These congregation points break up the slower speeds of the bars, following the logic of rocks in a river, and provide flexible rooms which the students and professors can activate collectively.
JM: *What's lovely is that you have a generic and highly pragmatic set of rules, generating what could be complex adjacencies and programmatic relationships. It's a really powerful idea.* CB: *Your way of thinking is structured, with variation, and makes a compact volume. That to me has a lot of credibility as a straightforward architectural proposition.*

Elaina Berkowitz 215
Instead of dividing studios into 'architecture' or 'design' students only, the plan is arranged around three pedagogical centers—the auditorium, the library, and the shop. These 'centers' are bracketed by two bars—one carries the studios, and the other carries the exhibition halls, which face Morris Avenue, acting as a public face to the university. The three centers allow students to focus on specific discourses within design.
AL: *It's so even-handed. It's almost too even-handed: everything has a place. In a school though, you need a place for things that don't have a place. A place where you are productive away from your desk, where you're not productive away from your desk. What happens in the interstitial spaces?*

Chad Greenlee 216, 217
This project sets out to simultaneously investigate two seemingly opposite 'camps' within architecture: the compositional and its arrangement of parts versus the systemic and its rigid ordering principles. Each grouping of program is assigned an individual system, long span, short span, field condition, and the last system functions as a shear wall. The project plays out to be a composition of systems, constantly re-proportioning and studying the intersections and junctions of the systems.
LH: *I see the logic of the plan very clearly, but what a perfect opportunity! Give me a plinth, give me a space, give me something else as you reinvent the parking!*

Wilson Carroll 218, 219
The Michael Graves College hosts both the School of Design and the School of Public Architecture. The dual nature of these programs shape the simple rectangular form that divides the site in two—the private park from the public parking. While the curves are only experienced in part from the interior, the fullness of the form is finally observed from the garden, described best by Melville in his poem "Art," "unlike things must meet and mate."
EJ: *What does that billboard say, what does it mean?* Wilson: *It means that the students and what they're doing has more value and purpose than people driving by would give them credit for.* MM: *That's weird.* [laughter]

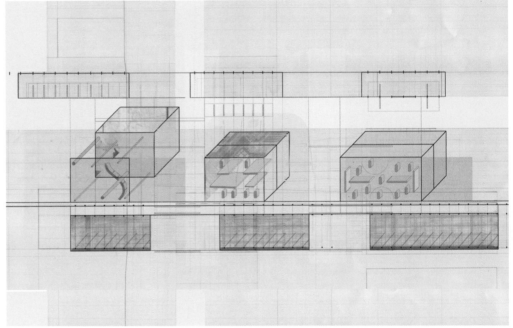

215

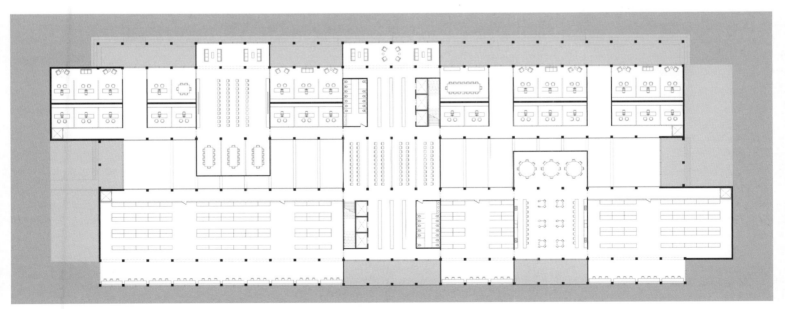

214

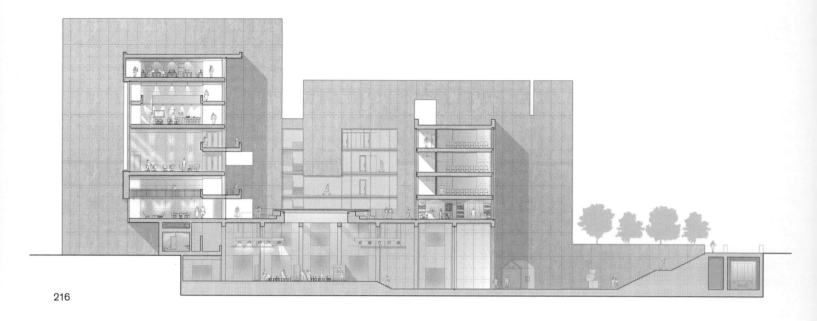

216

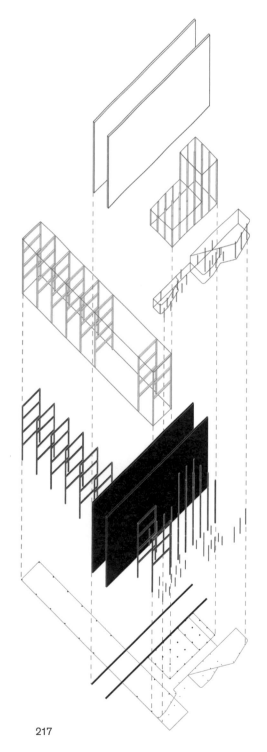

217

218

219

Drawing and Architectural Form

Design & Visualization

Victor Agran

With the emergence of increasingly sophisticated digital technologies, the practice of architecture is undergoing the most comprehensive transformation in centuries. Drawing—historically the primary means of generation, presentation, and interrogation of design ideas—is currently ill-defined and under stress. This course examines the historical and theoretical development of descriptive geometry and perspective through the practice of rigorous constructed architectural drawings. The methods and concepts studied serve as a foundation for the development of drawings that consider the relationship between a drawing's production and its conceptual objectives. Weekly readings, discussions, and drawing exercises investigate the work of key figures in the development of orthographic and three-dimensional projection. Ultimately, the goal is to engage in a focused dialogue about the practice of drawing and different methods of spatial inquiry.

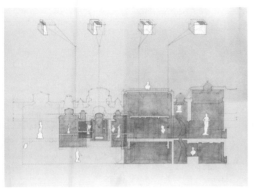

220

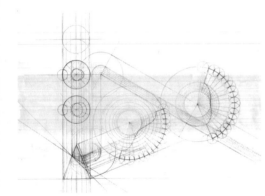

221

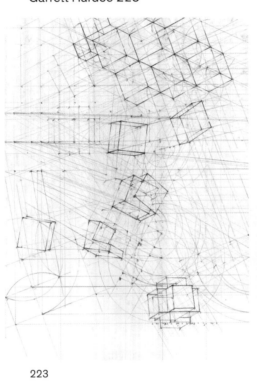

223

222

Ecological Urban Design

Urbanism & Landscape

Alexander Felson

This course lays the groundwork for students from the School of Architecture and the School of Forestry & Environmental Studies to collaboratively explore and define ecologically driven urban design. The course uses the Earth Stewardship Initiative, a large land-planning project developed for the Ecological Society of America in Sacramento, California to create a real-world project where interdisciplinary teams can work to combine ecological applications and design with the goal of shaping urban systems to improve the ecological, social, and infrastructural function of city components.

224

225

Peter Eisenman

Design & Visualization
Advanced Studio

with Miroslava Brooks

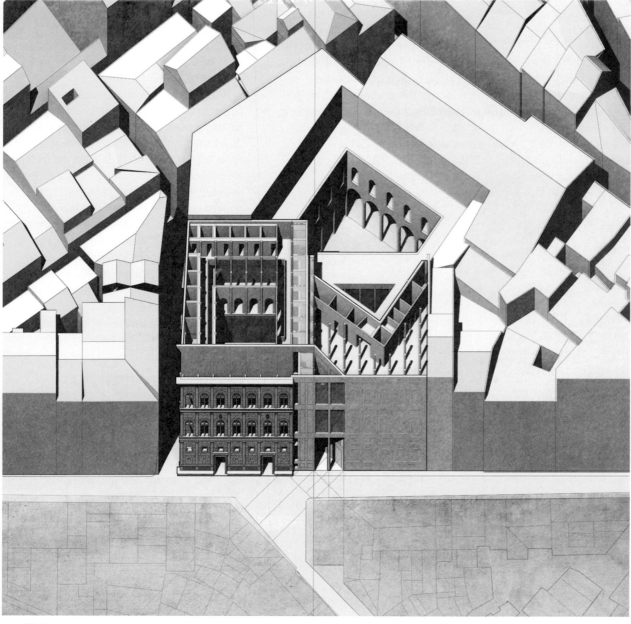

226

It is usually assumed that Palazzo Rucellai in Florence was designed as a symmetrical building, even though it was never completed as such. In its incomplete state, Palazzo Rucellai offers itself as an ideal subject for exploring the idea of a diptych in architecture. When making abstract schemata of architecture, the numbers three and nine are traditionally used, whether as a tripartite façade or a nine-square plan. Very rarely is a four-square plan or a two-part façade proposed, and when it is, it is as a two part opposition. Such a binary opposition, which has underpinned thought in most disciplines, seems today to be insufficient or inadequate to deal with the complexities of the built environment in the post-mechanical age. The idea is to mobilize, from an architectural practice, the possibility of a diptych in architecture. What that entails is a certain formalization of a diptych—traditionally a painterly idea that originated as celebratory artifacts in Roman and Byzantine times and gradually moved from a boxed horizontal surface to a framed vertical surface. The studio project is to design a structure on the site adjoining

Palazzo Rucellai in such a way that it becomes part of a new diptych composition. Although the idea of a diptych animates the theoretical discussion and analytic portion of the studio, it is up to the students to develop the analogical strategy of a diptych and how it manifests itself in their architectural proposals.

Critics

Harry Cobb (HC), Preston Scott Cohen (PSC), Cynthia Davidson (CD), Peter Eisenman (PE), Palmyra Geraki (PG), Jackie Hawkins (JH), Ingeborg Rocker (IR), Matthew Roman (MR), David Salle (DS), Brett Steele (BS), Robert A.M. Stern (RAMS), Anthony Vidler (AV), Elia Zenghelis (EZ), Guido Zuliani (GZ)

Sarah Kasper, Dima Srouji (Feldman Nominees) 226–228
In questioning how to join two to create one, only the façade of the Palazzo Rucellai, the single Albertian structure, is preserved. With this tabula rasa both adjacent to and behind Rucellai, a framework based on the prescripts of Alberti's text *Della Pittura*, and their manifestation in Sandro Botticelli's painting *Cestello*

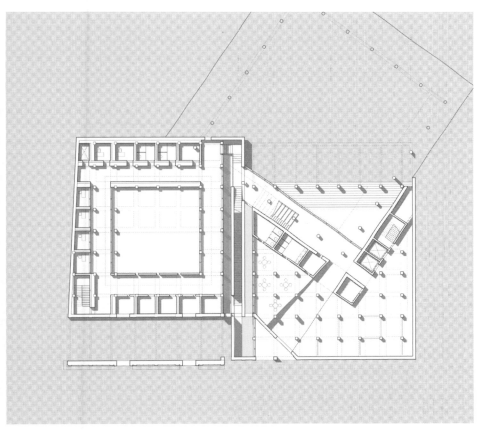

227

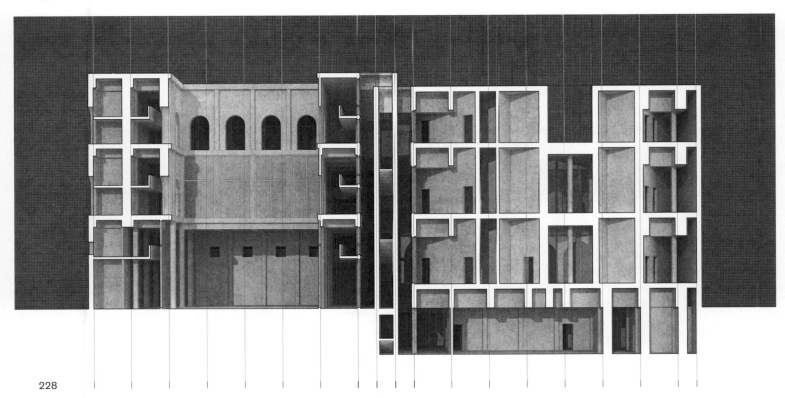

228

Annunciation (1489), allows for a choreography of forms that define a diptych composition. Oscillating between the rational and the pictorial, contextual forces shear the supplemental building, establishing a void at the hinge. This voided, weaving hinge reflects the tension between the hands of the angel Gabriel and the Madonna figure in the Annunciation; the two figures incline towards one another, but do not yet touch, signaling the imminent motion of the composition. From this initial framework, additional contextual reactions from the triangular piazza in front of Ruccelai and the monastery cortile behind signal entry along the diagonal and carve away at the mass beyond. Rucellai's original residential program is preserved, yet it is destabilized through the hinge as it intertwines with the new adjacent public institution. This conversation between existing and new, solid and void, ideal and destabilized, draws upon the call and response of the Annunciation, establishing forms in dialogue and poised for union, yet separated by the activated void of the hinge.

GZ: *I think it's a super project. It treats the original façade simply as a theme and isolates it as a phantom. And around that theme, you have variations. It generates a very powerful relationship between two parts. It is the only project that is not completely subservient to the original façade but provides a kind of a counter-façade so that you can see that the idea of the diptych is of two different parts that have a relationship with one another that is then reinforced by two very respectable plans. Two projects with beautiful plans make the hinge the really active element.* AV: *You've given us a modern courtyard and a Renaissance courtyard and you've brought them together. I think that the sliding is absolutely impeccable but what I love is the axon there—that is a fantastic drawing! It reminds me of drawings of [Constantino] Dardi in Venice: fantastic structural formalism which even Rossi didn't get to.* BS: *You begin to feel the tension between the two hands almost touching which is something very interesting. I don't know if it could be more successful.*

Alicia Pozniak, Caitlin Thissen 229, 230

The Palazzo Rucellai is an assemblage of seven medieval rowhouses unified by a monolithic stone façade attributed to Alberti. This project creates an architectural diptych by correcting the old palazzo structure and reproducing it in an 'ideal' rationalized form. In between the two parts is the 'hinge' which both divides and unites the overall composition. While the existing façade is incomplete, an early drawing shows Alberti's ideal proposal for the Palazzo Rucellai as a symmetrical five bay structure (AABAA). This is reinforced by his description of the 'Portico of the Highest Citizen' in *De Re Aedificatoria*. Our project mirrors this composition to create a three bay extension (BAA) to the existing building that overlaps the two residual bays of the unfinished façade. In plan, existing walls are removed from these bays to implement an 'ideal' palazzo structure. The trabeation of Alberti's flattened classical façade is abstracted and extruded to form an open modern post and beam system. The overlapping structural lines of old and new grids are mediated in the poché of the hinge, thickened façade members, and shifted wall openings. An internal stair forms the hinge joining the old and new palazzos. These separate vertically in section to read as two distinct parts of a larger whole. On the façade, the fifth bay is stripped of its stonework to reveal the hinge behind. This duly maintains the incomplete state of Alberti's façade and subsumes it in the architectural diptych. There are multiple dialectical relationships between the two parts of the diptych, the genesis of which is a reaction to the flattened classical façade. The project juxtaposes the old façade with a modern interpretation of Alberti's trompe l'oeil composition. It realizes the implied deep space collapsed within the façade and expands it into the building.

BS: *I think it's a terrific case on the terms that you present and argue with. It seems like the game would be how to not look at it like an architect and then to come back to architecture through the catalog of things discovered through a five hundred year history of split image—vertical surfaces that we think of as paintings. In that way, it seems like it might give you ways to argue the project in something other than this form, which in the end seems like a Trojan horse for Contextualism. That's the secret word. The diptych lets us think Contextualism without using that awful word that in the '70s was banned in this building… it seems what's at stake in this project is ultimately the singular architectural object and even the mastery of the autonomous architectural object, which has now a fifty year delivery. We're done with that. Architects make projects that make sense on their own. This is saying this project will make sense only in relation to another project, which in a way is really just a claim about the city, which is actually pretty impressive—that you're actually trying to say that the city might matter but certainly in a form very different than the way we're used to arguing it.*

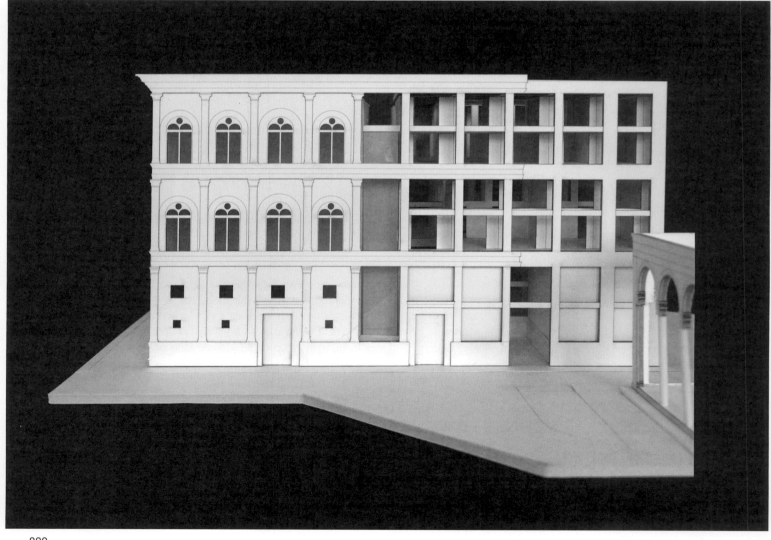

229

Eisenman, Peter

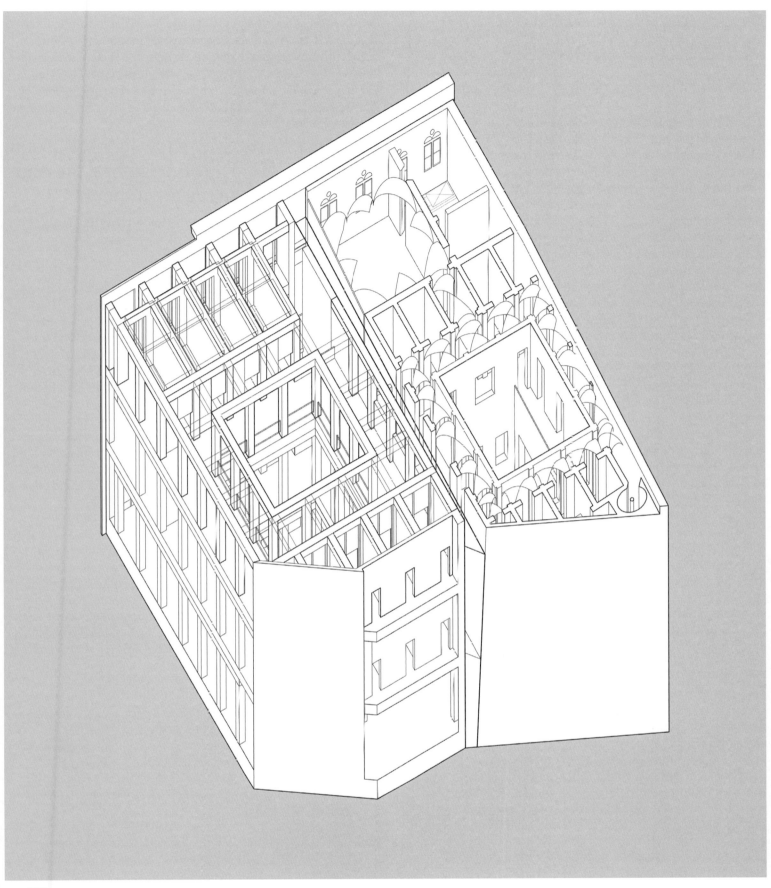

230

Peter Eisenman
Palladio Virtuel

with Matthew Roman

Upon my return to the States in 1963, I still did not understand what that lesson was. Today, I realize it was like reading a score in music. Composers don't need music to be played in order to hear it; they can hear it by reading the notes on a staff. Architecture is the same—one can know it by seeing what is not on the façade—for example, the plan. An architect sees differently than does an art historian or critic. Architects look for how buildings teach them to see through their facture. *Palladio Virtuel* is a book by an architect, not a historian or a critic. I wrote about Palladio in order to elaborate my own pedagogy in architecture, and perhaps to reaffirm the necessary authority of Palladio. The book is also an attempt to open architecture to investigations that promote change from the status quo, and propose a theoretical matrix from which to understand those changes.

In *Palladio Virtuel*, the 'virtuel' refers to architectural aspects that are implied by a condition of presence, but that exist beyond the literal or the ideal. These characteristics of Palladio's villas are not necessarily 'visible' in any one space, but their indeterminant qualities can be revealed through a close reading of the relationships between articulated architectural elements, such as porticos, arcades, cortiles, and staircases…

From one individual to another, from Frank Lloyd Wright to Le Corbusier, my own experience in the 1950s and 1960s, from Cornell to Cambridge to Princeton, is an interesting barometer of the changes in authority within the pedagogy of architecture. In 1960, when I began teaching at Cambridge, the authorial voice shifted from Frank Lloyd Wright to Louis Kahn. But for me, the important change in this context was my PhD dissertation written in the void of the early 1960s, before Rossi, Tafuri, Venturi, and Derrida. Looking back, it was important because it was an attempt at a different disciplinary authority to swerve away from the authorial legacy of the individual. It is this difference that is attempted in *Palladio Virtuel*; it is not your potted view of his work.

My interpretation of the events of the early 1960s did not become conscious until Venturi's book of 1966, *Complexity and Contradiction*, which precipitated quite conscious reactions within architecture circles in the US. While those thoughts on a revised disciplinary authority might have subconsciously powered my earlier dissertation, it did not at that time interrupt the sequence of Le Corbusian authority of an individual. His authorial voice was so virulent and persuasive, that students and faculty alike would converse in short hand in the schools where these ideas flourished, such as Princeton and Cornell. In fact, many students' desks had the five volumes of the *Oeuvre Complete* stacked on it for a quick reference. It was only after Venturi's book that it was possible to articulate two differing disciplinary authorities—American pragmatism and modernist ideology—putting to rest the notion of an individual dogma for the ensuing years.

These differing authorities spawned people like Aldo Rossi, who brought a new idea of architecture from continental Europe, called the *Tendenza*—an idea about the organization of the urban in relation to, what he called, urban artifacts. We were fascinated by Rossi's work from the Milan Triennale of 1973 and his book *The Architecture of the City*, first published in Italian in 1966.

Next came James Stirling's earlier projects, like the Churchill College Competition and the iconic Leicester Engineering Building of 1963. Again, this is something that came to the United States with a great flourish, because Stirling became a visiting professor here at Yale in 1959, and stayed here until 1983. He was one of those figures who taught, built, and thought about architecture—again, what was at the time one of the last individual voices of authority.

By 1980, things began to change again and postmodernism, as a style, if not an ideology, became the new authorial voice within the architectural pedagogy. Its most prominent manifestation was the *Strada Novissima*, the first international Architecture Biennale in Venice. This exhibition changed radically the idea of the façade and what constituted the architecture of the street, of the new street—*Strada Novissima*.

The Deconstructivist show in the Museum of Modern Art in 1988 hastened the end of postmodernism as an authorial idea, but what is important is that it did not replace it.

Thus, near the end of the last century, the idea of an internal disciplinary authority began to be eroded in academic circles. There could be several reasons for this situation. One would be the demise of disciplinary giants. While media named and then expanded the influence of 'starchitects,' few of these architects had any ideological or pedagogic project to compare with people like Aldo Rossi, Manfredo Tafuri, O.M. Ungers, and Robert Venturi. The demise of the influence of these figures, coupled with the proliferation of increasingly sophisticated computation and software, created a seemingly unbridgeable gap between a younger generation and their older mentors and colleagues. This gap, which is a new phenomenon, has often contributed to a generational disregard for any disciplinary authority, and has prioritized software as a driving force in architecture.

Whether this generational divide has any ultimate validity only the present future will be able to judge. Unmoored from any disciplinary concerns, not to mention the loss of authority, the digital software explosion has led to a virtual cacophony of work, with little ability to develop a corresponding critical apparatus to assess this production. The idea of a critical matrix seems more necessary today than ever before, since popular software is able to produce an infinite number of singular iterations, without any value system in place other than personal aesthetics or expression to validate any choice.

In a concluding paragraph to his book, *The Alphabet and the Algorithm*, Mario Carpo says:

> The modern process of architectural design and the architects authorial role in it may not survive the digital turn. Yet, as architecture pre-existed both the invention of the Albertian author and the rise of mechanical copies, neither may be indispensable to its future. The post-Albertian architecture of our digital future will have something in common with the pre-Albertian architecture.

Understanding the changes prefigured by Carpo will begin to help us shape a possible future for architectural pedagogy.

Palladio Virtuel begins with Alberti's implication of homogeneous space in his *De Re Aedificatoria*, (*On the Art of Building*, 1452), which originated the discourse about space and how to conceptualize it. After Bramante, much of what is known as architectural mannerism, including Palladio, is in fact a questioning of Albertian spatial principles. An important aspect of Palladio's work is the shift from the Albertian idea of homogeneous space to what might be called heterogeneous space. The evident conceptual transformation from homogeneous to heterogeneous space is variously referred to in *Palladio Virtuel* as the dissipation of a supposed 'ideal' toward 'virtual' spatial conditions. This brings us back to seeing the unseen and my first architectural lesson while encountering the Palladian villa in Italy. Although computation promised heterogeneous singular instances, the space today is understood in terms of parametrics, spatial or temporal, which translate into homogenizing data.

December 3, 2015
Eisenman, Peter *Lecture*

Environmental Design

Technology & Practice

Michelle Addington
with Eero Puurunen

This course examines the fundamental scientific principles governing the thermal, luminous, and acoustic environments of buildings, and introduces methods and technologies for creating and controlling the interior environment. Beginning with an overview of the Laws of Thermodynamics and the Principles of Heat Transfer, the course investigates the application of these principles in the determination of building behavior, and explores the design variables—including climate—for mitigating that behavior. The overarching premise of the course is that the understanding and application of the physical principles by the architect must respond to and address the larger issues surrounding energy and the environment at multiple scales and in domains beyond a single building.

Martin Finio

Design & Visualization
Second Year Studio

This third core studio concentrates on a medium-scale institutional building, focusing on the integration of composition, site, program, mass, and form in relation to structure and methods of construction. Interior spaces are studied in detail. Large-scale models and drawings are developed to explore design issues.

Critics
Emily Abruzzo (EA), Lee Altman (LA), Daniel Barber (DB), Stella Betts (SB), Gerald Bodziak (GB), Sara Caples (SC), Stephen Cassell (SCa), Peter de Bretteville (PdB), Martin Finio (MF), Mimi Hoang (MH), Mariana Ibañez (MI), Andrea Kahn (AK), Tessa Kelly (TK), Gordon Kipping (GK), Craig Konyk (CK), Joel Sanders (JS), Robert A.M. Stern (RAMS), Laetitia Wolff (LW)

Christopher Leung 231, 232
This project emphasizes the "between" spaces: between exterior edges and the interior spine, between large studio spaces and rows of individual desks, and between the building's arms. This concept is reflected by contrasting the monolithic central spine with the individualized scale of the building edge. The tripartite form stretches toward the site boundaries connecting to the university beyond, while also forming three distinct "neighborhoods" enclosed within the extended arms of the architecture school. These

231

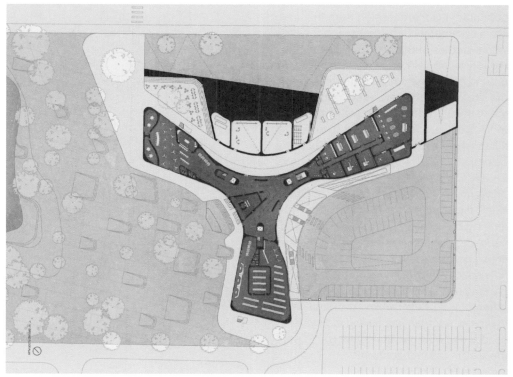

232

"neighborhoods" act as main entry points as well as interdisciplinary spaces bridging the different programs of each arm. The ebb and flow of movement funnels through a "neighborhood," enters into the central anchor, disperses to the arms, and exits back out the "neighborhoods" in constant harmonious motion. By defining edges and cultivating permeable "between" spaces, the school presents itself as public architecture that creates a diverse range of individual and collaborative learning opportunities for its students.

MI: *I find your take on the site very compelling. You're spatializing that line to create a hierarchy for your entrance, but when you enter the building, it's really the tripartite system that organizes it. So I find that it has that sophistication which works very well for you. You're doing something axial but at the same time introduces rotation, which is successful.* GB: *Why is it such an object? I think at architecture school there's this expectation that form has to trump all.* SB: *It's so diagrammatically strong and tight that we default to how we fill the program within that space. I'm just wondering if there's a way and opportunity where it could have inverted itself at one point and surprised us.*

Ilana Simhon 233

This design school for Kean University challenges the static nature of a singular working surface in favor of an activity based environment. Typically, each student claims ownership over one space that is forced to act as the social hub, lunch table, model-making workshop, discussion space, and the silent production zone. By acknowledging the range of activities and creating zones to accommodate each, the students are empowered to select a working environment based on their current stage of production.

The striated system—which begins with the commuter—is a procession from the larger scale community of the school to the individual studios at the water's edge. As the motion of the car constructs the pedestrian ground plane, the voids continue through the site changing scale to accommodate the various programs. The zones become more articulated and build up in density to establish an active community among the design students.

CK: *My first impression is that there's a kind of tyranny to your phasing. What I actually like is the atomization—you've put the galleries in the parking lot. You've reinvented parking.* SCa: *One interesting thing about architecture schools is they're running at full capacity twenty hours of the day. This is being used over the course of the day differently. So, how can you overlap spaces in time rather than just having individual spaces and how can that allow you to get more from the architecture?*

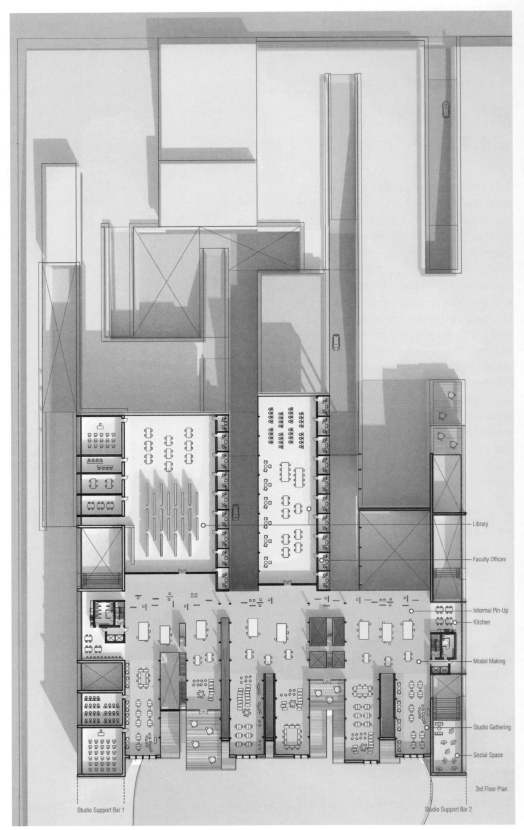

233

Formal Analysis
Design & Visualization

Peter Eisenman
with Miroslava Brooks

The first activity in this class is one of unlearning. I remember my shock when traveling with Colin Rowe in Italy in the summer of 1961, after my first year of teaching at Cambridge. Rowe said to me in front of my first Palladian villa, "Tell me something about the villa that you cannot see." He did not want me to tell him about its three stories, about its material rustication, about its symmetrical window arrangement; these were obvious and seeable. But an architect must learn to see beyond the facts of perception. An architect must see as an expert. This expertise implies two things. Firstly, being able to see, as a form of close reading, the not present—the unseen. Secondly, and more importantly, an architect is a maker, not just a reader. In order to make what contains "what cannot be seen," one has to know what that is. In order to make what can be close read, one has to know first how to close read. This is a class about that kind of learning. And its first and most basic form of close reading is formal analysis.

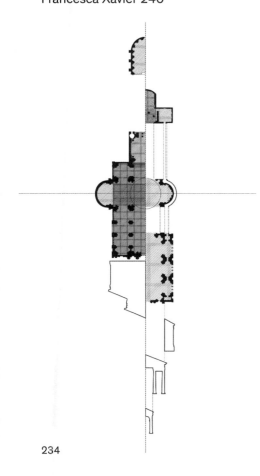

234

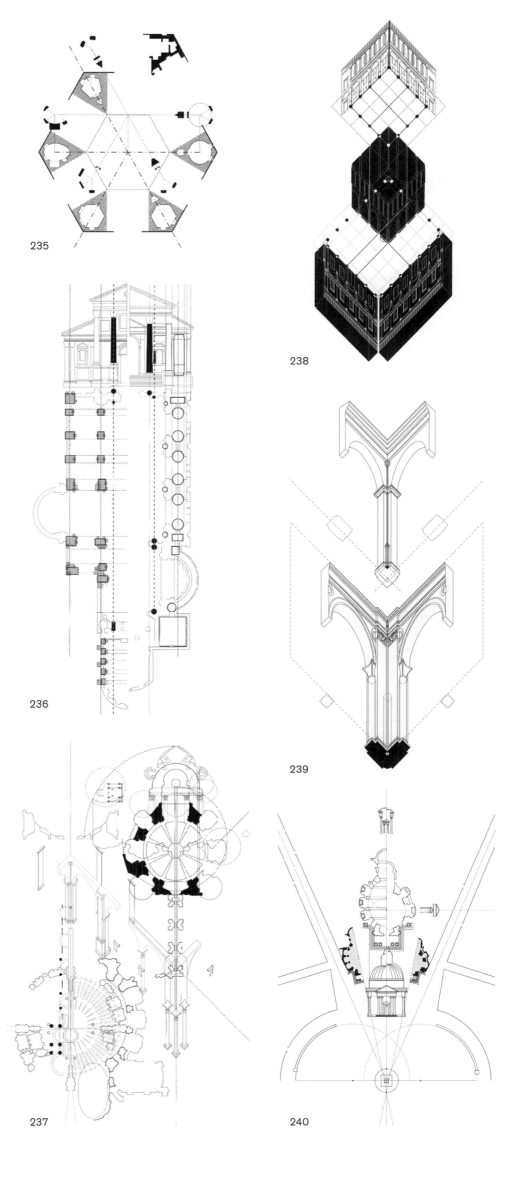

235

236

237

238

239

240

German Architecture since 1945

History & Theory

Kathleen James-Chakraborty

This seminar examines architecture in the Federal Republic of Germany and in the German Democratic Republic with particular attention paid to the city of Berlin and to the issue of representing a nation through buildings designed by both foreigners and its own citizens. Architects explored include Rudolf Schwarz, Egon Eiermann, Hermann Henselmann, Hans Scharoun, Ludwig Mies van der Rohe, James Stirling, O.M. Ungers, Daniel Libeskind, Zaha Hadid, and SANAA.

History of Landscape Architecture: Antiquity to 1700 in Western Europe

Urbanism & Landscape

Bryan Fuermann

This course presents an introductory survey of the history of gardens and the interrelationship of architecture and landscape architecture in Western Europe from antiquity to 1700, focusing primarily on Italy. The course examines chronologically the evolution of several key elements in landscape design: architectural and garden typologies, the boundaries between inside and outside, issues of topography and geography, various uses of water, organization of plant materials, and matters of garden decoration, including sculptural tropes. Specific gardens or representations of landscape in each of the four periods under discussion—Ancient Roman, medieval, early and late Renaissance, and Baroque—are examined and situated within their own cultural context. Throughout the seminar, comparisons of historical material with contemporary landscape design are emphasized.

John Chengqi Wan 241
Michelle Gonzalez, Clarissa Luwia 242
Anthony Gagliardi 243

241

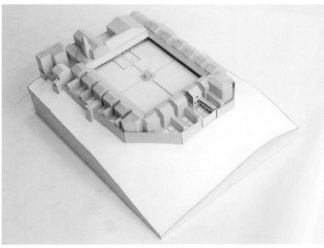

242

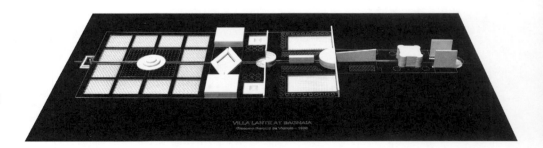

243

Joyce Hsiang

Design & Visualization
First Year Studio

In an era of information architecture, where the idea of virtual space is increasingly prevalent, this studio examines and reasserts the role of physical spaces, sites and structure. Three distinct projects explore the architectural potential of alternate modes of learning in contemporary culture. The first project asks students to design a study, a volume that contains, hosts or organizes alternate modes of learning. The second project for the design of a seed vault as an exterior study shifts focus towards site as a subject of study, informing the design approach as well as the literal program for the project. The third project examines the urban public library as a type that historically functioned as a container of books, social center and monument for a neighborhood but is recast in light of questions of the role of the library in a digital age. This project asks students to reinvigorate the public library as a universal cultural institution.

Critics
Sunil Bald (SB), Miroslava Brooks (MB), Brennan Buck (BB), Trattie Davies (TD), Rosetta Elkin (RE), Joyce Hsiang (JH), Nahyun Hwang (NH), Skender Luarasi (SL), Daniel Markiewicz (DM), Kyle Miller (KM), Alan Organschi (AO), Julia Sedlock (JS), Rosalyne Shieh (RS), Michael Szivos (MS), Irina Verona (IV), Elia Zenghelis (EZ)

Hyeree Kwak 244
DM: *There's an element of playfulness which is also kind of scary—a kind of [Antoni] Gaudí celebration of grotesqueness. Everything is kind of lumpy and dripping over itself, which I think is really fun and interesting.* MS: *The way you've presented it, the interventions look more like specimens than objects that you've created, almost cocoon-like. I wonder if there's a point in the project where you can remove yourself and look at these as found objects and learn from them.*

Claire Haugh 246
EZ: *Super project! I like very much that somehow the program transcends library.*

It's not just a library. Amongst other things it's also a place where you can get books and read. It's a club in a way. I'm not so sure how well it works as a library, but it works very much as a landscape that can be used as a place in the neighborhood, and kind of livens it up. I also like the effort you made in constructing these details of the project. I think this is the time, in first year, to go all out with one's imagination. MB: *It cannot happen in third year? It should!* EZ: *Unfortunately, by the time you get to third year things get boring…*

Timon Covelli 247
EZ: *The research is fantastic, the drawings are fantastic. The whole thing is dedicated to the process of digitizing so, therefore reading is primarily something you do online. There is no need to read there. It's a little factory. There is no reason for the public to visit it. The process is interesting and maybe even beautiful. Just scanning, nothing exciting. In many ways you can see this as the anti-library.* MB: *A cemetery of books, really, is how I see it.*

Jonathan Molloy 245

244

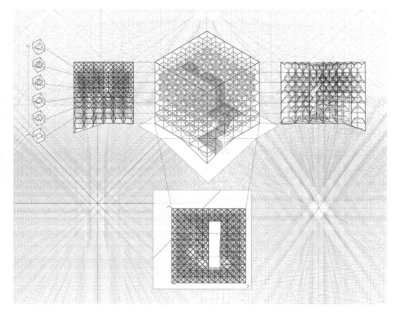

245

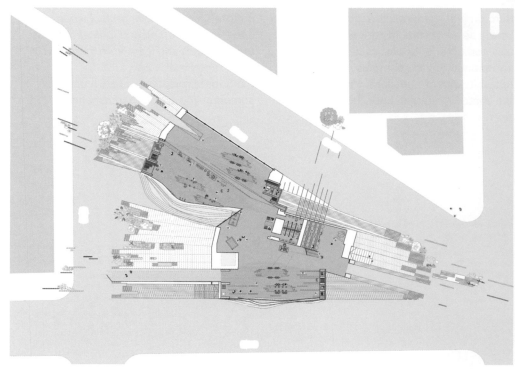

246

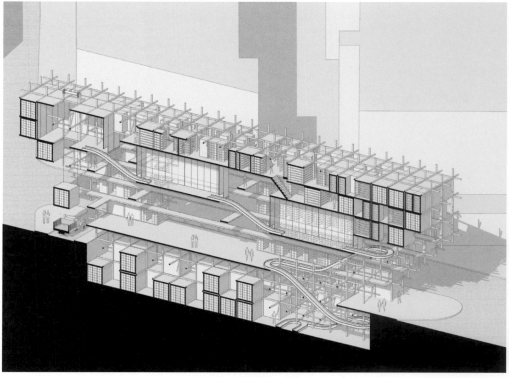

247

Fall
Hsiang, Joyce

Introduction to Commercial Real Estate

Urbanism & Landscape

Kevin Gray

This seminar introduces and examines five basic types of commercial real estate from the standpoints of the developer, lender, and investor. Principles of location, financing, timing of market cycles, leasing, ownership structure, and external factors are explored. Students are expected to evaluate assets, partnership interests, and other positions such as debtor interests through valuation measurement. Students also examine commercial deeds, leases, partnership agreements, and other legal documents. Each student selects a building or development site within New Haven County for a due diligence analysis of zoning, real estate taxes, deeds, liens, market supply and demand, projected income and expenses, and availability of debt.

Introduction to Planning and Development

Urbanism & Landscape

Alexander Garvin

This course demonstrates the ways in which financial and political feasibility determine the design of buildings and the character of the built environment. Students propose projects and then adjust them to the conflicting interests of financial institutions, real estate developers, civic organizations, community groups, public officials, and the widest variety of participants in the planning process. Subjects covered include housing, commercial development, zoning, historic preservation, parks and public open space, suburban subdivisions, and comprehensive plans.

Issues in Architecture and Urbanism

History & Theory

Edward Mitchell

Current issues in architecture and urbanism are explored through seminars and case studies, introducing methods and theories of architectural research.

Daphne Binder
Within extant urban design and practice, the prominence of the American town—in particular the resort town—is indicative of potential reciprocities of planning concepts between them and their urban counterpart. Urban design practice frequently aspires to the town or village model as an ideal spatial organization. Nevertheless, the resort town's accommodation of spatial transformation offers much more to be studied in relation to the urban environment. The disproportionately large number of visitors these small centers attract and expel annually places them at the extreme end of the spectrum of cyclical urban growth and shrinkage.

Abdulgader Naseer
A product of the orthodox nature of most Islamic schools of thought [is that] the notion of innovation is viewed as taboo; however, I would argue that the current image of the mosque is a product of innovation as the typology has undergone a series of transformations since the birth of Islam 1,437 years ago. Hence, the stereotypical image of the mosque can only be challenged by identifying the paradigm shifts in history. The design of mosques has undergone a series of changes, proving that the typology is not static. The mosque is a fluid condition.

Alicia Pozniak
As the 'Dream' fades, an after-image is left behind of an idealized time where the fantasy was possible in the land of suburbia. It is this image that remains pervasive and validates suburban life for most residents of American and Australian cities. For this reason the notion of suburbia cannot be cast aside in the densification and development of our cities. As architects we must work within it to understand and evolve its conditions as both part of the city and a still viable place to live.

Sofia Singler
Today's renderings are remarkably homogeneous in their uniform immaculacy; they create, sell, and reinforce images that deliver the promise of perfection and depict, in their shininess and splendor, states of idealized harmony where all the complexities and contrapuntal notes of urbanism have been resolved into an unblemished denouement. A sempiternal smile is a disquieting characteristic in a person; does architecture's uncompromising jolliness not also reek of ill?

Kathleen James-Chakraborty
The Architecture of Modern Memory: Building Identity in Democratic Germany

George Morris Woodruff, Class of 1857 Memorial Lecture

It was here at Yale that, inspired by Vincent Scully's passion for buildings, I became an architectural historian. One of Scully's many talents has been to rekindle an appreciation of how much architecture's past could contribute to its present. This evening I want to tease out the relationship between multiple pasts—including modernism's own history—in a series of German buildings whose occupation with precedent reinforces how right he was.

The key feature of the architecture of modern memory is the pairing of historic fabric with abstract form. Most of the historic architecture, although it often appears older, dates to the nineteenth century. Its modernist counterparts usually descend fairly directly from the Expressionism of the 1910s and the early 1920s, more than from what the Germans at the time termed the 'New Building,' and what is more often known elsewhere as the 'International Style.' Together the pairing is taken to suggest an acceptance of the past as well as the possibility of a better, and in the case of the Reichstag, a more democratic future.

Bruno Taut optimistically inscribed his little advertising pavilion for the glass industry on the grounds of the German Werkbund's 1914 exhibition in Cologne with an aphorism from the poet Paul Scheerbart, "colored glass destroys hate." The Glass House doubled as an effort to create a sense of community on the eve of World War I. This was to be accomplished through the shared empathetic reaction to the spectacles experienced within. Taut's overly optimistic sense of what architecture could achieve later extended to visions of crystalline cathedral-like structures set atop the Alps, where the spiritual unity of medieval piety was to be recast in utopian socialist terms. Foster's cupola, which sits atop the legislative chamber and allows the general public to ascend a spiral ramp within it, would be unthinkable without Taut's schemes.

Tessa Kelly

Design & Visualization
Second Year Studio

This third core studio concentrates on a medium-scale institutional building, focusing on the integration of composition, site, program, mass, and form in relation to structure, and methods of construction. Interior spaces are studied in detail. Large-scale models and drawings are developed to explore design issues.

Critics
Emily Abruzzo (EA), Daniel Barber (DB), Stella Betts (SB), Gerald Bodziak (GB), Peter de Bretteville (PdB), Martin Finio (MF), Mariana Ibañez (MI), Tessa Kelly (TK), Gordon Kipping (GK), Joel Sanders (JS), Robert A.M. Stern (RAMS), Laetitia Wolff (LW)

Benjamin Rubenstein 248, 249
As a commuter school, Kean experiences a tremendous pressure on its existing surface parking lots. These parking lots form a physical barrier between old and new campuses, including the site of the new design school. This challenge provides a great opportunity for the building—which will house the Michael Graves School of Public Architecture—to address this spatial issue by absorbing all of the university's parking needs into the program of the design school.
MI: *I welcome radicality in a proposal, but if we just take a school and put it in a parking structure, then there's nothing to talk about beyond if we accept the proposal or if we don't accept the proposal.* SB: *Once you couple those two programs then you should look at the metrics of how many students are actually driving to campus and is there an opportunity where you could practically drive up to your desk? How is the parking really interfacing with the program and are there weird kinds of illogical logics that come out of this new hybrid program? How has the architecture school transformed the parking and how has the parking transformed the architecture school?*

Cecily Ng 250
This project begins with the belief that activities within a design school are strengthened by their proximities to dissimilar activity types. The act of weaving is used as a strategy to mix the activity types. The program is divided into three primary categories: input, output and distribution. 'Input' includes classrooms and the library, 'output' includes studios and the shop and 'distribution' includes public interfacing programs such as the auditorium, administrative offices and exhibition space. By evenly distributing the program throughout the building, the weave diminishes hierarchy between program types and acknowledges that the design process is non-linear.

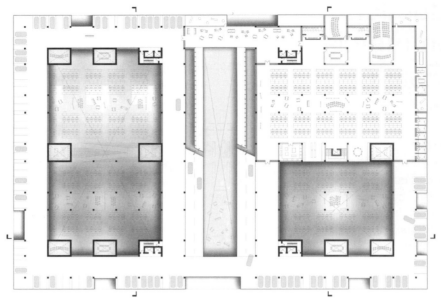

248

249

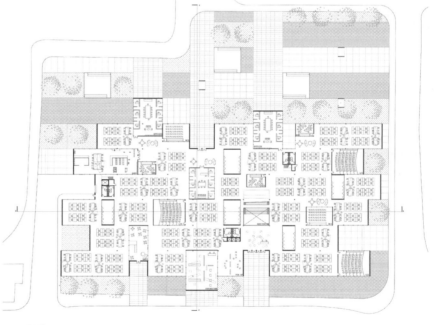

250

251

MI: *In the winter, once it snows, those screens will be closed and snow will accumulate on the ground. It is interesting that the same room that at one time of the year works as a connector—works as a divider at another. That can begin to inform how other spaces transform.* GK: *Know when to use your metaphor and know when to let go of your metaphor. Use your metaphor to create a distinctive architectural element that extends at the same scale and materiality onto the site.*

Lucas Boyd 251

With the future of design being undoubtedly collaborative, this project strives to perpetuate this by arranging the program not by discipline, but by building type. The result is a shift from separate heterogeneous buildings with a homogenous discipline to four homogeneous 'buildingettes' heterogeneously occupied by all the disciples. The four 'buildingettes' are the sloped (review spaces, classrooms), the ramp (studios, library), the grid (offices, classrooms, services), and the plenum (shops, fabrication, labs).

MF: *You've shown an amazing command of a certain framework, or even just a headspace, of being able to chart out how you want to deal with all of these issues, how you want to make these issues relevant to this program, and how you want to play those out in a way that is utterly convincing.* MI: *I think the interior is incredibly rich with spatial opportunity, but to contribute to this idea of differentiation, letting some of these internal conditions permeate all the way to the façade would have generated, naturally, a landscape of difference and would allow you to make decisions about how to orient the building.*

Margaret Tsang 252, 253

The Michael Graves College at Kean University put forth 'public architecture' as one of its main pedagogical ambitions. This proposal reflects on three interpretations of 'public:' as an academic resource, as a site for community engagement, and finally as an expression of identity for the school. The main gesture on the site is a generous public path situated between the programmed 'neighborhoods.' This path serves as part-park, part-unprogrammed area where the visitors can wander into the school or where students engage with the community or build large scale projects.

SB: *I don't mind the arbitrariness of the geometry. What I'm less convinced by is this path that feels domesticated, like an outdoor mall.* MF: *The idea that one needs to be a slave to one's own rhetorical logic—when does it makes sense to let go of that?* MI: *I want to go back to the title of your project* Inside/Out. *You started with that binary and the project I think stayed too close to it. I think the way elements are set, there is a lot of opportunity to expand on those formal moves.*

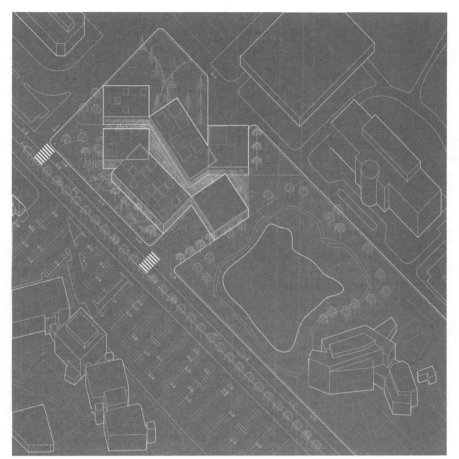

252

253

M.J. Long
Anatomy of a Shed

This search for a direct and real response to current architectural challenges in Cornwall is seen in my projects such as the Maritime Museum, Charlestown Harbour, and Studios in St. Ives. … Aalto has been a particular inspiration. At the Villa Mairea he incorporated a vernacular sauna seamlessly into a clearly modern building. His ability to quote directly from other architectural sources and from the vernacular produces a form of inclusive modern architecture—honest and authentic to the core—that makes postmodernism unnecessary. … In Cornwall, and elsewhere in this world of limited resources, I find myself increasingly engaged in making use of existing buildings—finding ways of transforming them to new uses without losing their individual architectural quality. At Porthmeor studios in St. Ives, we found ourselves working on a building with a long history serving both fishermen and artists. We managed to transform the building and give it new life while keeping its historical aura intact. We spent five years and several million pounds in the effort, and my favorite (and very un-Yale) comment was, "But you haven't done anything."

Edward Mitchell

Design & Visualization
M.Arch II Studio

The studio analyzes the historic development of the metro region of the city of Boston, studies these sites that are both products of contemporary infrastructure and possible paradigms of urban futures, researches new developments in green and sustainable urban design and building technology, and examines the conceptual development of both the urban 'parkscape' and the urban 'workplace' relative to the need for increased density in the communities. The studio examines three formerly industrial towns north of Boston—Charlestown, Lowell, and Lynn. Though the interstate highway system might have produced a more complex regional network reinforcing the historic strength of small town New England communities, it contributed to the drain on these towns.

Critics
Peter de Bretteville (PdB), Andrei Harwell (AH), Anne Haynes (AH), Brian Healy (BH), Kathleen James-Chakraborty (KJC), Tim Love (TL), Edward Mitchell (EM), Joseph Mulligan (JM), Carie Penabad (CP), Kim Polliquin (KP), Aniket Shahane (AS), Na Wei (NW), Elia Zenghelis (EZ)

Andreas De Camps,
Shreya Shah 254, 255
How to create a public space for Lynn by amplifying its existing characteristics through one of its greatest assets, the shoreline? The focus of the project is Route 1A, or the Lynnway, which is an area already targeted for development by the city.
BH: *You are presenting an ad-hoc, funky-town waterfront, a Jersey kind of place. So the car and how you get there and the destination are very important. It's not just convenience. It's a little Disneyland-ish. Some of the developments outside of cities use a stage-set quality to make you think of a Main Street, and it's so disturbing. As a snooty, snobby architect, with a nose onto what's fake, I do know that it's very popular. But you are doing that. It's very kitsch.*

Chris Hyun, Jiajin Min,
Gordon Schissler 256
Haverhill's greatest asset for its redevelopment is the Merrimack River. Yet, despite

254

255

256

their adjacency, physical and social barriers have historically separated the downtown from the river. This new development intends to break down the divide between the downtown and the river by reversing the existing condition so that the city faces the river.

AH: *We are walking into very specific decisions that you've made; you've illustrated a very intentional quality of the place, and that's very admirable. What's interesting is that you've actually designed two frameworks that are a kind of plug-in play, kit of parts that could frankly be left at that level.* TL: *Thinking more theoretically or pedagogically, this is a way to propose a vision for a district that has all kinds of pros and cons that are interesting above the specific questions about where you put the basketball court.*

Heather Bizon,
Patrick Kondziola 257, 258
Lynn, Massachusetts: once the "Shoe Capital of the World." The shoe industry attracted immigrants and migrant workers to Lynn, bringing with them their diverse backgrounds and rich cultures. Today's disparate communities are residual from the passing of this industry. Anchoring an annual schedule of events, we propose the Lynn Shoe Parade to establish a new identity for the city. We created a festival circuit: a 2.75-mile loop.
BH: *I buy it. The narrative is both whimsical and sincere, and the parade is inclusive but investive. I don't know why these things couldn't be permanent—a marker where other squares and streets we know are activated for particular occasions. I think they are also elegant and clever, and not outrageous.* PdB: *You guys are so deadpan, so non-performative.* [laughter] *I expect you to go dancing, flourish to show these things, to quickly show us all. If you present this to the city, you need a director, you need a choreographer!*

Matthew Bohne, Jamie Edindjiklian 259
Our ambition is to rethink the Merrimack River and reorient the region towards a revitalized resource. The project proposes a regional park system to create a regional identity in order to share, manage, and leverage resources. With a combined population approaching that of Boston, the new Merrimack River City has the potential to challenge how the scale and scope of a successful New England city performs.
TL: *You created from scratch a mythology which doesn't exist. I think it's a very interesting proposition, and does stake a claim for what design can do for political aims. This is propaganda, clear and simple.* KJC: *This reorients and conceptualizes in ways that are powerful for building a sense of community for places that have not had much of a sense of community within [themselves], much less with each other.*

257

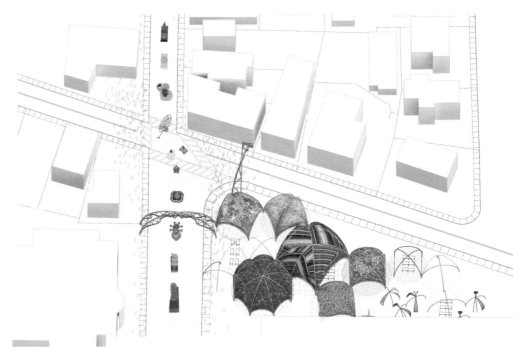
258

259

Modern Architecture

History & Theory

Kurt Forster

The course embraces the last century and a half's history of architecture, when traditional fables began to yield to more scientifically conceived ideas of architecture's role in the creation of civilizations. As architecture gained importance in advancing social and industrial agendas, it also built a basis for theoretical reflection and visionary aesthetics. The expanding print and media culture accelerated the migration of ideas and propelled architecture beyond its traditional confines. Discussion of major centers of urban culture and their characteristic buildings alternates with attention to individual concepts and their impact in an increasingly interconnected culture of design.

New England Domestic Architecture: 1870–1910

History & Theory

Kathleen James-Chakraborty

Sixty years after the publication of Vincent Scully's *The Shingle Style and the Stick Style*, this seminar revisits architect-designed suburban and resort housing in late-nineteenth and early twentieth-century New England. The role of the emergent architectural press in disseminating new approaches to these building types and of women in commissioning, decorating, and writing them is also addressed.

Daphne Binder
Today village greens serve as a symbol of a settlement's rootedness in regional and national history. These undisturbed garden landscapes are frozen in a state that harks back to a presumably shared New England past in colonial times. Yet the study of the green's origin in the village common, and the multiple transformations it underwent in the late 19th and early 20th [centuries], reveals it to be a modern construct rather than a remnant of colonial times. By tracing the history of the New England green, we may reframe our understanding of its contemporary condition. The connections established early on between the common and military,

industrial and commercial activity, as well as the progressive thinking of village improvement societies and architects such as Andrew Jackson Downing, situate the green as more than a signifier of the past. It has historically been used as a vehicle to reinvent the present and future.

Patrick Kondziola
Tiffany and the Power of Environment was the title of a research project that examined Gilded Age domestic interiors for their transformative and meaningful spatial experiences. Louis Comfort Tiffany's consummate project, his mansion in Long Island, New York, burned down in 1957. Its internal Fountain Court employed a dynamic spatial layering of light, color, material, exoticism, mysticism, decoration, artifact, landscape; the event and costume left its visitors in awe.

A 3D scan of the Tiffany stained-glass window titled "Education," [is located] in Yale's Chittenden Hall. The scans show the artist's complex understanding of glass and his experimentation in the glass making process. The thick modulating volume of the glass surface creates the ethereal effect of bending and reconfiguring light's color and consistency cast throughout a space. A giant stained-glass dome covered the Fountain Court interior and must have had a far more astonishing effect.

Parallel Moderns: The New Tradition

History & Theory

Robert A.M. Stern

This seminar puts forward the argument that what many have accepted as the mutually exclusive discourses of tradition and innovation in the modern architecture of the first half of the twentieth century—respectively identified as the "New Tradition" and the "New Pioneers" by Henry-Russell Hitchcock in his *Modern Architecture: Romanticism and Reintegration* (1929)—in fact share common genealogy and are integral to an understanding of modern architecture as a whole. The seminar explores in depth key architects working in the New Tradition and goes on to explore its impact for postmodernism in the 1970s and 1980s. The possible emergence of a new synthesis of seeming opposites in the present is also considered.

John Kleinschmidt 260
Throughout his long career, Ralph Erskine has maintained a complicated dual identity. He is resolutely British but speaks his native tongue with a lilting Swedish affect. He trained in London, but left for

Stockholm at the first chance he got, fascinated by Swedish housing design in the 1940s. Last year, he won Sweden's highest award for urban design—and promptly made a symbolic return to England at the ripe old age of fifty-nine. Today, this "English Swede" is leading the design of what may well be the United Kingdom's most significant contemporary residential development: the Byker Estate in Newcastle-Upon-Tyne. For his implementation of seminal theories of urbanism, his thoughtful responses to difficult housing problems, and his unwavering focus on people in his user-centered approach to design, I am delighted to present Ralph Erskine as an enthusiastic participant in this exhibition.

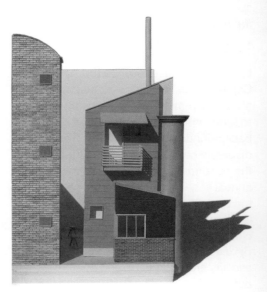

260

Participation in Diverse Communities

Urbanism & Landscape

Sara Caples and Everardo Jefferson

This case study seminar analyzes examples of cultural and public spaces in Asia, Africa, South America, Europe, and the United States that have involved local participation in their creation and, in some cases, in their ongoing space-making. By examining specific cultural strategies and resulting artifacts, the seminar attempts to identify a wide range of responses and strategies that can be used to generate cultural buildings and public spaces broadly under-stood in their communities as places of meaning.

Heather Bizon
The Makoko Floating School, by NLE Architects, created a dynamic public space for the illegal floating community of Makoko.

The structure was designed to serve the community as a small school (60–100 students) and establish a prototype for testing the strategies of urban infrastructure for rogue settlements. The resultant artifact became much more to the community; it established a constantly active, as well as flexible collective public space for the settlement, and provided a place of identity.

James Kehl

Francis Kéré's projects in Gando, Burkina Faso are consistently predicated [upon] community participation, and are lauded for their environmentally-based form and detail, as well as for their constructability with local materials and means. Although these regionalist qualities are typically celebrated as the forefront of Francis Kéré's work, they are actually only one side of the story. As Kéré's Gando projects were built in succession, a Burkinabé vernacular element—distinct from the modern regionalist approach—emerges in his work.

Red Location Museum of Struggle: Language of Reconciliation in Post Apartheid South Africa

Jenny Kim

Townships are prime examples of a marginalized population being forced into [an] urban condition that does not respond to their culture and way of life. Not only that but the severe imbalance of resources and complete lack of community engagement meant that the black population has never had the means to create spaces of their own or even spaces that reflect their culture. Instead [they] had to make do with what was given and re-appropriate found spaces, even structures, that bear a dark history.

The Women's Opportunity Center, Kayonza, Rwanda

Georgia Todd

Light plays an integral role in Sharon Davis' conception of non-intimidating classroom spaces that foster a sense of community for women in rural Rwanda. In order to create a safe, we coming, and secure environment, the scale and typology of the place were carefully considered. The brick patterning refers back to the permeable qualities of traditional Rwandan dwellings and is one of the key design moves in this project. Without natural light, these small classrooms would become claustrophobic, negating the original intention of the space.

Alan Plattus

Design & Visualization
Advanced Studio

with Andrei Harwell

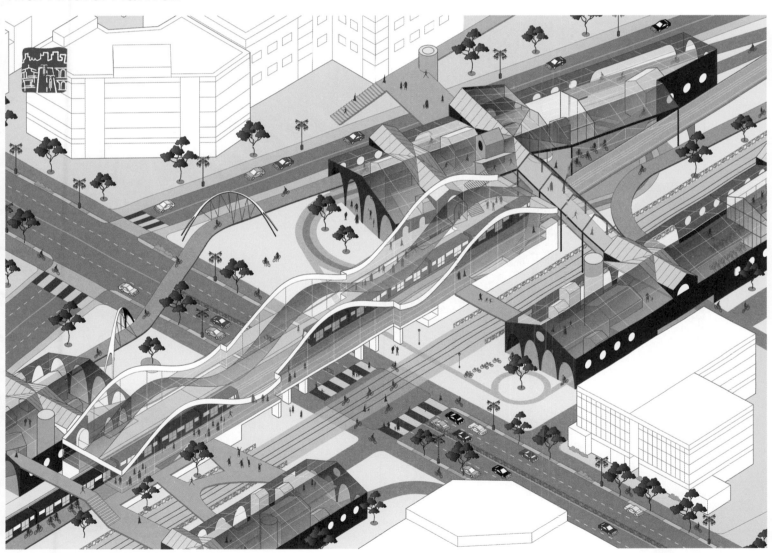

261

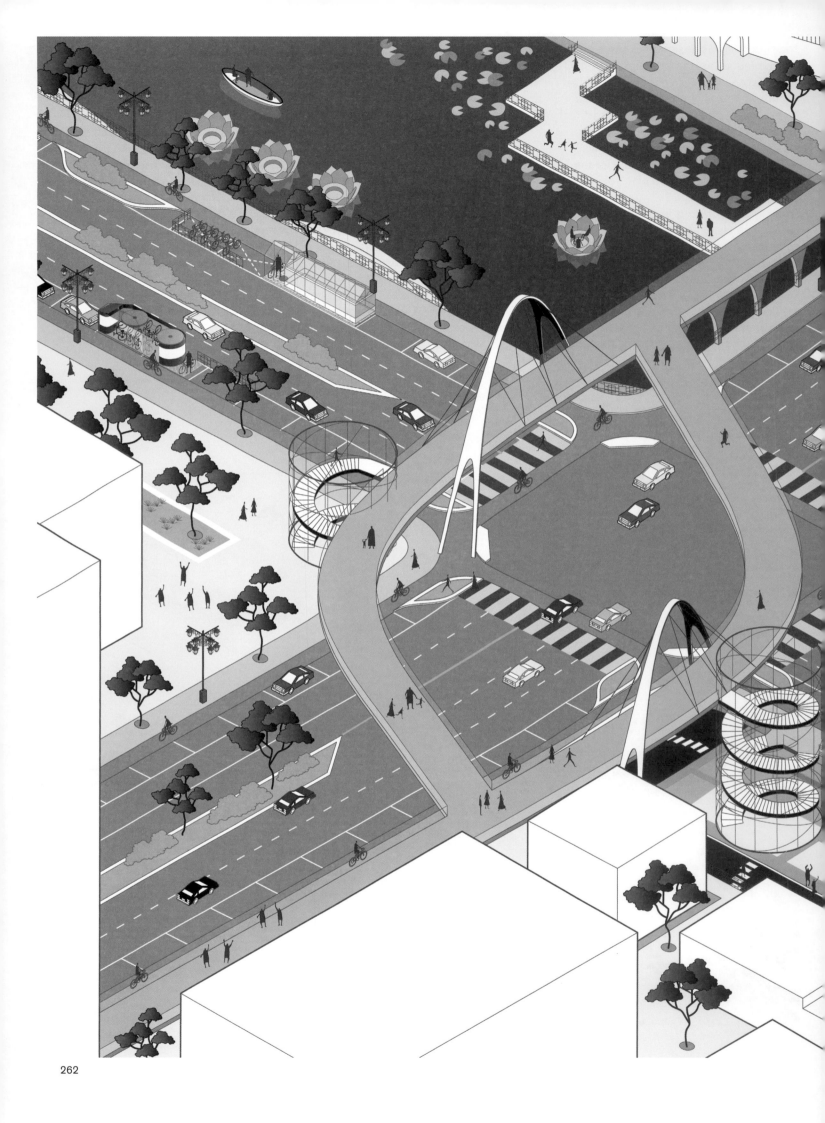

Fall
Plattus, Alan

This studio is in its sixteenth year of the Yale School of Architecture's China Studio, and the fifth year of the collaboration between Yale and Tsinghua University School of Architecture in Beijing. We continue an investigation of urban development and redevelopment in the historic and contemporary Chinese city, with a particular emphasis on models of sustainable mixed-use and neighborhood development. This year's studio continues a new line of investigation examining the development corridor that has recently been created by the high speed commuter rail connection from Beijing to the port city of Tianjin. The site considers the re-use of another historic shipbuilding factory complex directly to the east of the new CBD and located on a dramatic site where the Hai River flows into Tianjin Harbor and the Bohai Sea.

Critics

Naomi Darling (ND), Alexander Felson (AF), Andrei Harwell (AH), Jian Liu (JL), Edward Mitchell (EM), Carie Penabad (CP), Alan Plattus (AP), Robert A.M. Stern (RAMS), David Tseng (DT), David Waggonner (DW), Na Wei (NW), Wenyi Zhu (WZ)

Cynthia Hsu, Winny Tan 261, 262

Our visit promoted a close examination of contemporary transportation culture and infrastructure in Beijing. Once a city where the bicycle was an icon of the people, its rapid economic growth and population led to the steady decline of the bicycle in favor of the automobile. Although the streets are congested with people, the current infrastructure prioritizes vehicular over pedestrian traffic. Meanwhile, bicycles have all but vanished from the roads. Despite the current cultural pushback, interest in reviving bicycles as a major mode of urban transportation persists due to promising environmental and economic benefits combined with the frustration towards Beijing's overcrowded ring roads and subway stations.

CP: *Sign me up as a member of your club! I want to get one of the pins.* [laughter] *I think it's an incredibly important project for the city.*
NW: *There's so many people—even thousands of people—waiting at train stations. So imagine if everyone is riding bicycles to the station; you really need to figure out a way to make people love the bicycle because from your drawing it definitely doesn't work.*

Apoorva Khanolkar, Isaac Southard 263, 264

Our proposal breaks down Beijing's contemporary relationship with water through a comprehensive democratization of the Tonghui. This act begins by exposing new processes of water treatment and purification such that they are made visible to the public. A number of 'water towns' along the riverfront are linked not by a single spatial narrative, but by the instrumentalization of water as a productive landscape across varying degrees of rehabilitation and food production. Water is then the backbone of a new kind of fabric-making that promotes quality urbanism, ecological restoration, economic sustenance and social integration without resorting to the nostalgia of the *hutongs*. It breaks free of its current shackles in becoming both an amenity and a resource for a new and responsible Beijing.

AF: *[You have to consider the] whole range of engineering strategies which are some sort of callibration of building development, water management, and agriculture, which also have social dimensions to them.*

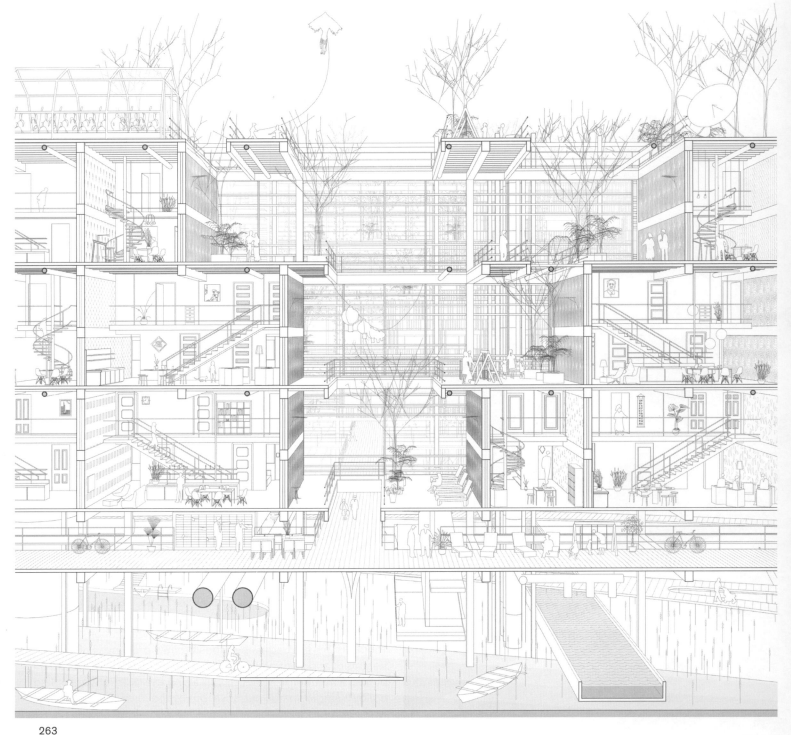

263

264

Anne Ma, John Chengqi Wan (Feldman Nominees) 265–268
The Tonghui riverfront in central Beijing is a difficult, forgotten post-industrial railway landscape, only because its latent potential has not been realized. These places can be the foundations for insurgent public spaces: self-made urban spaces that range from reclaimed and re-appropriated sites, to temporary events and informal gathering places. We approach the question of city-healing not through a singular top-down strategy, but instead through the analysis of site-specific, unique situations. We see program not as a singular, unyielding thing, but as a limitless list of possibilities generating a continuous urban laboratory in which both public and private are engaged in the process of urban development, represented through narratives that capture the intricacies of human inhabitation.

AP: *It's hard, as a critic, not to just stand back and see what happens next. You hesitate to intervene in the process. Part of it is that I have known in my work architects who are not conductors but listeners and ghostwriters. While everyone else is talking, [they are] listening but drawing at the same time. I've always imagined that figure—both of you—just keep drawing the story and it layers over time. So choices are not really being made but it's all piling up in the course of the semester. You didn't throw much out.* [laughter]

265

267

266

268

145
Plattus, Alan

Poets' Landscapes
Urbanism & Landscape

Dolores Hayden

This course is an introduction to techniques poets have used to ground their work in the landscapes and buildings of American towns and cities, including Chicago, New York City, and Los Angeles. Attention is paid to poems from a national automotive landscape as well as narrative poems about cities. Writing exercises include short essays and exercises in various poetic forms; readings from the works of Dickinson, Frost, Bishop, Lowell, Wilbur, Dickey, Pinsky, Cervantes, and Merrill.

Excerpt from "The Iron Twig"
Amra Saric
…The slopes collapse/in layers and sediments, and sometimes crumble/into one another—colliding, perhaps,/beneath the sheet of green; a landmass stumble./We glide along the road as it swerves,/until I see it: a synapse between two mounds,/a single line connecting two curves,/so fragile, yet so sternly it bounds/our path.…

Demetri Porphyrios
Design & Visualization
Advanced Studio

with George Knight

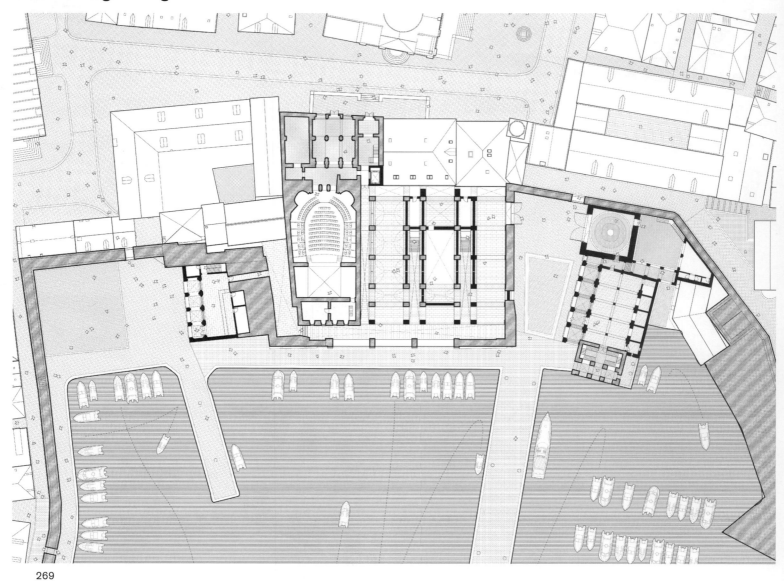

269

This studio focuses on the parallel trajectory that the 'city' and 'art gallery' follow in grappling to give visible form to absence. As such, it focuses on the meaningful contrast between the domestic and the industrial, suggesting as it may be that beauty and violence unfold as an implacable palimpsest.

Critics
Thomas Beeby (TB), Kent Bloomer (KB), Melissa DelVecchio (MD), Judy DiMaio (JD), Kyle Dugdale (KD), Ann Morrow Johnson (AMJ), Barbara Littenberg (BL), Demetri Porphyrios (DP), Alexander Purves (AP), David Schwarz (DS), Robert A.M. Stern (RAMS), Ellis Woodman (EW)

Justin Oh (Feldman Nominee) 269
The city of Dubrovnik, the "City of Stone and Light," enjoys an urban environment rich in culture, materiality, and intimacy. There is no shortage of urban variety or places to be. The city breathes. The Dubrovnik Gallery of Contemporary Art and Sculpture is not a single building, but a neighborhood of buildings. Built upon the existing structure of Dubrovnik's former arsenal—a building once used to build, repair, and store the city's four warships—the gallery must respect what is existing. Only when the gallery understands the language, character, and tectonic of its site, will the city give back to the gallery her diverse inventory of potential exhibition spaces. It will be a quiet set of buildings.
RAMS: *Well-orchestrated work. Your tower is wonderful. It's a marvelous project. Now, of course, when you get an applause before the jury begins to say anything, you're in trouble.* [laughter]

Michelle Chen 270

As a foreigner fares by sea to the coast of Dubrovnik, he would realize that his admittance into the city depends upon his confinement at the Lazareti. Within the fortified walls of this customs house, time will reveal his fitness, authority will ascertain his validity. No sight of the city is to be found: no ceremonious glimpse of the final destination, no promising view of purpose. Aside from an upward look to the sky, the sole aperture to the outside world frames a serene picture of the sea—a retrospective reminder of the undulating waves that brought one to the brink, but not quite to the finale. In this liminal space—sightless of any future, nostalgic for a past, and removed from the present by bastioned authority—one is withdrawn from any progression in time and place. Within this transitory place designated for the marginalized, the familiar and the foreign are brought to constant opposition. It is through their continual interaction that finite definitions of beauty and violence begin to lose distinction.

KB: *Sculpture has a history of its own, and architecture has a history of its own, and they work together, conceivably. When they work together, they inform each other. If you look at the history of architecture, you can see where sculpture has informed architecture and vice versa. I get the sense that the second track of history where the sculpture informs the architecture is so far not appearing as part of the argument.* KD: *It feels as if you're on the cusp of finding a way of communicating your ideas that is quite unique to you.*

Boris Morin-Defoy 271

This project takes root in the city of Korcula, a peninsular town on the coast of Croatia. The gallery complex engages in conversation with the town through a normative statement that incorporates or reinvents key elements of the city. Art is displayed in the complex in a variety of ways. One would experience the sculpture collection serially or axially in courtyards replicating the negative imprint of the city plots. Reflections accentuate the experience of art as some of these courtyards are flooded by the carving of the architectural envelope.

JD: *I think this is a beautiful project because it has allusions of taking the palace of Diocletian and interpreting it into a modernist grid. But within the grid you have placed these vignettes and set pieces that hark to Saint Ivo's and Hadrian's Villa with these objects floating in the water. I think it's beautiful. I only have one real problem, and I wish when the water was actually eating into it that this had changed the materiality so you can tell that the water mushes into the building.*

Sofia Singler 272, 273

The etymology of Hvar can be traced to the Greek word for lighthouse, *pharos*. The town's civic, religious and artistic institutions operate as independent beacons around the town square's perimeter that direct visitors in pursuit of particular rituals and conventions. Pharos Gallery situates itself in this string of institutions as a lighthouse that guides the art tourist's itinerary. The gallery's most intrinsic function—the display of art—is kept separate: the viewing galleries, organized around a central cortile, remain geometrically, axially, and spatially autonomous from the rest of the program. This nucleus of discrete viewing galleries unashamedly defends the significance of the individual's encounter with art as a necessarily intimate and subjective endeavor.

JD: *I like where you juxtapose the figural and the sculptural in these bare, empty, austere spaces. That is quite beautiful.* KD: *I feel as if your presentation comes at the cost of something such as the ability to study the light conditions. We look at these images and we recognize the type, but for me those types also come with certain relationships to the world outside them. That includes the question of how do you get light into that space. The reason the spaces that we think of are the way they are is in large part because of the question of how you bring light into the interior.*

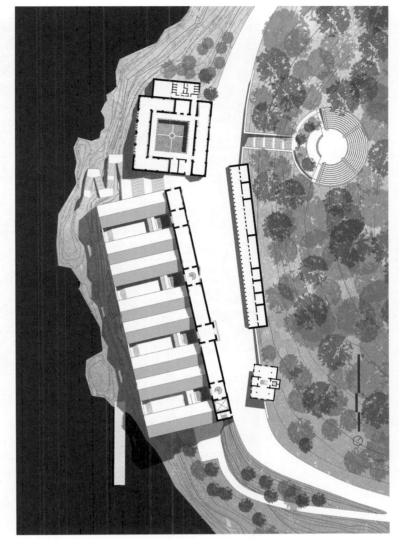

270

271

Porphyrios, Demetri

272

273

149
Porphyrios, Demetri

Rendered:
Architecture and
Contemporary
Image Culture

Design & Visualization

Brennan Buck

This course addresses the role of image
making in architecture at a time when
consumers of culture, including architects,
are inundated by images. While images
can never replace the experience of a
building in time and space, it is their
potential to circulate so seamlessly that
gives them undeniable power as our
discipline's primary means of engagement
with popular culture. The course questions
their status as solely representational, a
sign of some other, more 'real,' object. What
is the relationship they construct between
real and simulacrum? Can images produce
alternate realities rather than simulate our
own? Can they resist their own illusionary
function? The course revolves around
readings and discussion dealing with these
questions, but also deals directly with
techniques of image-making.

275

276

274

277

Jonathan Rose
Design Like You Give a Damn

The lecture tonight is called *Design Like You Give a Damn*, and
the title comes from a book that was published by Architects for
Humanity. It's a very interesting book. There are two versions of
this book, two editions, and they describe socially responsible
architecture from around the world. I love the phrase "design like
you give a damn" because the work that we do provides key DNA
to the evolution of cities. As you all know, by 2100, 80% of the
world's population is going to live in cities. And the difference

that we make with each building that we do—and actually each
room, each nuance of the building—contributes to what this
overall DNA is going to be, the metagenomics of cities. We can do
that well or we can do that poorly.

...One of the interesting things about this tension is that, as
all of these stresses are happening within cities, we're seeing fault
lines grow. In 2012, all of a sudden, riots broke out in London, a
place that one never would have thought… If you look at [the map],
riots are not in the poorest areas. They're actually near the fault line
where the lower middle class, who tend to be immigrants, could
not move into the middle class. They're places of frustration, where
people ran into the invisible lines of inequality and couldn't move
forward. It was out of that frustration that the riots really emerged.

Joel Sanders

Design & Visualization
Second Year Studio

This third core studio concentrates on a medium-scale institutional building, focusing on the integration of composition, site, program, mass, and form in relation to structure, and methods of construction. Interior spaces are studied in detail. Large-scale models and drawings are developed to explore design issues.

Critics

Emily Abruzzo (EA), Lee Altman (LA), Carol Burns (CB), Sara Caples (SC), Stephen Cassell (SCa), Peter de Bretteville (PdB), Martin Finio (MF), Louise Harpman (LH), Mimi Hoang (MH), Andrea Kahn (AK), Tessa Kelly (TK), Craig Konyk (CK), Amy Lelyveld (AL), David Mohney (DM), Joeb Moore (JM), Joel Sanders (JS), Robert A.M. Stern (RAMS), Claire Weisz (CW)

Nasim Rowshanabadi 278, 279
This project resolves the lack of connection of the site to the main campus and creates the sense of presence across Morrison Avenue. The architecture school's massing, which is formed by the environmental forces, shapes a gateway to a semi-private plaza that serves as an urban hub. A gradient-perforated skin filters light on the south and west sides, responding to parameters such as visibility and program. The surrounding skin then folds inside and creates the main interior cores that integrate circulations, enclosed programs, meeting spaces and services.
AL: *In terms of pedagogy I think it's really witty that you come in the front and you think you know what you're getting, and then it all flips on you.* JS: *The potential for your project is a new kind of pedagogy that suggests that there are these semi-enclosed cores that are catalysts. They're like magic rocks! It's a new relationship between public and private that allows for this very complicated sea of furniture.*

Robert Yoos 280
This proposal is at once a critique of the banal office park architecture of the site and the programmatic composition of Rudolph Hall. Rather than a traditional voided center such as in Rudolph Hall, the building is filled with a colored sculptural condenser of shared spaces that include auditoriums, classrooms, fabrication facilities and student lounges. This social center, conceivably caught in amber, is suspended from above and sculpts space throughout the box in order to maintain a dynamic visual connection to the open studios that surround it.
PdB: *I think the least convincing thing for me is the site plan, and I think the really big event is the underground cut. That should be dramatized in some way.*

Alexander Stagge 281
This project addresses the commuter campus by creating a linear connection from the parking garage to the pedestrian campus. The ground floor is made up of entirely of public programs, allowing the building to act as a continuation of the campus. The studio spaces above are housed in an inwardly-focused linear bar that wraps above. The conceptual front is a faceted surface that articulates a zone of stairs and critique spaces. The outer edge of the space is skylit; the structure divides the continuous space into zones that articulate the individual studios.
AK: *I think there is an opportunity to reflect on conventional terminologies associated with function, and projecting out further saying: If this is a project predicated on bringing a public through, what becomes public in design pedagogy?*

Paul Lorenz 282
This proposal for the Michael Graves School of Architecture seeks to extend a conception of the built environment to include the banal landscapes that often surround suburban and exurban developments. While these landscapes frequently become neglected and ignored, assumed to be in a primordial condition, they are truly as constructed as the rest of a project. As its starting point, this project admits the constructed nature of its context.
RAMS: *I looked at your scheme and thought it was a toll plaza on the Garden State Parkway. It's a completely mechanistic usurpation of the entire site.* Paul: *I will admit it is an aggressive intervention.* RAMS: *Well, I'll give you a high score for self-analysis.* [laughter] AK: *I think there needs to be a distinction between landscape and ground plane. This is a project that is 'architecting' a ground plane but is not working with what one fully understands to be the landscape, which is a great deal more than the surface.*

279

278

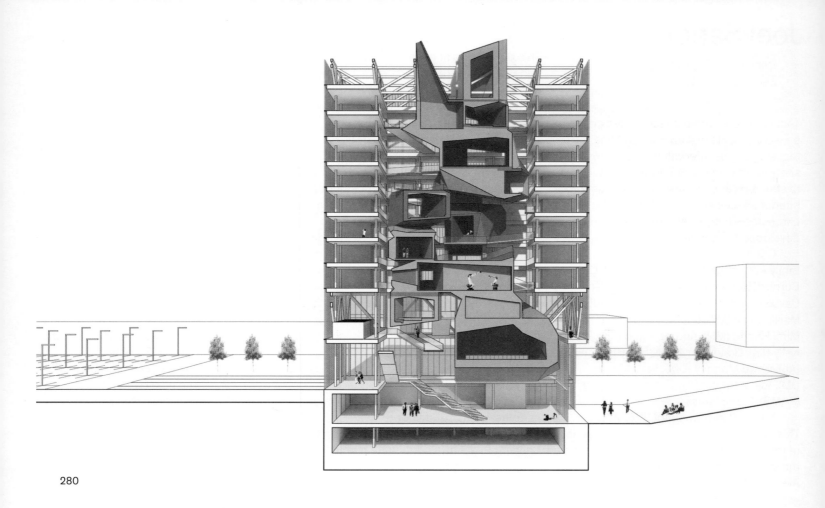

280

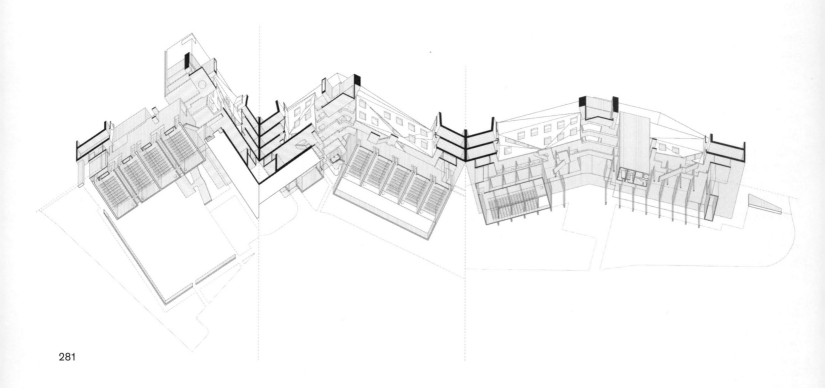

281

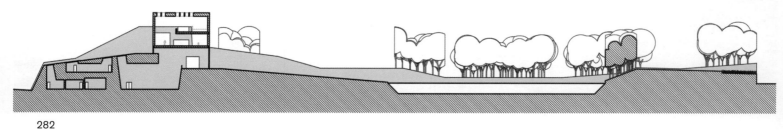

282

Fall
Sanders, Joel

Saskia Sassen
Expulsions

Myriam Bellazoug Memorial Lecture

It is really wonderful to be here, and thank you for that very kind introduction. I must also say that I was so impressed with the Yale Perspecta group. I don't know who was my editor there, but I wish that I could take her with me on every book that I'm working on. It was just great work. The idea, the imagination—I'm very honored to deliver this lecture, the Myriam Bellazoug Memorial Lecture....

I brought you two books for the organizers. My books tend to be quite boring, all of them, but they have some good stuff in there. [*laughter*]

I want to talk briefly about [my] book, Expulsions. In many ways, what I try to do there is to interpolate the category 'inequality.' Everybody is talking about inequality. I have been talking about inequality myself for thirty years. But inequality by itself is just a distribution. So you've got to interrogate it with something, and so I've done that with many questions of social justice. When does inequality become profoundly socially unjust? And when is it manageable inequality? Any complex system is going to have inequality. In this particular book,

I want to understand the moment when the familiar—not the monstrous—the familiar becomes so extreme that our categories, conceptual, statistical, of the imaginary, almost can no longer capture them.

It's a very specific zone, this "zone of expulsions." Most of our cities, for instance, are becoming more beautiful, redone, built up—and mind you, a lot of people are expelled and they become invisible—but if you look at the mainstream zone of our current world, you say, "Hey, what's wrong? New York looks more beautiful, cleaner, has more high rise buildings, out with the little old buildings." I hate that part....

My concern is with the very material conditions [of] dead land and dead water. I say in the book, I don't want to talk climate change—that language is almost too beautiful. "Climate change"—my God, it sounds beautiful. No. Dead land. Dead water. [Language] in its full materiality, it becomes invisible. A long-term, unemployed black man of Harlem, thirty-three years old, never held a job. Can you capture that with 'long-term unemployment?' No, we're on the other side of a curve. This is a radical situation that is not simply 'long-term unemployment.'

In my research practice I expose, I've understood that I've always been doing that. I call [my research 'zone'] the 'zone before method' to give it a name. Mind you, I've done whole lectures on this subject, and now a publisher has asked me to publish a little book called Before Method. Not 'After Method'—you know there is a famous book called After Method. 'Before Method' is the notion that the more interesting 'zone' of the paradigm, whatever the paradigmatic knowledge you are dealing with—I think it would hold for architecture as well—is actually where paradigm becomes weak: not the center, but the edges…

The core knowledge that we can accept as continuing—I'm sure you must have some version of that—is strong in the center, and then, what happens at the edges?

At the edges we can interrogate, interpolate, do away with, as something else is coming up there. To do that I engage the

social sciences—the imaginary plays a far smaller role than it does in architecture and design.

You have to use analytic tactics to clean it up a bit. So with the very strong category, and again, think about whatever category you may have or be working with, you can't quite throw it out of the window, even if you don't like it, but what you can do is sort of destabilize it. Actively destabilize it. Or ask 'what don't I see when I invoke this?' In the social sciences, 'the economy,' 'the middle class,' [there is a] whole range of terms that are invitations not to think....

This notion is actively destabilized, partly because we are actively living in a period of change, an unstable period.

I'm [currently] obsessing about the category 'territory,' which is not simply land: it's not terrain, it's not ground, it's not space. It is actually a rather complex condition that is partly made with embedded logics of power and embedded logic of claim-making.

In our western modernity the most accomplished forms of that were the state and citizenship. Again, I ignore domains—I don't know what the equivalent would be.

But I want to start with that final point: the making of it all. Emphasizing making is a partial approach. We don't make everything. We inherit a lot. A lot continues. But I want to sharpen the moment and say we make. We make that. We made that, you understand what we're talking about? The Barrow Sea in twenty years. One of the biggest inland water bodies to nothing. Clearly I'm not using capability as the notion of 'making' in the positive sense. I'm saying this is a capability. We made it—it didn't fall from the sky—we made it. Now one can see, one can take a whole range of these issues and say "We made it. It's all bad right now. But we were able to make that." What are the capacities that we mobilize? Can we give them another value? We made this. Millennia, millennia, millennia: it was fine. We managed to destroy that in twenty-five years. When you stand back, you say, this is actually amazing. So we are extreme makers. We've also made some good things. We've also made some good things.

October 8, 2015

Sassen, Saskia *Lecture*

Rosalyne Shieh

Design & Visualization
First Year Studio

In an era of information architecture, where the idea of virtual space is increasingly prevalent, this studio examines and reasserts the role of physical spaces, sites and structure. Three distinct projects explore the architectural potential of alternate modes of learning in contemporary culture. The first project asks students to design a study, a volume that contains, hosts or organizes alternate modes of learning. The second project for the design of a seed vault as an exterior study shifts focus towards site as a subject of study, inform- ing the design approach as well as the literal program for the project. The third project examines the urban public library as a type that historically functioned as a container of books, social center and monument for a neighborhood but is recast in light of questions of the role of the library in a digital age. This project asks students to reinvigorate the public library as a universal cultural institution.

Critics
Annie Barrett (AB), Phillip Bernstein (PB), Brennan Buck (BB), Abigail Coover (AC), Trattie Davies (TD), Dana Getman (DG), Eugene Han (EH), Andrew Holder (AH), Joyce Hsiang (JH), Kathleen John-Alder (KJA), Alfred Koetter (AK), Carrie McKnelly (CM), Marc McQuade (MM), Bimal Mendis (BM), David Moon (DM), Shane Neufeld (SN), Ben Pell (BP), Surry Schlabs (SS), Rosalyne Shieh (RS), James Slade (JS), Beka Sturges (BS), Michael Szivos (MS), Anthony Titus (AT)

Dylan Lee 283, 284

RS: *I want to commend you for being so tenacious in your study of the saw-tooth. The locus of the problem is precisely between the semantic and the formal. You have a real attachment to the sematic, but you've made huge strides to understand the performative aspects of that form.*

Alexis Hyman 286, 288

SS: *I'm not sure what is going on in this expertly composed array of gridded spaces. As a fiction I'm totally on board. Using the grid to distort is amazing.* TD: *This is two projects: one that is archeological and one that is territorial. It's about disorientation and illusion.*

Patrick Doty 287

BP: *As with any parametric design—what- ever the inputs are that you start with—it's a very willful moment. If you start with walls, you are going to get Mies. If you start with boxes, you're going to get Loos. You have to be aware—in the moment you decide to use walls—instead of volumes or poles, you have a very defined set of possibilities in terms of what the spatial implications are.*

Jack Lipson 285

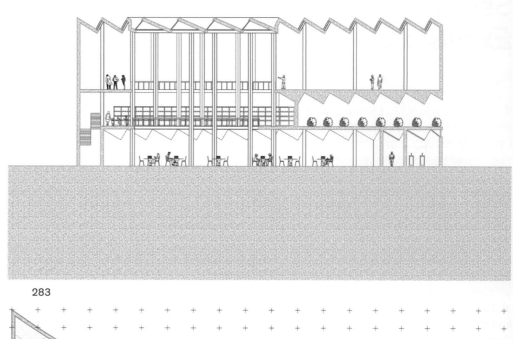

283

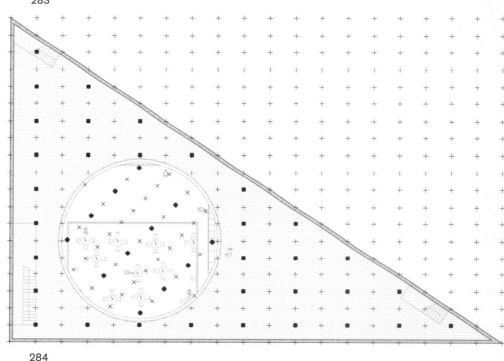

284

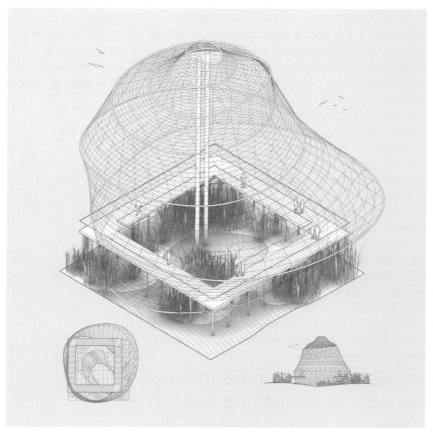

285

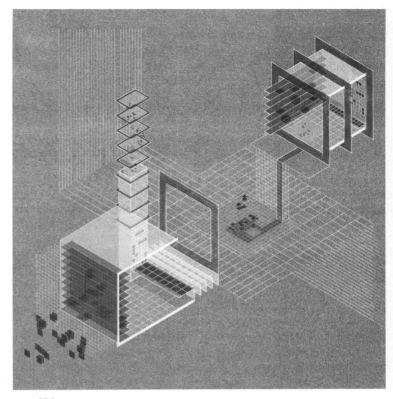

288

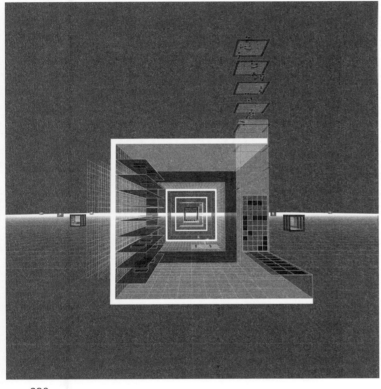

286

287

155
Shieh, Rosalyne

Spatial Concepts of Japan

History & Theory

Yoko Kawai

The seminar explores the origins and developments of Japanese spatial concepts and surveys how they help form the contemporary architecture, ways of life, and cities of the country. Many Japanese spatial concepts, such as *Ma*, are about creating time-space distances and relationship between objects, people, space, and experiences. These concepts go beyond the fabric of a built structure and encompass architecture, landscape, and city. Contemporary works studied include those by Maki, Isozaki, Ando, Ito, SANAA, and Fujimoto. The urbanism and landscape of Tokyo and Kyoto are discussed.

Slow Thresholds in Japanese Architecture
Graham Brindle

There is an interesting role played by the exterior façade within the genealogy of Japanese architecture. What I explore in particular is the cultural application of thickened envelopes. These are the diaphanous, peripheral spaces of verandas, sliding screens, entry halls, overhangs, and landscaping that divide interior space from exterior. The planar divide between opposing worlds (interior/exterior, public/private, nature/human) is given volume and depth—an inhabitable gap that slows and emphasizes the transition between environments. In each particular relationship, the tectonic elements that mediate the exchanges serve distinct purposes.

…The line between public and private may necessitate a visual mediation, while human space might demand a dry room separated from the wet natural environment. In the modern Western conception of architecture, these roles are all commonly served by a singular structural façade. But the distinctly Japanese preoccupation with layering and depth led to the delamination of these elements into their own discrete tectonic systems.

To understand the products of this spatial practice, it is important to first mention the Japanese concept of *Ma*. Through a basic translation *Ma* can be understood as a gap or interval. But *Ma* does not simply refer to the voids created amidst compositional elements. Instead, *Ma* refers to the conscious human differentiation between form and non-form, whether in time or in space. This spatial concept can be found embedded in the products of Japan's cultural history, whether through music, spoken verse, or structure. And when considered at the scale of architecture, *Ma* carries with it several interesting

connotations. *Ma* implies an interstice between two environments. But it also intrinsically refers to the motion of a person between those spaces. So the space of *Ma* can be understood as a node along a linear progression: a pause between forms that allows the occupant to become aware of that moment of change before proceeding. As important as *Ma* is in generating a quarantine between two worlds, it is also a critical space for guiding the transition between them.

Tadao Ando Vitra Conference Pavilion, 1993, Vitra Weil am Rhein, Germany
Andrew Dadds

Ando discusses his desire to penetrate to the root of an idea—in this case, western architecture—in search of the source. When comparing the plan of the Vitra Pavilion to that of the Parthenon and the Acropolis, it is clear that Ando is borrowing a sense of anticipation from the antiquities at the Acropolis as they unfold as a sequence in time and space. The Acropolis leads one through a winding path, whereby the Parthenon is not seen on a formal axis until the very end, hiding and revealing itself through extensions of landscape and building. The materiality of the building appears heavy, as if sculpted from the earth, growing out of the formation of the site, a large rocky hillside.

Ando, on the other hand, deploys a similar attitude towards materiality: stable, heavy concrete, notably in stark contrast to that of traditional Japanese architecture, such as the Ise Shrine, whose living quality is in harmony to the cedar forest site. Ise Shrine has its own lifecycle, decomposing and regenerating itself every twenty years. At Vitra—and characteristic of many of his projects—Ando builds in a monumental material of poured concrete, in stark contrast to the grassy orchard surrounding the pavilion. Ando describes his fondness for the "very hard and sharp" concrete forms that powerfully contrast and even enhance the qualities of nature: "I like the sharp edges and planes that can be made with concrete. When they come into contact with nature they are like a powerful foil. The precise order in contrast to nature can make both elements more dynamic." [1]

1. Ando, Tadao, and Michael Auping. *Seven Interviews with Tadao Ando*. Fort Worth: Modern Art Museum of Fort Worth, 2002. pg. 59

Rituals & Enclosures: Two Types of Sacred Space
Abdulgader Naseer

The *Chado* (way of the tea) itself, while frequently perceived as a secular activity, has been referred to as a religious ritual by many experts such as Sen Genshitsu, the previous grand master of the Urasenke School, who has stated, "Tea is the practice or realization of religious faith, no matter what you believe

in." Furthermore, Sen Rikyu, widely viewed as the most important tea master to date, has contextualized *Chado* within the quasi-religious disciple of Zen: "In Zen, truth is pursued through the discipline of meditation in order to realize enlightenment, while in Tea we use training in the actual procedures of making tea to achieve the same end."

From these quotes, it could be distilled that *Chado* has commonalities with all religious behavior that is not strictly dependent on doctrinal content. Therefore, identifying the essential religious characteristics of tea within its broad spectrum of ritual action, and relating these traits to various definitions of religions, can serve as the points of comparison between the *chashitsu* and the mosque. In both cases, a rigid boundary between the profane and the sacred cannot be drawn. It is through the performance of specific rituals, and the architectural manifestations that accommodate them, that one is able to attain a sense of sacredness.

Strange Forms in Strange Relationships

Design & Visualization

Nathan Hume

From simple cartoons to the intricacies of kitbashing, architectural form is in flux between extremes of simplicity and complexity. These new extreme states leave significant room to uncover new in-between territories for architecture, as its formal options have never been so great, or so widely accepted. This course investigates contemporary strategies and techniques through digital modeling, for developing innovative new languages that capitalize on these extremes. Precedents that similarly exhibit a curious and strange take on their historic architectural context are tracked throughout history and mined for the architectural qualities they produce. Associations that are derived from qualities of scale, posture, color, silhouette, and material are analyzed and cataloged in order to develop a lexicon of what might define an emerging formal direction in architecture.

289

290

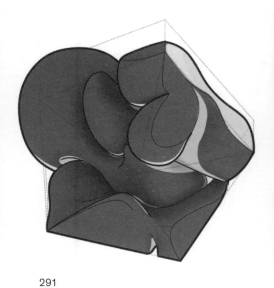

291

292

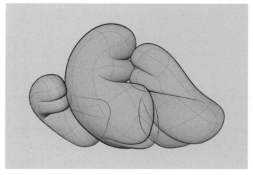

293

Structures I

Technology & Practice

Kyoung Sun Moon

The course introduces the analysis and design of building structural systems and the evolution and impact of these systems on architectural form. The course also covers structural classifications, fundamental principles of mechanics, computational methods, and the behavior and case studies of truss, cable, arch, and simple framework systems. Discussions explore the applications of structural theory to the design of wood and steel systems for gravity loads through laboratory and computational exercises and design projects.

Studies in Light and Materials

Technology & Practice

Michelle Addington

This seminar provides an overview of the basic characteristics and families of 'phenomenological' materials, with a special focus on materials and technologies that have a relationship to light and vision. Materials and technologies, such as LEDs, smart glazing, displays, and interactive surfaces, are examined in depth, and some of the contemporary experiments taking place in the architecture profession are explored. Throughout the term, students catalog relevant properties and begin to develop a mapping between behaviors and phenomena. Students have the opportunity to interact with some of the well-known architects who are at the heart of the current experimentation. Each student learns how to coherently discuss material fundamentals and comprehensively analyze current applications. The seminar culminates with each student focusing on a material characteristic with which to explore different means of technology transfer in order to begin to invent unprecedented approaches and applications.

Michael Szivos

Design & Visualization
First Year Studio

In an era of information architecture, where the idea of virtual space is increasingly prevalent, this studio examines and reasserts the role of physical spaces, sites and structure. Three distinct projects explore the architectural potential of alternate modes of learning in contemporary culture. The first project asks students to design a study, a volume that contains, hosts or organizes alternate modes of learning. The second project for the design of a seed vault as an exterior study shifts focus towards site as a subject of study, informing the design approach as well as the literal program for the project. The third project examines the urban public library as a type that historically functioned as a container of books, social center and monument for a neighborhood but is recast in light of questions of the role of the library in a digital age. This project asks students to reinvigorate the public library as a universal cultural institution.

Critics
Phillip Bernstein (PB), Miroslava Brooks (MB), Brennan Buck (BB), Abigail Coover (AC), Trattie Davies (TD), Rosetta Elkin (RE), Dana Getman (DG), Andrew Holder (AH), Joyce Hsiang (JH), Carrie McKnelly (CM), Kyle Miller (KM), Alan Organschi (AO), Rosalyne Shieh (RS), James Slade (JS), Michael Szivos (MS), Anthony Titus (AT), Irina Verona (IV), Elia Zenghelis (EZ)

Dimitri Brand 294
KM: *Ultimately a+x+3+! needs to add up to something that you can speak on behalf of.*

Ian Donaldson 295
AT: *It seems to me the big gestures that everyone is talking about are the strategy of carving the ground, touching the ground, and those points basically piercing the volume which you say are registered on top as this tense moment. I think [the object is] the strong point of your project.*

Kevin Huang 296, 297
AT: *Is what's most important the specific architectural expression, where the characteristics are at least momentarily less important? I think you have to ask yourself to what degree you consider that placement for something that is characteristically very different. I think you're not necessarily seeing how charged the specific forms you're reconfiguring are.*

Caitlin Baiada 298
JB: *You never know when you're in the building or out of the building. This whole precinct here becomes the building; once you're inside it becomes public. It's almost furniture within a larger room, which I think is a beautiful reading of the site and the idea of public spaces within a city.*

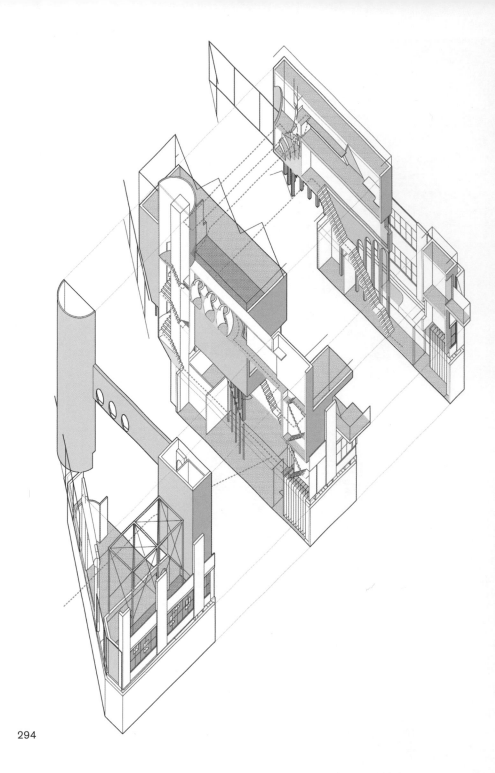

294

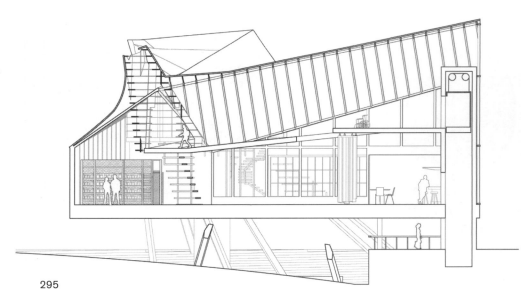

295

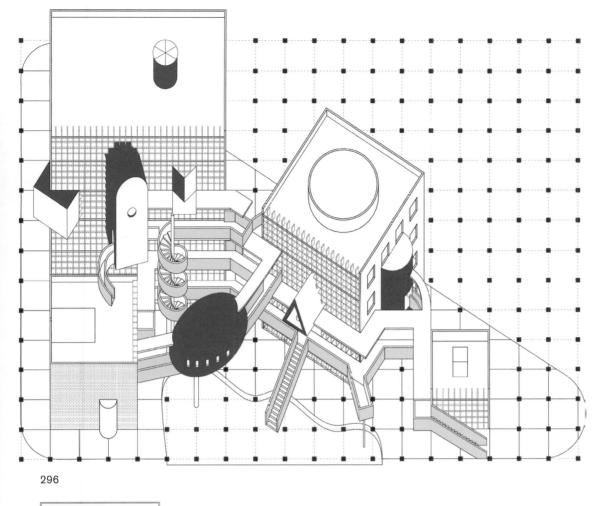

296

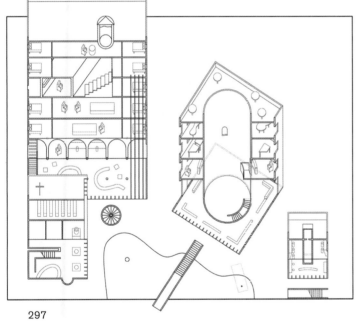

297

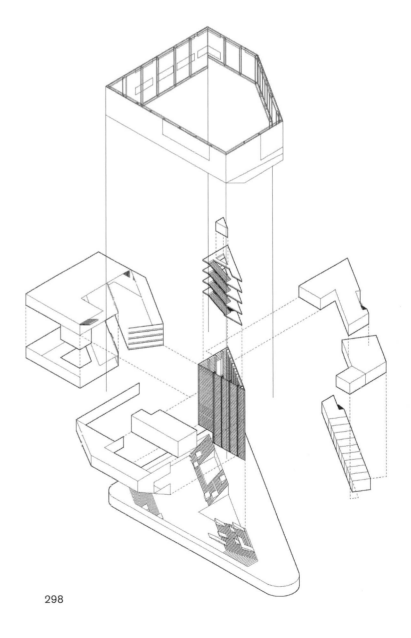

298

Techno-Sensations: Architecture, Technology, and the Body

History & Theory

Joel Sanders

This seminar explores the transformative impact of the digital revolution on architecture and the human senses. After exploring these contemporary developments through the lens of history and considering how the advent of audiovisual devices—from the camera obscura to the iPhone—have altered the design of the built environment and our sensory experience of space, the course speculates about the future.

Optics, Power and the Beheld Body: The Case of the Recumbent Venus
Cathryn Garcia-Menocal

When Michel Foucault concentrated on modern institutions of confinement—the asylum, the clinic, and the prison—he positioned Western oculocentrism and these institutional architectural spaces as the dialectic arbiters of the respective discourses of madness, illness, and criminality—a move that was a pointed reversal of spatial and phenomenal cause and effect. According to Douglas Crimp, "the other institution ripe for analysis in Foucalt's terms [is] the museum; and another discipline: art history." Art history is the interwoven practice of fabricating a historical past that could effectively be placed under systematic observation for use in staging and transforming the present. Indeed, it is Foucault who makes explicit that transitive properties of vision and power: if to see is to know, and to know is to empower, then to see is to empower. As such, the field of art history itself and its deference to vision as the supreme sense has shaped the space of the museum and especially its differentiation from the archive.

This course investigates drawing as a means of architectural communication and as a generative instrument of formal, spatial, and tectonic discovery. Principles of two-dimensional and three-dimensional geometry are extensively studied through a series of exercises that employ freehand and constructive techniques. Students work fluidly between manual drawing, computer drawing, and material construction. All exercises are designed to enhance the ability to visualize architectural form and volume three-dimensionally, understand its structural foundations, and provide tools that reinforce and inform the design process.

James Coleman 299
Valeria Flores 300
Alexandra Thompson 301
Timon Covelli 302

301

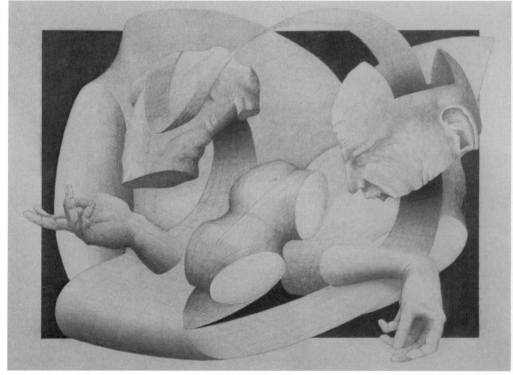

299

Visualization II: Form and Representation

Design & Visualization

Sunil Bald and Kent Bloomer

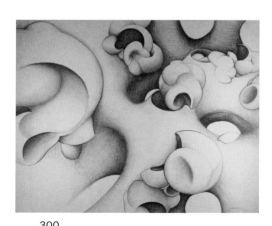

300

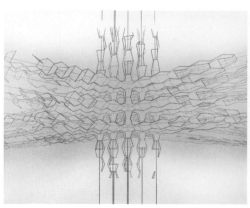

302

Marion Weiss and Michael Manfredi

Design & Visualization
Advanced Studio

with Britton Rogers

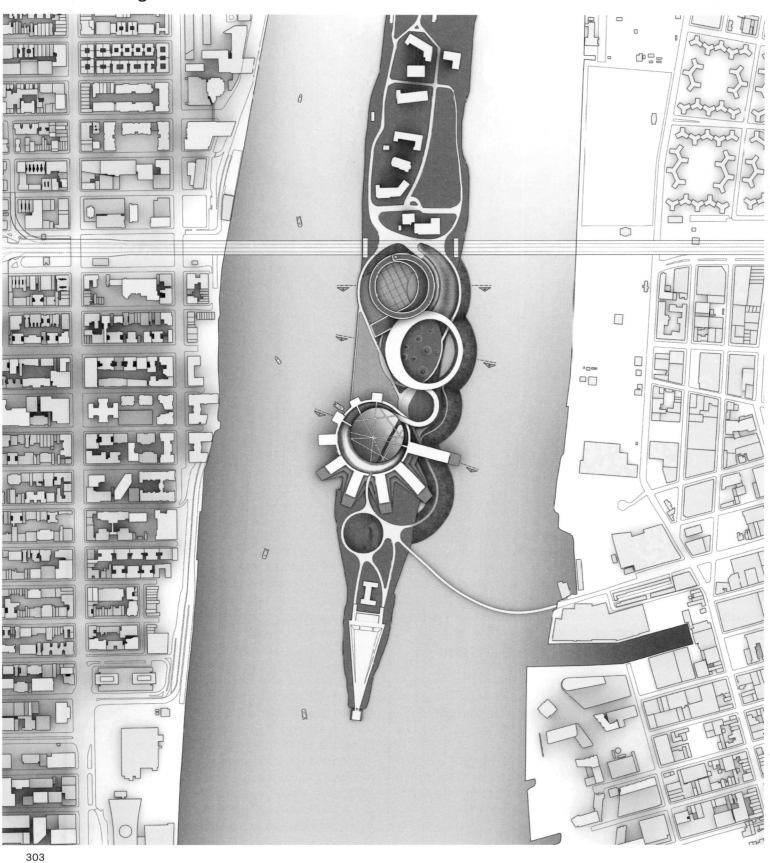

303

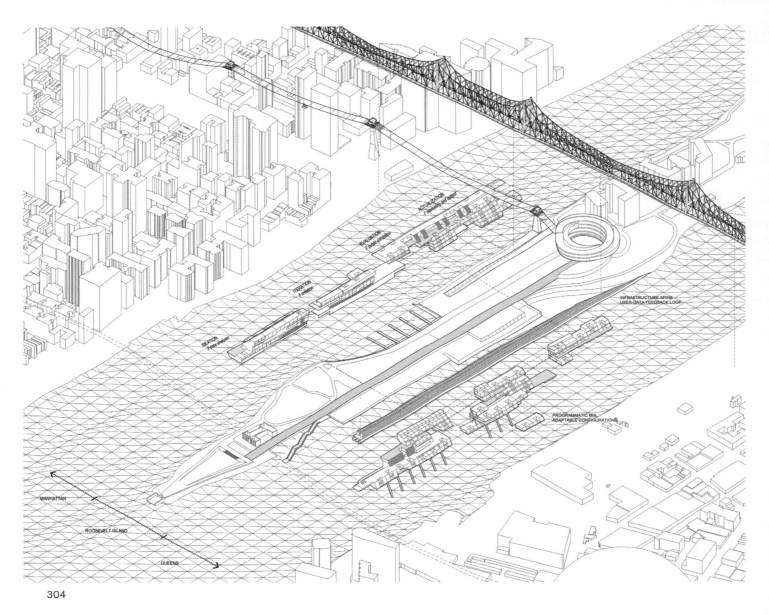

304

In 2011, New York City announced its partnership with Cornell University and Israel's Technion University to create "Cornell Tech," a pioneering plunge intended to recast New York City as a global technology hub. This two million square foot campus—an island incubator—is intended to forge vital connections between research and innovation and redefine Roosevelt Island as a vital urban character within the borough of Manhattan. Without predetermined answers, the creation of this new campus raises critical questions: How can we recast prior academic and corporate models to create a new academic/entrepreneurial ecosystem? What design strategies effectively resist or submit to predicted rising water levels and storm surges that could leave the land underwater by 2050? How can ecological aspirations inform the invention of a new academic infrastructure dedicated to catalyzing innovation?

Critics

Felipe Correa (FC), Joyce Hsiang (JH), Florian Idenburg (FI), Paul Lewis (PL), Michael Manfredi (MM), Thom Mayne (TM), Hilary Sample (HS), Joel Sanders (JS), Robert A.M. Stern (RAMS), Marion Weiss (MW), Allison Wicks (AW)

Eugene Tan 303

No longer just workplaces, tech campuses of today organize tours, host conferences, house hotels and public parks. Condensing life and labor, many also provide game rooms, in-house childcare, and daily dinners for the whole family. While outsiders see these amenities as absurdities, employees view them as part of the everyday culture in the world of technology. The design for a new Cornell Tech campus is prompted by this tension. Conceived as a series of ceaseless loops, each is crafted to 'serve' the respective type of user. By celebrating the desire to keep workers at the office and promoting the campus as a tourist destination, the project hopes to question the workings of such corporations and their role

in contemporary life. The formal exuberance attempts to reflect the campus' heterotopic conditions while giving imageability to a project that aims to emblematize the East Coast's new status as an innovation hub. For what is absurd? What is quotidian? And therefore, what is contextual within the metropolitan fantasy and urban incubator that is New York City?

FC: *It seems that the three programs could have benefitted enormously from your loop becoming more robust, infrastructurally. The moment you have a convention center, you'll need to bring in trucks and large elements. Maybe there is another scale of mobility to bring a level of urban life here that might justify the different scales. It gives it a structure to establish a new connectivity at a metropolitan scale that also redefines the island at large. Through an architectural intervention you can establish a new relationship with the two edges.* TM: *You wouldn't have to go too far to say that this is not the place to put a convention center. You need to go from being a designer to a thought leader. This is not a design problem. This is a thought leadership problem. Keep the implication of your project. Make it work.*

Anne Householder, Clarissa Luwia (Feldman Nominees) 304

As we delve deeper into the realm of the digital, the linear process of production is no longer relevant. Material goods have depreciated in value and knowledge has become the new currency. Innovations and ideas are bought and sold. Material manifestations are secondary and are often designed to provide even more data with which to generate ideas—through user generated content, user data, and other information-based inputs. Cornell Tech is in this business of knowledge creation. The long Main Street of this campus and large 'shopfronts' allow for connections to occur—not only with colleagues, but also with the public and the city of New York. The residential units and design labs are optimized in scale and arrangement to accommodate a new way of working and a connection with the living world. But perhaps most importantly, the campus is infrastructure—one that is adaptable to fluctuations in both ideology and climate change.

FI: *In a very effective way, you're able to create a double-loaded corridor that actually is able to bring in light on both sides. There is something quite powerful about how your module begins to aggregate to create a collective space that has a particular identity, but is also the residual space. What I would question is the limits of the aggregation of the module and how you would actually begin to introduce variation into it, because I think that view is great. Is there a way to make this very long corridor the aggregation of nine or ten different elements?*

Kiana Hosseini 305, 306

The Island Incubator explores the dialect between the academy and the tech industry. While aiming to generate a dynamic relationship between the two worlds, the project offers a critique of their increasingly blurred boundary, the integration of the employees' professional and personal life at corporate tech companies, and the isolation of these spaces from the surrounding context.

JS: *Some would say that we're living in an age when the boundaries between living and working and academia and incubators are changing—and the influence of digital culture would suggest that in the future we'll inhabit a similar version of a different bunch of spaces. Others would say, "No, there are still disciplinary distinctions." Different kinds of work require different kinds of cultures that would each have a spatial counterpart. Your project foregrounds that issue. You've made a very interesting distinction between the culture of industry and the culture of academia.*

RAMS: *What about the poor Franklin Roosevelt Monument? Some of us worked very hard...* Kiana: *It's integrated.* RAMS: *Yeah, that's the problem. It's integrated! It's become a little comfort station. The whole experience of getting there should be preparatory for a special experience.*

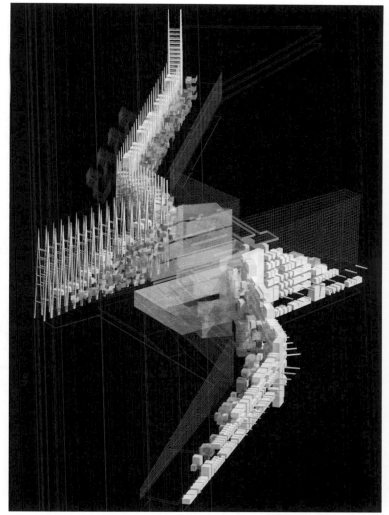

306

305

Weiss/Manfredi
Public Natures: Evolutionary Infrastructures

If 'infrastructure' has become the byword of so many practices that blur the boundaries between architectural and landscape practice, it is because it encapsulates the challenges of scale and complexity that are the preconditions of meaningful public design work today. Increasingly, we designers are operating in a global environment and discovering that the public realm is becoming heavily privatized and specialized, with short-term ambitions shaping long-term effects. And as the amount of public open space decreases, we must become increasingly inventive with compromised or orphan sites.

...If new forms of ecological and social systems are a hallmark of contemporary debates, both within the density of cities and at the fragile edges of natural realms, we believe the stakes of this debate resist oppositional clarity—nature versus city, individual versus collective—but instead suggests evolutionary forms of public nature.

Elia Zenghelis

Design & Visualization
Advanced Studio

with Andrew Benner

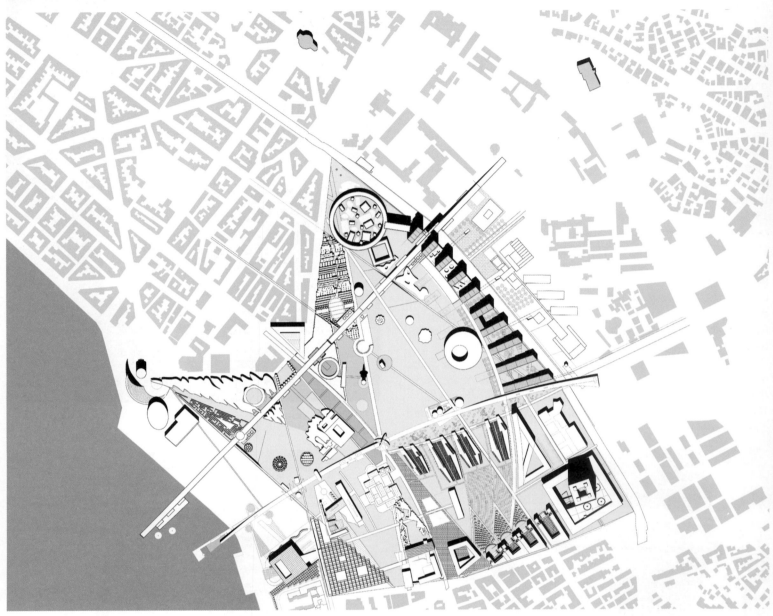

307

Architects have a critical role in shaping the future of civic space, supplying physical interventions that may set limits and shift centers of focus and activity. They also generate images that can serve as manifestos, rallying the will to realize new forms and spaces for civic participation. The studio rehearses that role while turning our attention to Thessaloniki. The studio proposes a critical intervention to a pivotal and central area in Thessaloniki's tissue. This area encompasses a number of major institutions. These constituents determine the area as the kernel of the city—albeit an insubstantial, incomplete, and rather incorporeal kernel—in need of an emblematic material presence and of paradigmatic reconfiguring. The expanded and unified site will be redesigned as an urban park incorporating selected cultural facilities and connections to the existing adjacent green areas, as well as the new waterfront redevelopment.

Critics

Ross Adams (RA), Andrew Benner (AB), Peter Eisenman (PE), Kenneth Frampton (KF), Theodossis Issaias (TI), Lydia Kallipoliti (LK), Alan Plattus (AP), Demetri Porphyrios (DP), Brett Steele (BS), Robert A.M. Stern (RAMS), Eirini Tsachrelia (ET), Anthony Vidler (AV), Marion Weiss (MW), Elia Zenghelis (EZ)

Studio Master Plan 307

Daphne Binder 308

This park and central axis for Thessaloniki's city center aims to stitch the fragmented territories of the surrounding city and frame its new city center. Extending the streets from the east and west edges of the site, a network of pathways transverses the different episodes of the city, and weaves the existing and proposed projects. The territories that began to emerge from this network create a thick edge, a softscape that would respect a central clearing, a large central room in the midst of the city center. This central lawn is surrounded by smaller vegetal rooms, where a sense of interiority could be achieved through a definition of edge and canopy. The Hebrard axis—a major pedestrian artery that traverses the city from mountains to sea—intersects and connects these urban rooms and widens and thickens to introduce programs into them.

RA: *I think the ambition of your project is really profound. It's the first one today saying that the territorial aspect of what it means to craft a park is only know through local moments that have intensely distinct personalities. In a sense the idiosyncrasies of these configurations lend themselves to this differentiation. You've chosen or elected to differentiate through, as you've said, the orchard, the wetland, the forest, the vegetation. So this kind of* botanic folly that you've unmasked is recast now as something that can be understood at once on an urban scale. You can just bypass it, or [create] a place of discovery where you could slow down: you can go into the garden. I think that the ambition is beautiful and poetic, but I think it could be stated very simply with one drawing, which is probably an axonometric.

Andrew Dadds (Feldman Nominee) 309

The 1950s in Greece saw rapid socioeconomic changes and urbanization; under such urgency that there was no time for theory or planning. The resulting typology from this urbanization was the *polykatoikia*, a five to seven story private block development which forms a relentless datum across the ever-expanding city. As a result, public and green space is in crisis in Thessaloniki. The premise of the studio aims to densify the center, consolidating the borders of the city while gifting the city with new public park space. The project tests ambitious design merged with contextual specificity, engaging with 'Greekness' as an expression of democratic design. The *polykatoikia* is met with a provocative extension of its type, a new datum for the city of Thessaloniki.

AP: *You're using a typological form that we recognize—the slab with repetitive cellular housing units—but you're using it in an urbanistic way that is maybe not so compatible or familiar, let's say. If you think about canonical versions of Unité-type compositions— Roehampton for example—the slabs echelon to demonstrate their independence or autonomy within the landscape and the landscape proceeds beneath them. But we find this project doing a couple of things that are not natural to their typological nature: defining a street edge on the short end, trying to define the edge of the parking in conjunction with other things, and then just coincidentally [forming] a very formalized gateway where they suddenly turn into a match set and define an axis. There are no rules written anywhere that says you can't do those things, but I think you have a burden of proof when you use that formal language to do the things you're trying to do.*

Andrew Sternad 310

The project is a negotiation between city and park, street scale and skyline. The collection of buildings attempts to seamlessly integrate with the existing urban fabric at the pedestrian level, while emerging from dense, homogenous *polykatoikia* to mark the extents of an urban meadow along the skyline. A bazaar anchors the complex along Via Egnatia, a thriving commercial corridor that once linked ancient Byzantium to Rome. The high-rise tower above it punctuates a line of other towers along the north edge of the park, while low-rise, townhouse-style residences enclose a sequence of elevated gardens.

DP: *I'm really encouraged and I applaud the fact that you are taking up the challenge of looking at the* polykatoikia *and reinterpreting it twice. I'm saying that because not only in Athens but the whole of Greece is based on that typology. I'm not saying that only for formal reasons, but because that typology works hand-in-hand with the financial possibilities of building in that part of the world. Nobody has the capital, so someone has to provide the land. Someone has to provide the construction. It is really quite an important thing and I'm glad that I see that.*

Jessica Angel 311, 312

In this project, infrastructure becomes architecture. It is an attempt to have infrastructure and architecture form a coherent whole to shape this new part of the city at various scales. The design efforts particularly concentrate on the *hammam*. Connected to a new archaeology site, the whole building is underground except the circular *frigidarium* that is visible from the upper level. The building is envisioned as a hybrid between a Roman bath and a *hammam*.

BS: *The idea that it's converting infrastructure into architecture and doing it in a place that cuts the site in half makes me wish Bob was here—this is a really traumatic thing that you've done.... This is a way as an architectural project to ruminate on the larger condition of the city without trying to correct it.*

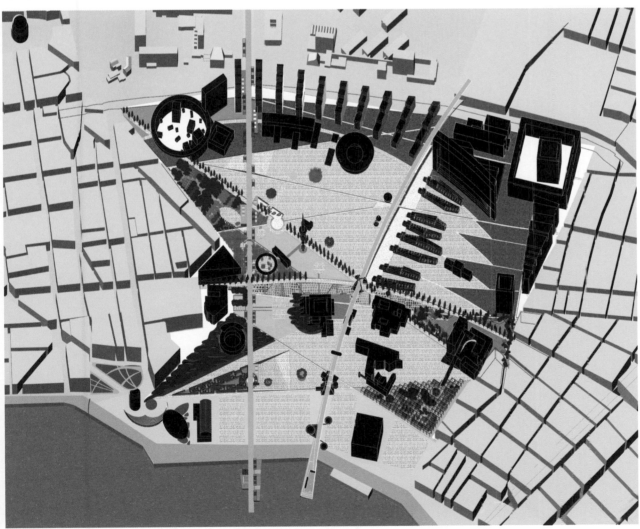

308

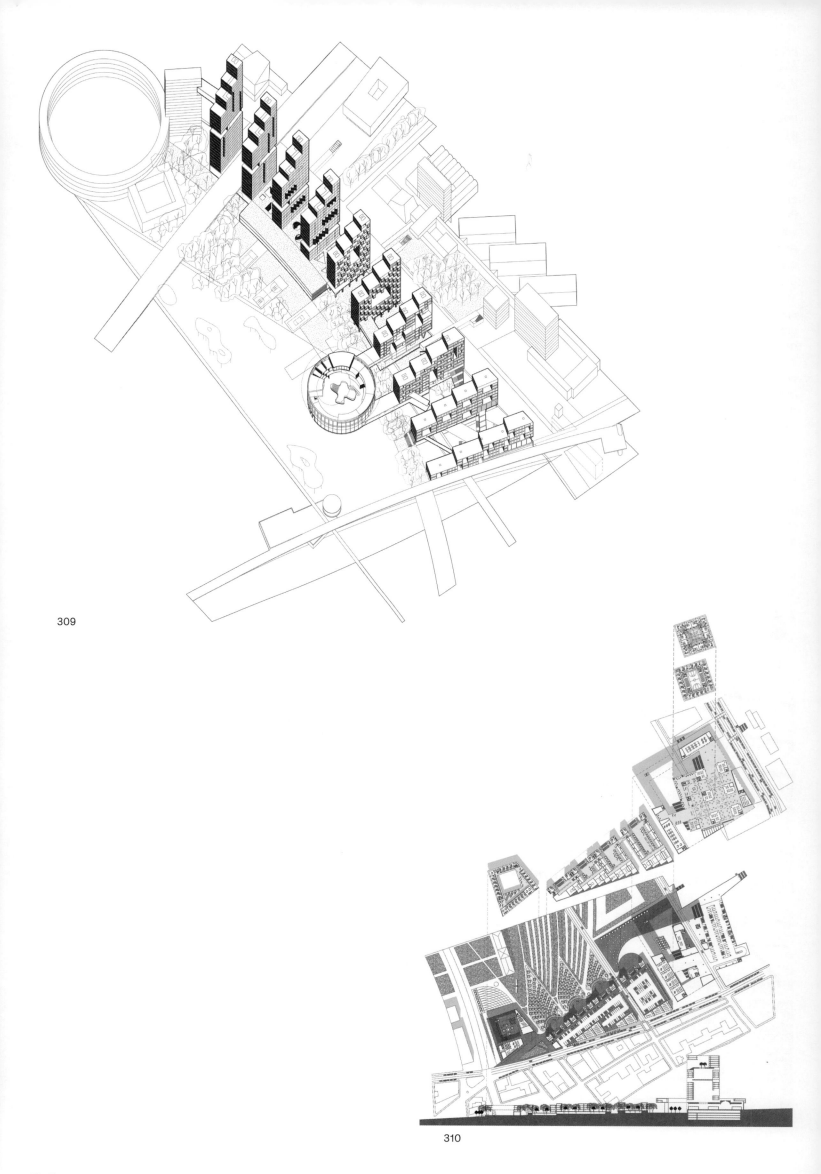

309

310

Fall
Zenghelis, Elia

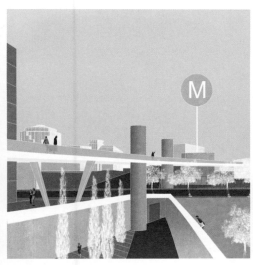

311

312

Zenghelis, Elia

Awards

A. Whitney Murphy
Scholarship
Dima Srouji

Alexander Gorlin Scholarship
Meghan Lewis

Alpha Rho Chi Medal
Daphne Binder

American Institute
of Architects Henry Adams
Certificate
Justin Oh

American Institute of Architects
Henry Adams Medal
Dorian Booth

Anne C.K. Garland Fund
Shayari De Silva

Anne Kriken Mann Scholarship
Madelynn Ringo

Arcus Scholarship
Caitlin Thissen

Bass Fellow in Architecture
Sofia Singler

Carol Ann Rinehart
Scholarship
Anne Householder

Carroll L.V. Meeks Memorial
Scholarship
Dante Furioso

Cesar Pelli Scholarship
Jack Bian

Charles Gwathmey
Scholarship
Dov Feinmesser

Charles O. Matcham
Scholarship
Eugene Tan

Christopher Tunnard Memorial
Scholarship
Kirk Henderson

Clarke Family Scholarship
Anne Ma
Meghan McDonough

David C. Morton II Scholarship
Michael Harrison

David M. Schwarz /
Architectural Services Good
Times Award
Winny Tan

David M. Schwarz /
Architectural Services Summer
Internship and Traveling
Fellowship
Rashidbek Muydinov

David M. Schwarz Scholarship
est. by Ken Kuchin
Geneva Morris

David Taylor Memorial Prize
Shivani Shedde

Dilworth Family Scholarship
Kiana Hosseini

Drawing Prize
Anne Ma

Eero Saarinen Memorial
Scholarship
Isaac Southard

Elisabeth Nan Martin and
Michael Coleman Duddy
Scholarship
Alicia Pozniak

Enid Storm Dwyer Scholarship
Anna Meloyan

Everett Victor Meeks
Fellowship
Shayari De Silva

Faith Lasser Memorial
Scholarship
Lisa Albaugh

Frank D. Israel Scholarship
Elizabeth LeBlanc

Franklin U. Gregory Memorial
Scholarship
Anthony Gagliardi

Frederick Bland Scholarship
Sarah Kasper

Frederick T. Ahlson Scholarship
Benjamin Bourgoin

Frederick W. Hilles Scholarship
Preeti Talwai

Gene Lewis Book Prize
Andrew Dadds

George Nelson Scholarship
Cathryn Garcia-Menocal

Gertraud A. Wood Traveling
Fellowship
Margaret Tsang

Gilbert and Ann Maurer
Scholarship
Katarzyna Pozniak

Harvey R. Russell Scholarship
Michelle Chen

Henry Pfisterer Scholarship
Kristin Nothwehr

Herman D.J. Spiegel
Scholarship
Dorian Booth

H.I. Feldman Nominees
Charlotte Algie, F '14
Lisa Albaugh, S '16
Luke Anderson, F '15, S '16
Heather Bizon, F '15, S '16
Benjamin Bourgoin, S '16
Gina Cannistra, S '16
Andrew Dadds, F '15
Jamie Edindjiklian, S '16
Dante Furioso, S '16
Anne Householder, F '15
Cynthia Hsu, S '16
Shuangjing Hu, S '16
Roberto Jenkins, S '16
Lila Jiang Chen, S '16

Sarah Kasper, F '15
Apoorva Khanolkar, S '15
Patrick Kondziola, F '15
Clarissa Luwia, F '15
Anne Ma, F '15
Kristin Nothwehr, S '16
Justin Oh, F '15, S '16
Dima Srouji, F '16
John Chengqi Wan, F '15
Xinyi Wang, F '15

H.I. Feldman Prize
Luke Anderson, F '15

Hilder Family Scholarship
Karl Karam

James Gamble Rogers
Scholarship
Lucas Boyd
Anny Chang
Wes Hiatt
Samuel King
Paul Lorenz
Brittany Olivari
Nasim Rowshanabadi
Robert Yoos

Janet Cain Sielaff Alumni Award
Pearl Ho

John A. Carrafiell Scholarship
Luis Salas Porras

John W. Storrs Scholarship
Lila Jiang Chen

Kenneth A. Householder
Memorial Scholarship
Apoorva Khanolkar

Kenneth A. Householder
Scholarship
Timon Covelli

Kenneth S. Kuchin Scholarship
Cynthia Hsu

Lord Norman R. Foster
Scholarship est. by the Hearst
Corporation
Charles Kane

Maya Lin Art/Architecture
Scholarship
Seokim Min

Moulton-Andrus Award
Boris Morin-Defoy

Ng Chi Sing Scholarship
Jingwen Li

Pickard Chilton Fellowship
John Kleinschmidt

Professor King-lui Wu
Scholarship
Adil Mansure

Professor King-lui Wu
Teaching Award
Trattie Davies
Kyle Dugdale

Richard D. Cohen Scholarship
Jared Abraham

Robert Allen Ward Scholarship
Fund
James Kehl

Robert Leon Coombs
Scholarship
Richard Mandimika

Ruesch Family Scholarship
Dima Srouji

Sam's Fund Scholarship
Michelle Gonzalez

Samuel J. Fogelson
Memorial Fund
Sarah Kasper

Sonia Albert Schimberg Prize
Samantha Jaff

Stanley Tigerman Scholarship
Cynthia Hsu

Takenaka Internship
Cecilia Hui

Tang Family Scholarship
Shuangjing Hu
Xinyi Wang

Ulli Scharnberg Scholarship in
memory of Carroll L.V. Meeks
Dante Furioso

Wendy Elizabeth Blanning Prize
Tess McNamara

William and Gertrude B. Lowry,
Class of 1947 Scholarship Fund
Mengshi Sun

William Edward Parsons
Memorial Medal
Andrew Sternad

William G., '30, and Virginia
Field Chester Scholarship Fund
Hugo Fenaux

William Wirt Winchester
Traveling Fellowship
Vittorio Lovato

Yen and Dolly Liang
Scholarship
Jenny Kim

Donors

Friends
Nancy Alexander '79 B.A.,
'84 M.B.A.
ASSA ABLOY
Charles L. Atwood
Ellen Ball
Penelope Bellamy
Deborah L. Berke
A. Robert Bissell '72 B.S.
Howard M. Brenner '54 B.A.
Brookfield Office Properties Inc.
John A. Carrafiell '87 B.A.
Centerbrook Architects
and Planners
James C. Childress
Elisha-Bolton Foundation
Graham Foundation for
Advanced Studies in the
Fine Arts
M. Ian G. Gilchrist '72 B.A.
Carolyn Greenspan
Julia & Seymour Gross
Foundation Inc.
Steven Harris
HBRA Architects
Andrew Philip Heid '02 B.A.
Judith T. Hunt
James L. Iker
Elise Jaffe + Jeffrey Brown
Ken Kuchin
Elizabeth Lenahan
Keith G. Lurie '77 B.A.
Anne Kriken Mann
Roger Matthews
Wendy Matthews
Ann Maurer
Gilbert Maurer
Peter D. McCann
Margaret McCurry
Nathan F. Moser
Linda Nelson
Helen W. Nitkin
Hayes Nuss
Hilda Ochoa-Brillembourg
Michael A. Pearce '09 B.A.
Richard B. Peiser '70 B.A.
Cesar Pelli '76 M.A.H., '08
D.F.A.H.
Kathryn L. Perkins
William K. Reilly '62 B.A., '94
M.A.H.
Joseph B. Rose '81 B.A.
Joel Rosenkranz
Robert Rosenkranz '62 B.A.
Marshall S. Ruben '82 B.A.
Brenda Shapiro
Jon Stryker
The BPB & HBB Foundation
The Maurer Family
Foundation, Inc.
The New York Community Trust
David Taylor Memorial Fund
The Robert A.M. Stern
Family Foundation
Gina Tso
Elpidio R. Villarreal '85 J.D.
Betty L. Wagner
Margo G. Walsh
Anne C. Weisberg
Ann E. Wolf
Mathew D. Wolf
Timothy E. Wood '72 M.F.,
'80 Ph.D.
Pei-Tse Wu '89 B.A.

1944
Leon A. Miller

1949
Frank S. Alschuler
Theodore F. Babbitt
Charles H. Brewer, Jr.
George D. Waltz

1950
Henry E. Martens

1951
Ross H. De Young

1952
Frank C. Boyer, Jr.
Paul E. Buchli
James A. Evans
George C. Holm
Donald C. Mallow
Lawrence Frederick Nulty

1953
Milton Klein
Julian E. Kulski
John V. Sheoris

1954
Charles G. Brickbauer
George R. Brunjes, Jr.*
James D. Gibans
Boris S. Pushkarev
Roger L. Strassman
Thomas R. Vreeland

1955
John L. Field
James Leslie

1956
Richard W. Chapman
Walter D. Ramberg
Stanley B. Wright

1957
Ernest L. Ames
Edwin William de Cossy
James H. Handley
Clovis B. Heimsath
Richard A. Nininger
William L. Porter
Richard Elliott Wagner
Mary S. Winder

1958
Arthur H. Corwin
James S. Dudley
Harold D. Fredenburgh*
Mark H. Hardenbergh
Allen Moore, Jr.
Malcolm Strachan, 2d
Michael W. Stuhldreher
Harold F. VanDine, Jr.

1959
Bernard M. Boyle
Frank C. Chapman
Louis P. Inserra
Robert M. Kliment
Earl A. Quenneville
Bruce W. Sielaff
Donald W. Velsey
Carolyn H. Westerfield

1960
Lawrence N. Argraves
James B. Baker
Thomas L. Bosworth
Richard S. Chafee
Bryant L. Conant
John K. Copelin
Michael Gruenbaum
Julia H. Keydel

James D. McNeely
Oscar E. Menzer
Robert A. Mitchell
Konrad J. Perlman
Walter Rosenfeld

1961
Edward R. Baldwin
Paul B. Brouard
Robert W. Carington
Peter Cooke
Warren Jacob Cox
Francis W. Gencorelli
Charles T. Haddad
William J. Hawkins
Lewis S. Roscoe
W. Eugene Sage
Bradford P. Shaw
Stanley Tigerman
Yung G. Wang

1962
George E. Buchanan
David W. Fix
Richard A. Hansen
Tai Soo Kim
Keith R. Kroeger
James Morganstern
Leonard P. Perfido
Renato Rossi-Loureiro
Meredith M. Seikel
Ming-Hsien Wang
Donald R. Watson
Myles Weintraub

1963
Austin Church III
Howard H. Foster, Jr.
John M. Lee
Ward Joseph Miles
F. Kempton Mooney
Louis H. Skidmore, Jr.
William A. Werner, Jr.
John V. Yanik

1964
Philip Allen
Theoharis L. David
Peter J. Hoppner
Charles D. Hosford
Judith A. Lawler
Charles L W. Leider
Robert J. Mittelstadt
Joan F. Stogis

1965
Michael J. Altschuler
Thomas Hall Beeby
Richard C. Fogelson
Peter L. Gluck
Neil Goodwin
Norman E. Jackson, Jr.
Kenneth H. Kaji
Arthur A. Klipfel
Isidoro Korngold
Thai Ker Liu
Gary L. Michael
John I. Pearce, Jr.
Alexander Purves
Elliot A. Segal
Robert A.M. Stern
Frederick C. Terzo
Leonard M. Todd, Jr.
Jeremy A. Walsh
Arnold N. Wile

1966
Andrew Andersons
Emily Nugent Carrier
Richard C. Carroll, Jr.
James Scott Cook

John S. Hagmann
William F. Moore
Myron B. Silberman
W. Mason Smith III

1967
William H. Albinson
Edward A. Arens
Robert A. Bell
R. Caswell Cooke
Charles M. Engberg
Alexander D. Garvin
Howard E. Goldstein
Glenn H. Gregg
Walter A. Hunt, Jr.*
Simon Lazarus
Chung Nung Lee
John W. Mullen III
Annette B. Ramirez de Arellano
Charles S. Rotenberg
Ongard Satrabhandhu
Theodore Paul Streibert
Darius Toraby

1968
Frederick S. Andreae
Robert A. Busser
Gail H. Cooke
Peter de Bretteville
David M. Dickson
John Fulop, Jr.
Christopher C. Glass
John Holbrook, Jr.
Edward T. Johnson
Peter C. Mayer
Peter Papademetriou
Franklin Satterthwaite
Donald R. Spivack
Salvatore F. Vasi
James C. Whitney

1969
Stephen H. Adolphus
James E. Caldwell, Jr.
Samuel R. Callaway
Robert J. Cassidy
David B. Decker
James M. Gage
George T. Gardner
Harvey R. Geiger
Jane L. Gilbert
Edward J. Gotgart
William H. Grover
Eric R. Hansen, Jr.
Roderick C. Johnson
Raymond J. Kaskey, Jr.
David H. Lessig
William B. Richardson
John H. Shoaff
Kermit D. Thompson
Robert W. White

1970
Richard F. Barrett
Roland F. Bedford
Paul F. Bloom
F. Andrus Burr
Roc R. Caivano
Thomas Carey
Michael G. Curtis
Ronald C. Filson
Brin R. Ford
Joseph A. Middlebrocks
Laurence A. Rosen
Daniel V. Scully
Marilyn Swartz Lloyd
Walter C. Upton
Jan A. Van Loan
Jeremy S. Wood
William L. Yuen
F. Anthony Zunino

1971
John R. Benson
William A. Brenner
An-Chi H. Burow
Rockwell J. Chin
Edward F. Cox
John Jayner
Humberto L. Rodriguez-
Camilloni
Susan St. John

1972
Paul E. Bailey
Edward P. Bass
Frederick Bland
Stephen J. Blatt
Philip Mack Caldwell
Roberta Carlson Carnwath
Heather Willson Cass
William A. Davis
John L. Delgado
John H. T. Dow, Jr.
Joseph A. Ford III
Coleman A. Harwell
Mark L. Hildebrand
Roberta D. Lawrence
William H. Maxfield
Joshua D. Morton
Keiichi Okamoto
David B. Peck, Jr.
Barton Phelps
Jefferson B. Riley
Robert L. Robinson
Paul W. Scovill III
Mark Simon
Carl H. Wies
Roger Hung Tuan Yee

1973
Hobart Fairbank
J.P. Chadwick Floyd
Stephen R. Holt
James O. Kruhly
Nancy Brooks Monroe
Robert D. Orr
Robert S. Page
Karen Rheinlander-Gray
Steven C. Robinson
William A. Sterling
J. Lawrence Thomas
R. Jerome Wagner
John W. Whipple
Robert J. Yudell

1974
Gordon M. Black
Jonathan G. Boyer
Andres M. Duany
William E. Odell
Thomas C. Payne
Patrick L. Pinnell
Elizabeth M. Plater-Zyberk
Barbara J. Resnicow
David M. Schwarz
Richard A. Senechal
George E. Turnbull

1975
Tullio A. Bertoli
Martha A. Burns
Douglas J. Gardner
Karyn M. Gilvarg
Stephen A. Glassman
Margaret R. Goglia
Susan E. Gocshall
Susan L. Keeny
Edwin R. Kimsey, Jr.
Francis C. Klein
Larry W. Richards
Andrew K. Stevenson
J. David Waggonner III

1976
Benjamin M. Baker III
Shalom Baranes
Henry H. Benedict III
Anko Chen
Barbara R. Feibelman
Daniel F. Kallenbach
James R. Kessler
Roy T. Lydon, Jr.
Eric Jay Oliner
Herschel L. Parnes
Adrienne K. Paskind
Barbara Sundheimer-Extein

1977
Yeshaya D. Ballon
Calvert S. Bowie
Louise M. Braverman
Peter D. Clark
Bradley B. Cruickshank
W.J. Patrick Curley
Carl M. Geupel
Jonathan S. Kammel
James Hirsch Liberman
Kevin P. Lichten
Randall T. Mudge
Andrew K. Robinson
Charles B. Swanson
Alexander C. Twining

1978
Philip H. Babb
Frederic M. Ball, Jr.
Paul W. Bierman-Lytle
Judith M. Capen
Kenneth H. Colburn
Kathleen A. Dunne
Ralph A. Giammatteo
Cynthia N. Hamilton
Kaspar A. Kraemer
Kevin R. O'Connor
Daniel Arthur Rosenfeld
Julia Ruch
David Spiker
Leonard Taylor

1979
Steven W. Ansel
Jack Alan Bialosky, Jr.
James Leslie Bodnar
Richard H. Clarke
Bradford W. Fiske
John Charles Hall
Kevin E. Hart
Michele Lewis
Gavin A. Macrae-Gibson
George R. Mitchell
Thomas N. Patch
Miroslav P. Sykora

1980
Jacob D. Albert
J. Scott Finn
Alexander C. Gorlin
Stephen W. Harby
Robert S. Kahn
Mariko Masuoka
Ann K. McCallum
Reese T. Owens
William A. Paquette
Beverly F. Pierz
Joseph F. Pierz

1981
Richard L. Brown
Michael B. Cadwell
Mitchell A. Hirsch
T. Whitcomb Iglehart
Michael G. Kostow
Jonathan Levi
Robin L. Meierding

Jane Murphy
Frances H. Roosevelt
Daniela H. Voith
Spencer Warncke
Diane L. Wilk

1982
Michael B. Burch
Domenic Carbone, Jr.
David P. Chen
Bruce H. Donnally
Eric J. Gering
Raymond R. Glover
Kay Bea Jones
John E. Kaliski
Thomas A. Kligerman
John C. Locke
Charles F. Lowrey, Jr.
Theodore John Mahl
Donald C. McBride
Paul W. Reiss
Constance A. Spencer
R. Anthony Terry

1983
Anthony S. Barnes
Phillip G. Bernstein
Carol J. Burns
Margaret D. Chapman
Stuart E. Christenson
Ignacio Dahl-Rocha
Jane B. Gelernter
Stefan Hastrup
Erica H. Ling
Elisabeth Nan Martin
Elizabeth Ann Murrell
Jacques M. Richter
Gary Schilling
Brent Sherwood
Sonya R. Sofield
Robert J. Taylor
Nell W. Twining
David M. Walker

1984
Paul F. Carr, Jr.
Marti M. Cowan
Teresa Ann Dwan
Ruth S. Harris
Blair D. Kamin
Elizabeth M. Mahon
Michael L. Marshall
David Chase Martin
Kenneth E. McKently
Scott Merrill
Jun Mitsui
Lawrence S. Ng
David L. Pearce
John R. Perkins
Jennifer C. Sage
Kevin M. Smith
Mary E. Stockton
Marion G. Weiss
Sherry L. Williamson
Sarah E. Willmer

1985
Barbara A. Ball
Rasa Joana Bauza
Bruce R. Becker
William Robert Bingham
Robert L. Bostwick
M. Virginia Chapman
Michael Coleman Duddy
Jonathan M. Fishman
Kristin E. Hawkins
Lucile S. Irwin
Andrew M. Koglin
Chariss McAfee
Richard G. Munday
Joseph A. Pasquinelli

Mark D. Rylander
Roger O. Schickedantz
Christine Theodoropoulos
R. David Thompson

1986
Margaret J. Chambers
Carey Feierabend
David J. Levitt
Nicholas L. Petschek
Whitney F. Sander
J. Gilbert Strickler
John B. Tittmann

1987
Mary Buttrick Burnham
William D. Egan
R A. Garthwaite
Elizabeth P. Gray
Andrew B. Knox
Douglas S. Marshall
Timothy D. Mohr
Craig D. Newick
Lilla J. Smith
Duncan Gregory Stroik
William L. Vandeventer

1988
Atowarifagha I. Apiafi
Hans Baldauf
Cary Suzanne Bernstein
John David Butterworth
Allison Ewing
Stephen C. Fritzinger
Natalie C. Gray-Miniutti
Drew H. Kepley
Ann Lisa Krsul
Thomas F. Marble
Oscar E. Mertz III
David H. Must
Kathryn B. Nesbitt
Nicholas A. Noyes
Kevin V. O'Brien
Alan W. Organschi
Elaine M. Rene-Weissman
William Taggart Ruhl
Gilbert P. Schafer III
Danna S. Sigal
Matthew Viederman
Li T. Wen

1989
Larry G. Chang
Darin C. Cook
John DaSilva
Steve Dumez
Thomas J. Frechette
Jennifer A. Huestis
Kevin S. Killen
Amy H. Lelyveld
Aari B. Ludvigsen
Stephen D. Luoni
David J. Rush
Cherie H. Santos-Wuest
Margaret S. Todd
Robert Ingram Tucker
Claire Weisz
Randy Wilmot
Koichi Yasuda

1990
Patricia Brett
Stephen Brockman
Elizabeth A. Danze
Kristen L. Hodess
Jeffrey E. Karer
David M. Levine
Marc D. L'Italien
David Clayton Miller
Robin E. Osler
Deborah R. Robinson

Scott Wood
Mark A. Yoes

1991
David M. Becker
John C. Gilmer
Linda Stabler-Talty
Alexander M. Stuart
Lindsay S. Suter
Claire E. Theobald
Michael W. Wetstone
Kevin Wilkes

1992
Andrew James Abraham
Peter K. Blackburn
Kelly Jean Carlson-Reddig
Betty Y. Chen
Frances Douglas Corzine
Perla Jeanne Delson
Alisa R. Dworsky
Frederick Adams Farrar, II
Bruce M. Horton
Maitland Jones III
Douglas Neal Kozel
James A. Langley
Elia Messinas
Daniel P. Towler-Weese
Marc A. Turkel
Marion C. Winkler

1993
Sari Chang
Richard G. Grisaru
Louise J. Harpman
Michael A. Harshman
Celia C. Imrey
Charles Lazor
Jordan J. Levin
Gitta Robinson
Allen D. Ross
Evan Michael Supcoff
Carl F. Svenstedt

1994
Brendan Russell Coburn
Mark C. Dixon
Pamela J. Fischer
Benjamin J. Horten
Paul W. Jackson
Mark R. Johnson
Thomas A. Kamm
Stephanie Kim
William J. Massey
Tania K. Min
Sergey Olhovsky
Edward B. Samuel
Albert J. Tinson, Jr.
Mimi H. Tsai

1995
Carolyn A. Foug
George Craig Knight
Johannes M. Knoops
Michael Henry Levendusky
John Christopher Woell

1996
Douglas C. Bothner
Russell S. Katz
Michael V. Knopoff
Chung Yin J. Lau
Arthur J. Lee
Alexander F. Levi
Thomas A. Lumikko
Richard J. Moschella
Nancy Nienberg
Steven A. Roberts

1997
Patrick Bleckwedel

Richard Kasemsarn
Drew Lang
Peter D. Mullan
Samuel E. Parker
David J. Pascu
Jeffery Ryan Povero
Ian M. Smith
Catherine M. Truman
William James Voulgaris
Shawn Michael Watts
Andrew Paul Wolff

1998
Holly M. Chacon
Thalassa A. Curtis
Melissa L. Delvecchio
Marjorie K. Dickstein
Clifton R. Fordham
Edward B. Gulick
Karl A. Krueger
Marc A. Roehrle
Faith Rose
Elizabeth P. Rutherfurd
Paul D. Stoller
Maureen R. Zell

1999
Jonathan D. Bolch
Kimberly Ann Brown
Yoonhee Choi
Bruce D. Kinlin
Hong-Chieh P. Lu
Aaron W. Pine

2000
Benjamin Jon Bischoff
Dominique D. Davison
Joseph Shek Yuen Fong
Oliver E. Freundlich
Donald W. Johnson
Thomas Matthew Morbitzer
Byung Taek Park
Ron M. Stelmarski
Jennifer L. Tobias
Cheng-Hsun Wu

2001
Ghiora Aharoni
Natalie S. Cheng
Mark Foster Gage
Christopher M. Pizzi
Adam J. Ruedig
Timothy A. Sullivan
Elizabeth W. Tilney
Can M. Tiryaki
Juliana Chittick Tiryaki
Laura L. Zaytoun
Zhonggui Zhao

2002
Noah K. Biklen
Pengzhan Du
Sarah Marie Lavery
Yansong Ma

2003
Andrew William Benner
Marcos Diaz Gonzalez
Li-Yu Hsu
Dongyeop Lee
Sangmin Lee
Igor P. Siddiqui
William L. Tims

2004
Abir Ahmad
Graham W. Banks
Valerie Anne Casey
Leejung Hong
Teresa H. Jan
Janny H. Kim

Michael E. Kokora
James C. Nelson III
Adam Sokol
Na Wei
Damian D. Zunino

2005
Brent A. Buck
Jennifer N. Carruthers
Ruth Shinenge Gyuse
Diala Salam Hanna
Derek J. Hoeferlin
Brandon F. Pace
Brett Dalton Spearman
Nicholas Martin Stoutt
Yory Teperman

2006
Angel Paolo Campos
Jennifer A. DuHamel
Michael J. Grogan
Sean A. Khorsandi

2007
Sandra Arndt
Gabrielle E. Brainard
Brook G. Denison
Geoffrey R. Lawson

2008
Michael B. Crockett
Jennifer J. Dubon
Marc Charles Guberman
Gabrielle K. Ho
Kathleen L. John-Alder
Whitney M. Kraus
Yichen Lu
Leo Rowling Stevens IV

2009
Lauren J. Mishkind
Matthew A. Roman

2010
Brett Patrick Appel
Daniel D. Colvard
Jacquelyn P. Hawkins
Jang Hyung Lee
Scott Brandon O'Daniel

2011
William Grandison Gridley
Elijah W. Porter

2012
Cotton B. Estes
Jeremy D. Steiner
Laura C. Wagner

2013
Antonia M. Devine
Altair L. Peterson
Ryan Salvatore
Paul C. Soper

2014
Mary F. Burr
John V. Farrace
C. Chessin Gertler
Kate M. Warren

2015
Elena R. Baranes
Hyeun J. Lee
Mark W. Peterson
Lauren E. Raab
Zachary A. Veach
Matthew H. White

*deceased

Faculty

Emily Abruzzo
Critic

Michelle Addington
Hines Professor of
Sustainable Architectural
Design

Victor Agran
Lecturer

John Apicella
Lecturer

Pier Vittorio Aureli
Louis I. Kahn Visiting
Assistant Professor

Sunil Bald
Associate Professor
Adjunct

Thomas Beeby
Professor Adjunct

Anibal Bellomio
Lecturer

Andrew Benner
Critic

Deborah Berke
Professor
Adjunct

Phillip Bernstein
Lecturer

John Blood
Critic

Kent Bloomer
Professor
Adjunct

Kyle Bradley
Critic

Karla Britton
Lecturer

Miroslava Brooks
Critic

Turner Brooks
Professor
Adjunct

Brennan Buck
Critic

Luke Bulman
Lecturer

Marta Caldeira
Lecturer

Sara Caples
Louis I. Kahn Visiting
Assistant Professor

Trattie Davies
Critic

Peggy Deamer
Assistant Dean and
Professor

Peter de Bretteville
Critic

Kyle Dugdale
Critic

Keller Easterling
Professor

John Eberhart
Critic

Peter Eisenman
Charles Gwathmey
Professor in Practice

Jonathan Emery
Edward P. Bass
Distinguished Visiting
Architecture Fellow

Alexander Felson
Assistant Professor

Martin Finio
Critic

Kurt Forster
Emeritus
Visiting Professor

Bryan Fuermann
Lecturer

Mark Foster Gage
Assistant Dean
and Associate
Professor

Alexander Garvin
Professor Adjunct

Kersten Geers
Louis I. Kahn Visiting
Assistant Professor

Martin Gehner
Professor Emeritus of
Architectural Engineering

Frank Gehry
Eero Saarinen Visiting
Professor

Kenneth Gibble
Lecturer

Kevin Gray
Lecturer

Sean Griffiths
Bishop Visiting Professor

Zaha Hadid
Norman R. Foster Visiting
Professor

Steven Harris
Professor Adjunct

Andrei Harwell
Critic

Robert Haughney
Lecturer

Dolores Hayden
Professor of Architecture
and Professor of
American Studies

Kristin Hawkins
Lecturer

Adam Hopfner
Critic and Director of the
Building Project

Joyce Hsiang
Critic

Nathan Hume
Critic

Sam Jacob
Bishop Visiting
Professorship

John Jacobson
Associate Dean and
Professor Adjunct

Kathleen James-Chakraborty
Scully Visiting Professor
of Architectural History

Everardo Jefferson
Louis I. Kahn Visiting
Assistant Professor

Larry Jones
Lecturer

Yoko Kawai
Lecturer

Tessa Kelly
Critic

George Knight
Critic

Alfred Koetter
Critic and Director of
Exhibitions

Hans Kollhoff
William B. and Charlotte
Shepherd Davenport
Visiting Professor

Amy Lelyveld
Critic

M.J. Long
Critic

Ariane Lourie Harrison
Critic

Greg Lynn
William B. and Charlotte
Shepherd Davenport
Visiting Professor

Michael Manfredi
Eero Saarinen Visiting
Professor

Nicholas McDermott
Critic

Bimal Mendis
Assistant Dean, Director
of Undergraduate Studies
and Assistant Professor
Adjunct

Edward Mitchell
Associate Professor
Adjunct

Kyoung Sun Moon
Associate Professor

Joeb Moore
Critic

Herbert Newman
Critic

Timothy Newton
Critic

Alan Organschi
Critic

Eeva-Liisa Pelkonen
Associate
Professor

Miriam Peterson
Lecturer

Laura Pirie
Lecturer

Alan Plattus
Professor

Victoria Ponce de Leon
Lecturer

Demetri Porphyrios
Stern Visiting Professor

Wolf Prix
Norman R. Foster Visiting
Professor

Alexander Purves
Professor Emeritus of
Architecture

Eero Puurunen
Lecturer

Craig Razza
Lecturer

Todd Reisz
Daniel Rose, 1951,
Visiting Assistant
Professor

Pierce Reynoldson
Lecturer

Britton Rogers
Critic

Jonathan Rose
Edward P. Bass
Distinguished
Visiting Architecture
Fellow

Kevin Rotheroe
Lecturer

Elihu Rubin
Associate Professor

Austin Samson
Critic

Joel Sanders
Professor Adjunct

Patrik Schumacher
Norman R. Foster Visiting
Professor

Aniket Shahane
Critic

Amir Shahrokhi
Lecturer

Daniel Sherer
Lecturer

Rosalyne Shieh
Critic

Edward Stanley
Lecturer

Philip Steiner
Lecturer

Robert A.M. Stern
Dean and J.M. Hoppin
Professor

Michael Szivos
Critic

Adam Trojanowski
Lecturer

Anthony Vidler
Vincent Scully Visiting
Professor

Marion Weiss
Eero Saarinen Visiting
Professor

Carter Wiseman
Lecturer

Michael Young
Louis I. Kahn
Visiting Assistant
Professor

Elia Zenghelis
William B. and Charlotte
Shepherd Davenport
Visiting Professor

Paprika!

Paprika! is a student weekly fold produced by and serving the arts and architecture community at Yale. Founded in the summer of 2014, the name comes from the color of the blazing '60s era carpets in the review spaces and auditorium of Rudolph Hall: focal points for discourse—our ground. A single 24-inch square sheet of newsprint distributed on Thursdays, a different team edits each issue, and a different graphic designer designs it. The editors hail from every year and program. A team of semesterly-elected editors, led by two coordinating editors, ensures quality and continuity.

We worked together over the past year to create a truly open and student driven platform for collaboration, work, debate, and investigations.

Submissions are open to the public, as are our weekly meetings. We receive no fiscal support from the university, and they exercise no editorial control. This year we made our content available online through a new website, raised more than $15,000 of funds through a Kickstarter, and became a non-profit organization to guarantee our fiscal and legal autonomy from the school.

All content is student-generated. Over the past year we published 25 issues, elevating the voices and work of over 200 contributors. Our issues included dispatches from Seattle, Switzerland, and Chicago, analyses of the migrant crisis in Lesbos, critiques of competitions and clients, and debates as to the future of our school, the nature of our pedagogy, and the purpose of our profession.

We have come a long way, but it is also clear the work has only just begun.

Coordinating Editors 2015–2016
  Nicolas Kemper
  Tess McNamara
  Andrew Sternad
  Margaret Tsang

Issue Advisors 2015–2016
  Francesca Carney
  Ian Donaldson
  Daniel Glick-Unterman
  Jacqueline Hall
  Charles Kane
  Nicolas Kemper
  John Kleinschmidt
  Madison Sembler
  Andrew Sternad

V
Second Year Fold
September 3, 2015
Edited by Caroline Acheatel, Elaina Berkowitz, Francesca Carney, Daniel Glick-Unterman, Garrett Hardee, Robert Hon, and Rashidbek Muydinov.
Designed by Rashidbek Muydinov.

VI
Competitons are for Horses not Artists
September 10, 2015
Edited by Charles Kane.
Designed by Anne Householder.

VII
Hands On
September 18, 2015
Edited by Dorian Booth and Jessica Angel.
Designed by Martin Bek.

VIII
Screens
October 2, 2015
Edited by Edward Wang and Amra Saric.
Designed by Cindy Hwang.

IX
Publics and Their Problems
October 8, 2015
Edited by Surry Schlabs.
Designed by Christopher Paolini.

X
VALUE
October 15, 2015
Edited by Elaina Berkowitz with Assistant Editors, Jacqueline Hall, and Benjamin Rubenstein.
Designed by Laura Coombs and Cary Potter.

XII
Perceptions
November 5, 2015
Edited by Caroline Acheatal, Garrett Hardee, and Georgia Todd.
Designed by Chase Thomas Booker.

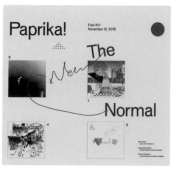

XIII
The New Normal
November 12, 2015
Edited by Pearl Ho and Jenny Kim.
Designed by Laura Foxgrover and Maziyar Pahlevan.

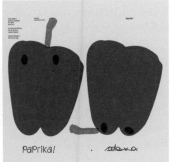

XIV
Formalists
December 3, 2015
Edited by Anthony Gagliardi, Wes Hiatt
and Robert Yoos.
Designed by Moonsick Gang.

XVIII
Home
January 28, 2016
Edited by Charlotte Algie, Sarah Kasper,
and Dima Srouji.
Designed by Seokhoon Choi.

XXII
(De)Natured
March 28, 2016
Edited by Dimitri Brand, James Coleman,
and Jonathan Molloy.
Designed by Seokhoon Choi.

XV
What Are You Doing?
December 17, 2015
Edited by Charles Kane and John Kleinschmidt.
Designed by Marta Galaz and Chris Rypkema.

XIX
Residue
February 4, 2016
Edited by Dante Furioso.
Designed by Sasha Portis.

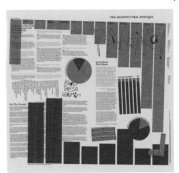

XXIII
Architectural Mystique
April 7, 2016
Edited by Cathryn Garcia-Menocal, Hannah Novack,
and Gentley Smith.
Designed by Dora Godfrey and Jerome Harris.

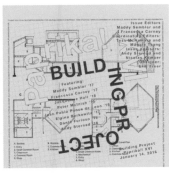

XVI
Building Project
January 14, 2016
Edited by Madison Sembler and Francesca Carney.
Designed by Erik Freer.

XX
Metrics
February 25, 2016
Edited by Caitlin Thissen, Daniel
Glick-Unterman, and Ethan Fischer.
Designed by Benjamin Ganz and Allyn Hughes.

XXIV
Masters
April 14, 2016
Edited by Samantha Jaff and Tim Altenhof.
Designed by Carr Chadwick.

XVII
Food
January 21, 2016
Edited by Juan Pablo Ponce de Leon
and Natalina Lopez.
Designed by Oliver Preston.

XXI
Historical Projections
March 7, 2016
Edited by Daphne Agosin, Preeti Talwai,
and John Chengqi Wan.
Designed by Rosen Tomov.

XXV
Visual Narrative
May 2, 2016
Edited by Hugo Fernaux, Anne Ma,
and Seokim Min.
Designed by Ana Pinto and Asad Pervaiz.

Publications

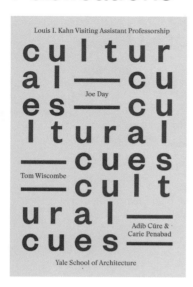

Cultural Cues: Joe Day, Adib Cure & Carie
Penabad, Tom Wiscombe (Louis H. Kahn Visiting
Assistant Professorship of Architectural Design)
July 1, 2015
Edited by Nina Rappaport.

The Louis I. Kahn Visiting Assistant
Professorship brings young innovators
in architectural design to the Yale School
of Architecture. This book, *Cultural Cues*,
includes the studio research and projects
of Joe Day of Deegan Day Design in
"NOWplex," a cinema in Los Angeles, Tom
Wiscombe of Tom Wiscombe Architecture
in "The Broad Redux," for a new interpretation of the Broad Museum in Los Angeles,
and Adib Cúre and Carie Penabad of Cúre
Penabad in the studio "Havana: Housing
in the Historic Center." The studios explore
contemporary interpretations of the
implications of cinema, the museum, and
housing, taking cues from their complex
cultural and urban contexts.

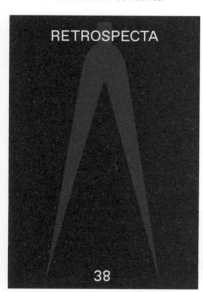

Retrospecta 38
August 2015
Edited by Cathryn Garcia-Menocal, Wes Hiatt,
Laura Meade and Margaret Tsang.

Retrospecta is the annual journal of
student work at the Yale School of
Architecture. Part-historical record, part-
monograph, *Retrospecta* seeks to capture
and record the current life of the school.
Documenting one academic year, each
issue contains exemplary work from both
the design studios and supporting courses.
The daily activities of the school, including
lectures, symposia, exhibitions, and studio
reviews, are highlighted.

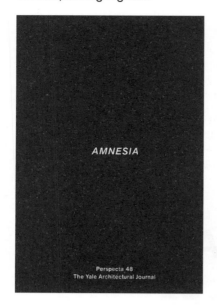

Perspecta 48: Amnesia
August 14, 2015
Edited by Aaron Dresben, Edward Hsu, Andrea
Leung, and Teo Quintana.

This issue of *Perspecta* proposes that
amnesia, often seen as a destructive force,
might also be understood as a productive
one: that the gaps it creates might also
provide spaces for invention. Contributions
from a diverse group of scholars, artists,
and practitioners explore the paradoxical
nature of amnesia: How can forgetfulness
be both harmful and generative? What will
we borrow or abandon from yesterday to
confront tomorrow? What sort of critical
genealogies can be repurposed, sup-
pressed, or manufactured to reenergize
current practice? How might we construct
counter-narratives, rebel histories, and
alternative canons that are relevant to our
present moment?

Constructs
Fall 2015
Edited by Nina Rappaport.

Constructs is a bi-annual news magazine
highlighting activities and events at
the Yale School of Architecture. The
large-format, 28-page publication features
interviews with visiting professors, pre-
views, and reviews of exhibitions, symposia,
and lectures sponsored by the school, as
well as faculty and alumni news. It also
has feature articles on issues relevant
to discussions in the design studios and
on architectural events worldwide. The
magazine is edited by Nina Rappaport and
designed by Jeffrey Ramsey. It is distributed
for free to alumni and Yale affiliates and
sold internationally.

Exhibiting Architecture: A Paradox?
September 1, 2015
Edited by Eeva-Liisa Pelkonen, Carson Chan,
and David Andrew Tasman.

As the title of the book suggests, the ambition to exhibit architecture always entails
a paradox: how to exhibit something as
large and complex as a building or a city,
and how to communicate something as
elusive as an architectural experience
that unfolds in space and time? *Exhibiting
Architecture: A Paradox?* brings together,
in print form, the lectures, paper presentations, and panel discussions that took
place at the eponymous symposium at the
Yale School of Architecture in Fall 2013.

Analytic Models in Architecture
October 1, 2015
Edited by Emmanuel Petit.

Analytic Models in Architecture documents
YSoA student work from the undergraduate

studio course "The Analytic Model: Descriptive and Interpretive Systems in Architecture," taught by Emmanuel Petit from 2005 to 2014. The projects are organized according to varying strategies of formal analysis.

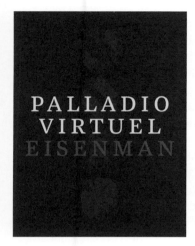

Palladio Virtuel
December 15, 2015
Peter Eisenman with Matthew Roman.

In this groundbreaking new study, American architect and educator Peter Eisenman analyzes twenty of Palladio's villas, offering a radical interpretation of the Renaissance master's work. Working from an architect's perspective, Eisenman, with Matthew Roman, shows the evolution of Palladio's villas from those that exhibit classical symmetrical volumetric bodies to others that exhibit no bodies at all, just fragments in a landscape. This conclusion stands in stark contrast to studies that emphasize principles of ideal symmetry and proportion in Palladio's work. Featuring more than 300 new analytic drawings and models, this handsome book is an important addition to the corpus of Palladian studies and a testament to Palladio's lasting place in contemporary architectural thought.

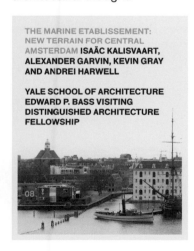

THE MARINE ETABLISSEMENT: NEW TERRAIN FOR CENTRAL AMSTERDAM **ISAÄC KALISVAART, ALEXANDER GARVIN, KEVIN GRAY AND ANDREI HARWELL**

YALE SCHOOL OF ARCHITECTURE EDWARD P. BASS VISITING DISTINGUISHED ARCHITECTURE FELLOWSHIP

The Marine Etablissement: New Terrain for Central Amsterdam
May 14, 2016
Edited by Isaäc Kalisvaart, Alexander Garvin, Kevin Gray and Andrei Harwell.

The Marine Etablissement: New Terrain for Central Amsterdam presents the studio of the ninth Yale Edward P. Bass Distinguished Visiting Architecture

Fellowship taught by Isaäc Kalisvaart, CEO of MAB Development, with Alexander Garvin (B.A. '62, M.Arch '67, M.S.U. '67), Kevin D. Gray (lecturer in real estate at the Yale School of Management), and Andrei Harwell ('06) of the Yale faculty. The studio proposed designs for the Marine Etablissement, Amsterdam's former military installation for over 350 years, which is currently undergoing a regeneration plan to open to varied public uses. The students' projects imagine numerous approaches with housing, schools, universities, tech centers, and infrastructural links to the city's core.

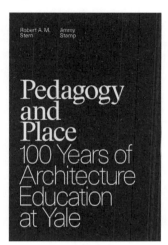

Pedagogy and Place: 100 Years of Architecture Education at Yale
May 17, 2016
Robert A.M. Stern and Jimmy Stamp.

Marking the centennial of the 1916 establishment of a professional program, *Pedagogy and Place* is the definitive text on the history of the Yale School of Architecture. Robert A.M. Stern, departing dean of the school, and Jimmy Stamp examine its growth and change over the years, and they trace the impact of those who taught or studied there, as well as the architecturally significant buildings that housed the program, on the evolution of architecture education at Yale. Owing to the impressive number of notable practitioners who have attended or been affiliated with the school, this book also contributes a history, beyond Yale, of the architecture profession in the twentieth century.

Against the Grain: Louis I. Kahn Visiting Assistant Professorship
July 1, 2016
Marcelo Spina and Georgina Huljich, Lisa Gray and Alan Organschi, and Dan Wood.

Against the Grain, features the work of three studios of the Louis I. Kahn Visiting Assistant Professors at Yale—Marcelo Spina and Georgina Huljich, Dan Wood, and Lisa Gray and Alan Organschi.

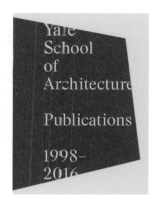

Yale School of Architecture Publications: 1998–2016
July 27, 2016
Edited by Nina Rappaport.

The school published its first brochure of all of the books and journals it has published from 1998 to 2016, both independently and with other book publishers and distributors. The brochure was presented at a book party in New York on July 27, at the office of Robert A.M. Stern Architects.

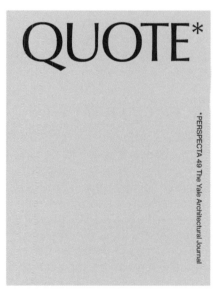

Perspecta 49: Quote
August 12, 2016
Edited by AJ Artemel, Russell LeStourgeon and Violette de la Selle.

This issue of *Perspecta* explores the uneasy lines between quotation, appropriation, and plagiarism, proposing a constructive reevaluation of the means of architectural production and reproduction. Although architecture is a discipline that prizes originality and easily-ascribed authorship, quotation and its associated operations are ubiquitous, intentional, and vital, not just palliatives to the anxiety of influence. These are perhaps the most potent tools of cultural production, yet also the most contested.

Student Organizations

Architecture Club

We are disciplinarians. We hope to be in no way exclusive of ideas from outside of architecture's traditional definition, but are dedicated to seeing how different interests—whether formal, social, ecological, political, etc.—are made manifest only in the built and the drawn. We believe that the freedom provided by this limited view of architecture's scope will generate a rich discourse on architecture and its value in a changing world.

Architecture Club was born out of what was seen as a lack of critical discussion of architecture in the studio culture at the Yale School of Architecture. Through architecture tours, social events, and public crits, we hope to fill this gap while also asserting architecture as a relevant, fresh, principally cultural discipline.

Badminton Tournament

It happens twice a year. During the wee hours of the night the fourth floor pit transforms into a stage for a semester long battle to achieve total victory….

The champions of the 2015 Fall Rudolph Open were the Dukes of York (Benjamin Rubenstein and Michael Loya). The 2016 Spring Rudolph Open champions were Tama the Cat (Winny Tan and Xiao Wu).

The Christian Fellowship

The Christian Fellowship at the Yale School of Architecture meets weekly over coffee and muffins. The gathering's purpose is to both encourage community and provide a venue for conversation on topics related to Christianity, Faith, and Architecture. All, not only Christians or those of faith, are welcome and encouraged to attend. We aim to alternate between meeting in a group setting and holding broader series of discussions with guest speakers as opportunities for interfaith discussions within the arts.

Each year we host a retreat at the Kipling House in Vermont. This past year we extended our participation to Harvard GSD. Together we explored how our Christian faith intersects with the profession and practice of architecture. Our underlying belief as a fellowship is that our faith can, and should, impact the way we care, design, think, and collaborate as architects, across all building types and projects. Our hope is that we can learn from each other and share our experiences as architecture students and as fellowship communities.

Equality In Design

Equality in Design is a coalition of students committed to expanding access to the discipline and profession of architecture as well as critically engaging with architecture's social and political context and implications. Our group holds discussions and lectures with the student body and faculty, and takes on other advocacy campaigns and events at the school. Our aim is to make architecture a more inclusive and equitable field for those who study and practice it. We also want to engage with related disciplines to better understand architecture's place in fostering a more ethical and just world. We believe that our studies at YSoA can and should expand the purview of architectural studies to question the prevailing social, cultural and ethical questions of our time, and are excited to host a wide variety of discussions about issues of inequality. Thanks to our funding from the Office of the Provost, EiD had an exciting line-up of speakers for our spring Brown Bag Lunch Series, including some events co-hosted by Outlines, YSoA's LGBTQ student group.

This year EiD held discussions which included such guests as urban planner and political scientist J. Phillip Thompson of MIT's Department of Urban Studies and Planning and sculptor Jilaine Jones.

Film Series

The School of Architecture's student-run film series hosts bi-weekly screenings of emerging and celebrated cinematic works every semester. The Series is based on the premise that cinema has a resounding and symbiotic relationship with architectural design, one that merits exploration both inside and outside the studio environment. Although many of the films selected have some clear link to the study of the built environment, the YSoA Film Series has a broad reach, often selecting movies for reasons like rich visual effects, phantasmagoric sequencing, or twisted psychological landscapes. Furthermore, the YSoA Film Series is inclusive not just in terms of subject matter, but also in terms of constituency. Any student is welcome to submit a sequence of films to be viewed in Rudolph Hall, and faculty members also view and nominate movies for public screening. Last semester, the Film Series screened movies by celebrated auteurs including Billy Wilder, Andrei Tarkovsky, and the Brothers Quay, as well as works by emerging talent Paweł Pawlikowski.

Outlines

Outlines is a social and advocacy group for lesbian, gay, bisexual, transgender, queer, and allied students at Rudolph Hall.

Established this year, Outlines functions as a support system, discussion group, advocacy platform, and social network focusing on the exploration of LGBTQ issues within the YSoA, Yale University at large, and future professional settings.

A lunchtime visit on April 6th by Samuel Knight Professor of History and American Studies George Chauncey marked Outlines' kick-off event, hosted in partnership with Equality in Design. Chauncey led attendees in a discussion of public space and sexual culture, focusing particularly on the urban geography of New York City. Chauncey drew on his work as a cultural historian to interrogate the role of the built environment in the formation of minority enclaves and safe havens.

On April 15th, Outlines and Equality in Design jointly hosted Graeme Reid, director of the Lesbian, Gay, Bisexual and Transgender Rights Program at Human Rights Watch and Lecturer in Women's, Gender, and Sexuality Studies, for a talk entitled "The Political Use of Homophobia." Reid led an interdisciplinary discussion on the political use of homophobia in global politics, citing examples of ruling elites in Gambia, Indonesia, Egypt and Russia employing anti-LGBT crackdowns for short-term political gain.

Soccer Club

FC YSoA is the school of architecture's intramural soccer team. We play against other graduate and professional students at Yale. It is a great opportunity to get out of studio and to be able to play a friendly game. It is one of the few organized activities in our school that allows students to get outside, do some physical activity, and interact with students from the other schools. It also helps to build camaraderie amongst architecture students from the different classes. But most importantly, we have awesome t-shirts.

Students

Jared Matthew Abraham
B.Arch. Univ. of Oregon '07
Portland, OR
M.Arch. II '16

Azza Alaa Eldin Abou Alam
B.I.Arch. American Univ. of
Sharjah '13
Sharjah, UAE
M.Arch. I '18

Caroline L. Acheatel
B.A. Univ. of Pennsylvania '12
Poway, CA
M.Arch. I '17

Daphne Manuela Agosin Orellana
B.Arch. Pontificia Univ. Católica
de Chile '12
Santiago, Chile
M.E.D. '17

Melinda Marlén Agron
B.A. Dartmouth College '14
Miami, FL
joint-degree program,
M.B.A., School of Management
M.Arch. I '19

Lisa Ning Albaugh
B.S. U.S. Naval Academy '06
Essex, CT
M.Arch. I '16

Mohammad Abdulatif Alothman
B.S. King Fahd Univ. of
Petroleum and Minerals '08
Dhahran, Saudi Arabia
on leave, '15–'16
M.Arch. I '16

Charlotte Leonie Algie
B.Arch. RMIT Univ. '11
Hawthorn, Australia
M.Arch. II '16

Tim Steffen Altenhof
M.Arch. Acad. of Fine Arts
Vienna '09
Vienna, Austria
Ph.D. (Fourth Year)

Ava Amirahmadi
B.A. Columbia Univ. '13
Kansas City, MO
M.Arch. I '17

Luke Alan Anderson
B.S. Ohio State Univ. '13
Cincinnati, OH
M.Arch. I '16

Jessica Flore Angel
B.S. École Polytechnique
Fédérale de Lausanne '11
Paris, France
M.Arch. I '16

Ioanna Angelidou
M.Arch. Columbia Univ. '09
New York, NY
Ph.D. (Fourth Year)

Caitlin Elizabeth Baiada
B.S. Cornell Univ. '10
M.A. Cornell Univ. '12
Moorestown, NJ
M.Arch. I '18

Elaina Diane Berkowitz
B.Des. Univ. of Florida '12
Seminole, FL
M.Arch. I '17

Li De Jack Bian
B.S. McGill Univ. '13
Toronto, Canada
M.Arch. I '16

Daphne Binder
B.Arch. Cooper Union '11
New Haven, CT
M.Arch. II '16

Heather Jean Bizon
B.Arch. Cornell Univ. '08
Morrisville, PA
M.Arch. II '17

Matthew James Bohne
B.Arch. Rhode Island School
of Design '15
Pasadena, CA
M.Arch. II '17

Anna Bokov
M.Arch. Harvard Univ. '04
Calverton, NY
Ph.D. (Fifth Year)

Abena Akyiaa Konadu Bonna
B.A. Wellesley College '13
Burlington, NJ
M.Arch. I '18

Dorian Ascher Booth
B.A. Univ. of Pennsylvania '12
Ogunquit, ME
M.Arch. I '16

Benjamin Stuart Harlan Bourgoin
B.A. Univ. of Washington '12
Lake Forest Park, WA
M.Arch. I '16

John Lucas Zechariah Boyd
B.A.S. Carleton Univ. '13
Toronto, Canada
M.Arch. I '17

Dimitri Brand
B.F.A. Maryland Institute
College of Art '11
Storrs, CT
M.Arch. I '18

Graham Stuart Brindle
B.A.S. Univ. of Waterloo '11
Toronto, Canada
M.Arch. I '17

Andrew Wayne Busmire
B.E.D. Texas A&M Univ. '14
Houston, TX
M.Arch. I '18

Denisa Ana-Maria Buzatu
B.S.E. Princeton Univ. '15
Slatina, Romania
M.Arch. I '18

Gina Christine Cannistra
B.Arch. Univ. of Notre Dame '13
Elk Grove Village, IL
M.Arch. II '17

Francesca Lena Carney
B.F.A. Savannah College
of Art & Design '14
Bryn Mawr, PA
M.Arch. I '17

Henry Wilson Carroll
B.S. Georgia Institute of
Technology '10
Lakeside, MT
M.Arch. I '17

Gregory Elia Cartelli
B.A. Bard College '12
Milford, NJ
M.E.D. '17

Guillermo Ignacio Castello Oliva
B.S. McGill Univ. '14
Barcelona, Spain
M.Arch. I '18

Pauline Jeanne Caubel
B.Arch. Pratt Institute '15
Easton, PA
M.Arch. II '17

Hsi ning Anny Chang
B.F.A. Parsons School
of Design '12
Fremont, CA
M.Arch. I '17

Ling Jun Chen
B.A. Princeton Univ. '12
Huntsville, Canada
joint-degree program,
M.B.A., School of Management
M.Arch. I '16

Lila Jiang Chen
B.S. McGill Univ. '11
Panama City, Panama
M.Arch. I '16

Tianhui Michelle Chen
B.A., B.F.A. Cornell Univ. '13
Gaithersburg, MD
M.Arch. I '16

Eunil Cho
B.Arch. Cooper Union '10
Louisville, KY
M.Arch. II '16

Sungwoo Matthew Choi
B.A. Washington Univ. '12
Gwangju, South Korea
on leave, '15–'16
M.Arch. I '16

James Douglas Coleman
B.S. Univ. at Buffalo SUNY '10
Endicott, NY
M.Arch. I '18

Dakota Anderson Cooley
B.F.A. Univ. Texas at Austin '12
Houston, TX
M.Arch. I '17

Robert Johannes Cornelissen
B.A.S. Univ. of Auckland '14
Auckland, New Zealand
M.Arch. I '17

Carl David Cornilsen
B.S. Univ. of Michigan '05
Houghton, MI
joint-degree program,
M.B.A., School of Management
M.Arch. I '16

Timon David Covelli
B.A. Univ. of Calif. Berkeley '12
Los Angeles, CA
M.Arch. I '18

Andrew Eric Dadds
B.A.S. Univ. of Waterloo '12
Oakville, Canada
M.Arch. I '16

Alexander James Davies
B.A. Brown Univ. '15
Los Angeles, CA
M.Arch. I '18

Andreas Salomé De Camps German
B.Arch. Pontificia Univ. Católica
Madre y Maestra '13
Santo Domingo, DR
M.Arch. II '17

Shayari Hiranya De Silva
B.A. Yale Univ. '11
Colombo, Sri Lanka
M.Arch. I '16

Ian Cameron Donaldson
B.S. Univ. of Michigan '14
Ann Arbor, MI
M.Arch. I '18

Patrick Thomas Doty
B.A. Carleton College '12
White Bear Lake, MN
M.Arch. I '18

Jamie Ann Edindjiklian
B.Arch. CUNY the City
College of NY '13
Long Beach, NY
M.Arch. II '17

Jessica Lynn Elliott
B.Des. Univ. of Florida '13
Sarasota, FL
M.Arch. I '16

Dov Feinmesser
B.A.S. Ryerson Univ. '11
Jerusalem, Israel
M.Arch. I '16

Hugo Gregory Fenaux
B.S. Univ. of Virginia '12
Dillwyn, VA
M.Arch. I '16

Daniel Xu Fetcho
B.A. Univ. of Calif. Berkeley '13
Los Angeles, CA
M.Arch. I '18

Ethan Fischer
B.A. Vassar College '11
Brooklyn, NY
M.Arch. I '17

Valeria Flores Vargas
B.F.A. Savannah College
of Art and Design '15
Escazu, Costa Rica
M.Arch. I '18

Jennifer Catherine Fontenot
B.Arch. Pratt Institute '13
Jakarta, Indonesia
M.Arch. II '17

Spencer Joseph Fried
B.A. Claremont McKenna
College '15
West Hills, CA
M.Arch. I '18

Dante T.H. Furioso
B.A. Wesleyan Univ. '07
Washington, D.C.
M.Arch. I '16

Casey M. Furman
B.Des. Univ. of Florida '14
Oviedo, FL
M.Arch. I '17

Anthony Vincent Gagliardi
B.S. Ohio State Univ. '13
Parma, OH
M.Arch. I '16

Rachel McKenzie Gamble
B.A. Clemson Univ. '14
Elgin, SC
M.Arch. I '17

Cathryn Alexandra Garcia-Menocal
B.F.A. Washington Univ. '12
Miami, FL
M.Arch. I '17

Daniel Marcus Glick-Unterman
B.S. Univ. of Michigan '14
Evanston, IL
M.Arch. I '17

Christian Ireland Golden
B.S. Ohio State Univ. '14
Bellefontaine, OH
M.Arch. I '18

Michelle Jennifer Gonzalez
B.S. Univ. of Michigan '13
West Orange, NJ
M.Arch. I '16

Richard Christopher Green
B.A. Univ. of Cambridge '12
Jarrow, UK
M.Arch. II '17

Chad Andrew Greenlee
B.S. Ohio State Univ. '14
Uniontown, OH
M.Arch. I '17

Jacqueline Elizabeth Hall
B.A. New York Univ. '12
Topsfield, MA
joint-degree program,
M.E.M., School of Forestry
& Environmental Studies
M.Arch. I '17

Eugene Han
M.Arch. ArtCenter College
of Design '05
London, England
Ph.D. (Second Year)

Claudia Garrett Hardee
B.A. Univ. of Texas '13
Beatrice, AL
M.Arch. I '17

Michael Edward Harrison
B.S. Univ. of Michigan '13
Grosse Pointe Park, MI
M.Arch. I '16

Claire Louise Haugh
B.Arch. Univ. College London '14
London, UK
M.Arch. I '18

Gary Huafan He
B.Arch. Cornell Univ. '09
La Mirada, CA
Ph.D. (First Year)

Kirk McFadden Henderson
B.A. Yale Univ. '05
Washington, D.C.
M.Arch. I '16

Wesley Michael Hiatt
B.S. Ohio State Univ. '13
Pickerington, OH
M.Arch. I '17

Ting Ting Pearl Ho
B.S. Univ. of Virginia '11
Hong Kong
M.Arch. I '16

Zachary Kyle Hoffmann
B.E.D. Texas A&M Univ. '14
Spicewood, TX
M.Arch. I '18

John Cameron Holden
B.A. Yale Univ. '12
Dallas, TX
M.Arch. I '18

Robert M. Hon
B.F.A. Savannah College
of Art & Design '14
Columbia, MO
M.Arch. I '17

Seyedeh Kiana Hosseini
B.A. Tehran Univ. '13
Karaj, Iran
M.Arch. I '16

Yue Hou
B.A., B.S. Univ. Toronto '13
Shijiazhuang, China
on leave, '15–'16
M.Arch. I '17

Anne Lawren Householder
B.S. Univ. of Illinois '13
Park Ridge, IL
M.Arch. I '16

Cynthia Hsu
B.A. Univ. of Calif. San Diego '12
Yorba Linda, CA
M.Arch. I '16

Shuangjing Hu
B.Arch. Tsinghua Univ. '12
Changsha, China
M.Arch. II '16

Kevin Ting-yu Huang
B.A. Univ. of Hong Kong '13
Taipei, Taiwan
M.Arch. I '18

Hunter T. Hughes
B.A. Denison Univ. '14
Grosse Pointe, MI
M.Arch. I '18

Heung-Sum Cecilia Hui
B.A. Univ. of Toronto '11
Toronto, Canada
M.Arch. I '17

Alexis Hyman
B.Des. Univ. of Florida '15
Palm Beach Gardens, FL
M.Arch. I '18

Chris K. Hyun
B.Arch. Univ. Southern
California '11
La Mirada, CA
M.Arch. II '17

Amanda Lara Iglesias
B.A. Wheaton College '14
Albuquerque, NM
M.Arch. I '18

Theodossios Issaias
M.Arch. MIT '11
Athens, Greece
Ph.D. (Third Year)

Samantha Leigh Jaff
B.A. Colby College '11
Newton, MA
M.Arch. I '16

Roberto Jenkins
B.Arch. Pratt Institute '13
San Jose, Costa Rica
M.Arch. II '16

Ha Min Joo
B.Arch. Univ. of Notre Dame '14
Seoul, South Korea
M.Arch. II '17

Matthew Charles Kabala
B.A. Univ. of Calif. Davis '14
San Mateo, CA
M.Arch. I '17

Charles Anderson Kane
B.A. Clemson Univ. '11
Lake Wylie, SC
M.Arch. I '16

Karl Elie Karam
DIPL Architectural Association
School '13
Beirut, Lebanon
M.Arch. II '16

Sarah Elizabeth Kasper
B.S. Univ. of Illinois '13
Crete, IL
M.Arch. I '16

John-Thaddeus Keeley
A.B. Harvard Univ. '07
Morristown, NJ
on leave, fall '15–'16
M.Arch. I '16

James E. Kehl
B.S. Univ. of Cincinnati '10
Newark, OH
M.Arch. I '16

Nicolas Thornton Kemper
B.A. Yale Univ. '11
Kansas City, MO
M.Arch. I '16

Apoorva Gurunath Khanolkar
B.Arch. Univ. of Mumbai '13
Mumbai, India
M.Arch. II '16

Jenny Kim
B.A.S. Univ. of Waterloo '12
Calgary, Canada
M.Arch. I '16

Samuel Redell King
B.A. Washington Univ. '12
Saint Louis, MO
M.Arch. I '17

John Walker Kleinschmidt
B.A. Washington Univ. '08
Fort Atkinson, WI
M.Arch. I '16

Patrick Dillon Kondziola
B.Arch. Florida Atlantic Univ. '11
Vero Beach, FL
M.Arch. II '17

Alexander Oleg Kruhly
B.A. Univ. of Pennsylvania '13
Radnor, PA
M.Arch. I '17

Jason Kurzweil
B.Arch., M.S. New Jersey Institute
of Technology '11
Staten Island, NY
M.Arch. II '16

Hyeree Kwak
B.A. Univ. of Hong Kong '13
Seoul, South Korea
M.Arch. I '18

Justin Kitsing Lai
B.A.S. Univ. of Waterloo '15
Winnipeg, Canada
M.Arch. I '18

David Alston Langdon
B.A. Yale Univ. '13
Indianapolis, IN
M.Arch. I '18

Elizabeth Ann LeBlanc
B.A.S. Univ. of Texas '13
San Antonio, TX
M.Arch. I '16

Aaryoun Lee
B.F.A. Rhode Island
School of Design '12
Tenafly, NJ
on leave, '15–'16
M.Arch. I '17

Dylan Seoyoon Lee
B.A. Univ. of Southern
California '14
Los Angeles, CA
M.Arch. I '18

Jeremy Caldwell Leonard
B.Arch. North Carolina
State Univ. Raleigh '13
Raleigh, NC
M.Arch. II '17

Christopher Haiman Leung
B.S. Univ. College London '10
Hong Kong
M.Arch. I '17

Meghan Lewis
   B.S. Washington Univ. '11
   Denver, CO
   joint-degree program,
   M.E.M., School of Forestry
   & Environmental Studies
   M.Arch. I '16

Jingwen Li
   B.Arch. Xian Jiaotong Univ. '11
   Changsha, China
   M.Arch. II '16

Xiaomeng Li
   B.A. Washington Univ. '13
   Shijiazhuang, China
   M.Arch. I '18

Audrey Yifei Li
   B.A. Hobart and William Smith
   Colleges '15
   Beijing, China
   M.Arch. I '18

Jack Meyer Lipson
   B.A.S Univ. of Waterloo '15
   Toronto, Canada
   M.Arch. I '18

Jizhou Liu
   B.Arch. Tsinghua Univ. '13
   Beijing, China
   M.Arch. II '16

Ziyue Liu
   B.A.S Univ. of New South
   Wales '11
   Nanjing, China
   M.Arch. I '18

Paul Jacob Lorenz
   B.S. Univ. of Wisconsin '06
   Madison, WI
   M.Arch. I '17

Vittorio F. Lovato
   B.S. Univ. of Michigan '12
   Berkley, MI
   M.Arch. I '16

Michael Loya
   B.A. Columbia Univ. '12
   New York, NY
   joint-degree program,
   M.B.A., School of Management
   M.Arch. I '17

Skender Luarasi
   M.Arch. Massachusetts Institute
   of Technology '05
   Somerville, MA
   Ph.D. (Third Year)

Clarissa Astrid Luwia
   B.Des. Univ. of Sydney '12
   New South Wales, Australia
   M.Arch. I '16

Anne Wing Yan Ma
   B.A.S. Univ. of Waterloo '11
   Toronto, Canada
   M.Arch. I '16

Richard David Mandimika
   B.A. Univ. of Miami '12
   Harare, Zimbabwe
   M.Arch. I '16

Adil Mansure
   B Arch. Univ. of Mumbai '11
   Toronto, Canada
   M.Arch. II '16

Tara Suzanne Marchelewicz
   B.A. Univ. of Toronto '14
   Missississauga, Canada
   M.Arch. I '18

Alexandra Mikaela Maria
Karlsson-Napp
   B.S. Royal Institute of
   Technology '12
   El Paso, TX
   M.Arch. I '18

Margaret Marsh
   B.A. Princeton Univ. '13
   New York, NY
   M.Arch. I '18

Daniel S. Marty
   B.S. Univ. of Michigan '13
   Cincinnati, OH
   M.Arch. I '17

Aymar Mariño Maza
   B.Arch. Cornell Univ. '15
   Potomac, MD
   M.Arch. II '17

Larkin Patrick Daniel McCann
   B.A. Harvard Univ. '15
   Tulsa, OK
   M.Arch. I '18

Megan Elizabeth McDonough
   B.S. Georgia Institute of
   Technology '13
   Ambler, PA
   M.Arch. I '16

Stephen A McNamara
   B.S. Ohio State Univ. '14
   Brewster, NY
   M.Arch. I '17

Tess Kathleen McNamara
   B.A. Princeton Univ. '12
   New York, NY
   joint-degree program,
   M.E.M., School of Forestry
   & Environmental Studies
   M.Arch. I '17

Laura E. Meade
   B.S. Ohio State Univ. '12
   Pickerington, OH
   M.Arch. I '17

Stephanie Medel
   B.A. Barnard College '13
   Searcy, AR
   M.Arch. I '18

Adam Thomas Meis
   B.Des. Univ. of Colorado '15
   Boulder, CO
   M.Arch. I '18

Anna Meloyan
   B.A. Univ. of Calif. Los Angeles '13
   Glendale, CA
   M.Arch. I '16

Maxwell T. Mensching
   B.A. Hobart and William Smith
   Colleges '11
   New Canaan, CT
   M.Arch. I '17

Jiajian Min
   M.Arch. Tsinghua Univ. '15
   Beijing, China
   M.Arch. II '17

Seokim Min
   B.S. Korea Advanced Institute of
   Science and Technology '13
   Seoul, Republic of Korea
   M.Arch. I '16

Jonathan Charles Arthur Molloy
   B.A. Swarthmore College '14
   Nyack, NY
   M.Arch. I '18

Boris Morin-Defoy
   B.S. McGill Univ. '11
   Montreal, Canada
   M.Arch. I '16

Geneva Morris
   B.A. Loyola Univ. '11
   Chicago, IL
   M.E.D. '16

Rashidbek Muydinov
   B.A. Tashkent State Technical
   Univ. '07
   New Haven, CT
   joint-degree program,
   M.E.M., School of Forestry
   & Environmental Studies
   M.Arch. I '17

Elizabeth G. Nadai
   B.A. Yale Univ. '10
   Essex, MA
   M.Arch. I '17

Ali Naghdali
   B.Arch. Rice Univ. '10
   Sugar Land, TX
   M.Arch. II '17

Abdulgader Samier Naseer
   B.Arch. Univ. of Miami '14
   Jeddah, Saudi Arabia
   M.Arch. II '16

Anna Alexandrovna Nasonova
   B.A. Yale Univ. '13
   Voronezh, Russia
   M.Arch. I '17

Cecily Maria Ng
   B.A. Univ. of Calif. Berkeley '12
   San Francisco, CA
   M.Arch. I '17

Kristin Louise Nothwehr
   B.A. Yale Univ. '10
   Clarinda, IA
   M.Arch. I '16

Hannah L. Novack
   B.A. Barnard College '13
   Saint Louis, MO
   M.Arch. I '17

Justin David Oh
   B.A.S. Ryerson Univ. '13
   Calgary, Canada
   M.Arch. I '16

Brittany Paige Olivari
   B.S. Univ. of Virginia '12
   Castine, ME
   M.Arch. I '17

Ronald V. Ostezan
   B.S. Univ. of Michigan '15
   Lake Orion, MI
   M.Arch. I '18

Andrew Bryan Padron
   B.Des. Univ. of Florida '12
   Loxahatchee, FL
   M.Arch. I '17

Jeannette Kittredge Penniman
   B.A. Yale Univ. '12
   Essex, CT
   M.Arch. I '16

Luis Enrique Salas Porras
   B.A. Rice Univ. '11
   Chihuahua, Mexico
   M.Arch. I '16

Alicia Pozniak
   B.A., B.Arch. Univ. of
   Technology Sydney '05
   Sydney, Australia
   M.Arch. II '16

Katarzyna Magdalena Pozniak
   B.Arch. Cornell Univ. '13
   Gdansk, Poland
   joint-degree program,
   M.B.A., School of Management
   M.Arch. II '16

Xiaoyi Pu
   B.S. McGill Univ. '12
   Beijing, China
   on leave, Fall '15
   M.Arch. I '16

Feng Qian
   B.E. Southeast Univ. '13
   Nanjing, China
   on leave, '15–'16
   M.Arch. I '16

Laura Yue Quan
   B.E. Cooper Union '15
   Edison, NJ
   M.Arch. I '18

Yazma Rajbhandary
   B.Arch. Cornell Univ. '12
   Kathmandu, Nepal
   M.Arch. II '17

Paul Lloyd Rasmussen
   B.S. Brigham Young Univ. '13
   San Jose, CA
   M.Arch. I '17

Madelynn Christine Ringo
   B.A. Univ. of Kentucky '12
   Bardstown, KY
   M.Arch. I '16

Meghan Stratton Royster
   B.S. Univ. of Michigan '14
   Williamston, MI
   M.Arch. I '18

Nasim Rowshanabadi
   B.Arch. Bahai Institute for Higher
   Education '11
   Hamden, CT
   M.Arch. I '17

Benjamin Frank Rubenstein
   B.S. Univ. of Illinois '13
   Glencoe, IL
   M.Arch. I '17

Gordon Daniel Schissler
B.Arch. Univ. of North Carolina
Charlotte '13
Swannanoa, NC
M.Arch. II '17

Surry Schlabs
M.Arch. Yale Univ. '03
New Haven, CT
Ph.D. (Fifth Year)

Danielle Schwartz
B.A. Univ. of Pennsylvania '14
Old Westbury, NY
M.Arch. I '18

James Schwartz
B.F.A. New York Univ. '12
Old Westbury, NY
M.Arch. I '17

Madison Sembler
B.F.A. Washington Univ. '12
Pinellas Park, FL
M.Arch. I '17

Misha Semenov
B.A. Princeton Univ. '15
San Francisco, CA
joint-degree program,
M.E.M., School of Forestry
& Environmental Studies
M.Arch. I '19

Matthew Dean Shaffer
B.A. Univ. of Pittsburgh '08
Lewisburg, PA
M.Arch. I '18

Shreya Hasmukh Shah
B.Arch. Syracuse Univ. '12
Rochester, NY
M.Arch. II '17

Shivani Umesh Shedde
B.Arch. Univ. of Mumbai '12
Mumbai, India
M.E.D. '16

Ilana R. Simhon
B.S. Univ. at Buffalo SUNY '14
Plainview, NY
M.Arch. I '17

Sofia Anja Singler
B.Arch. Univ. of Cambridge '13
Jyväskylä, Finland
M.Arch. II '16

Gentley Noelle Smith
B.S. Ohio State Univ. '14
West Windsor, NJ
M.Arch. I '18

Robert Charles Smith Waters
B.S. Ohio State Univ. '14
Canton, OH
M.Arch. I '18

Jeongyoon Isabelle Song
B.A. Princeton Univ. '14
Chuncheon, South Korea
M.Arch. I '18

Melody J. Song
B.A. New York Univ. '11
Seoul, South Korea
M.Arch. I '16

Isaac Philip Southard
B.Arch. Drexel Univ. '11
Philadelphia, PA
M.Arch. II '16

Dima Ramzi Srouji
B.A. Kingston Univ. '12
Bethlehem, Palestine
M.Arch. I '16

Alexander Stagge
B.S. Ohio State Univ. '14
Cincinnati, OH
M.Arch. I '17

Katherine Rose Stege
B.E.D. Univ. of Colorado '12
Leadville, CO
joint-degree program,
M.E.M., School of Forestry
& Environmental Studies
M.Arch. I '17

Andrew John Sternad
B.A. Washington Univ. '09
Norcross, GA
M.Arch. I '16

Mengshi Sun
B.Arch. Tsinghua Univ. '14
Beijing, China
M.Arch. II '16

Preeti Murali Talwai
B.A. Univ. of Calif. Berkeley '13
Folson, CA
M.E.D. '16

Winny Windasari Tan
B.A. Carnegie Mellon Univ. '12
Jakarta, Indonesia
M.Arch. I '16

You Zhi Eugene Tan
B.A. National Univ. of
Singapore '12
Singapore
M.Arch. I '16

Phineas Urban Taylor-Webb
B.A. Carnegie Mellon Univ. '15
Los Angeles, CA
M.Arch. I '18

Pierre Thach
B.S. McGill Univ. '13
Montreal, Canada
M.Arch. I '18

Caitlin Mory Thissen
B.S. Univ. of Utah '13
Kodiak, AK
M.Arch. I '16

Alexandra M. Thompson
B.A. Yale Univ. '11
Guilford, CT
M.Arch. I '18

Georgia Mohr Todd
B.A. Colgate Univ. '10
Charlottesville, VA
M.Arch. I '17

Margaret Jau-ming Tsang
B.A. Yale Univ. '11
Bethesda, MD
M.Arch. I '17

Julie Turgeon
B.A. Univ. of Calif. Berkeley '14
Hinsdale, IL
M.Arch. I '18

David Turturo
M. Des. Harvard Univ '11
Auburn, NY
Ph.D. (First Year)

John Chengqi Wan
B.S. Univ. College London '13
Singapore
M.Arch. I '16

Shuo Wang
B.A.S. Univ. of Waterloo '13
Kitchener, Canada
joint-degree program,
M.B.A., School of Management
M.Arch. I '16

Xinyi Wang
B.Arch. Tsinghua Univ. '13
Beijing, China
M.Arch. I '16

Dylan K. Weiser
B.Des. Texas A&M Univ. '13
Los Angeles, CA
M.Arch. I '18

Xiao Wu
B.S. Univ. of Virginia '12
Hangzhou, China
joint-degree program,
M.B.A., School of Management
M.Arch. I '17

Francesca Xavier
B.S. Ohio State Univ. '14
Longwood, FL
M.Arch. I '18

Robert J. Yoos
B.S. Univ. at Buffalo SUNY '14
Kings Park, NY
M.Arch. I '17

Samuels Franklin Zeif
B.A. Brown Univ. '14
Brooklyn, NY
M.Arch. I '18

Alison M. Zuccaro
B.Des. Univ. of Florida '15
Hollywood, FL
M.Arch. I '18

Matthew Glen Zuckerman
B.A. Yale Univ. '11
Mamaroneck, NY
M.Arch. I '17

End with a Bang! exhibition reception.

Dean Stern dedicates the Jim Vlock Building Project house.

Spring Advanced Studio lottery presentations.

Badminton tournament.

Prom.

PoMo Party: students roasting Dean Stern.

May 19, 2016
Graduating Class of 2016

Travel Week

Each semester students in the Advanced Studios spend a week traveling at and around the location of their studio project with their class and professors. It is a time that allows for both research and the forming and strengthening of personal relationships.

Spring

Pier Vittorio Aureli
    San Francisco, California
Kersten Geers
    Milan, Italy
    Vicenza, Italy
    Venice, Italy
Frank Gehry 314
    Los Angeles, California
    Berlin, Germany
    Munich, Germany
    Paris, France
Sean Griffiths and Sam Jacob 313
    London, United Kingdom
Zaha Hadid and Patrik Schumacher
    London, United Kingdom
    Cambridge, United Kingdom
Hans Kollhoff
    Berlin, Germany
Greg Lynn
    Amazon Fulfillment Center
    Louisville, Kentucky
Wolf Prix
    Vienna, Austria
    Frankfurt am Main, Germany
    Paris, France
    Lyon, France

Fall

Sunil Bald
    Edinburgh, Scotland
    Glasgow, Scotland
Sara Caples and Everardo Jefferson
    Paris, France
    Le Havre, France
Peter Eisenman 316
    Florence, Italy
    Arezzo, Italy
    Sansepolcro, Italy
    Urbino, Italy
    Milan, Italy
Alan Plattus 315
    Beijing, China
Demetri Porphyrios 318, 319
    Dubrovnik, Croatia
    Venice, Italy
Marion Weiss and Michael Manfredi
    San Francisco, CA
Elia Zenghelis 317
    Thessaloniki, Greece
    Athens, Greece

314

313

315

316

317

319

318

September 26–October 4, 2015
Fall Travel Week

Dean Stern, PoMo Party.

Index

Students

Faculty & Critics

Electives

Design & Visualization

History & Theory

Technology & Practice

Urbanism & Landscape

Lectures

Studios

Advanced Studios

First Year Studios

Post-Professional Studio

Second Year Studios

Retrospecta 39
    2015–2016. Celebrating 100 years of architecture at Yale.

Published by the Yale School of Architecture
    Dean Robert A.M. Stern, 2015–2016
    Dean Deboarah Berke, 2016–

Editors
    Dimitri Brand
    James Coleman
    Amanda Iglesias
    Jeongyoon Song

Graphic Designers
    Seokhoon Choi
    Laura Coombs

Editorial Assistants
    Caroline Acheatel
    Melinda Agron
    Elaina Berkowitz
    Francesca Carney
    Anny Chang
    Spencer Fried
    Wes Hiatt
    Kevin Huang
    Alexandra Karlsson-Napp
    Apoorva Khanolkar
    Samuel King
    Hyeree Kwak
    Jeremy Leonard
    Jack Lipson
    Margaret Marsh
    Jonathan Molloy
    Laura Quan
    Madison Sembler
    Gentley Smith
    Robert Smith Waters
    Julie Turgeon

Photography
    Lisa Albaugh
    Jack Bian
    Matthew Bohne
    John Jacobson
    Benjamin Rubenstein
    Shayari Shah
    Isaac Southard
    John Chengqi Wan

Design Consultant
    Pentagram, New York

Printer
    Allied Printing Services, Manchester, CT

Typeface
    Theinhardt by François Rappo, Optimo Type Foundry

Paper
    Soporset Text 60lb. and Cover 111lb.

We would like to extend our most sincere gratitude to:
    Michael Beirut, Pentagram
    Deborah Berke
    Sheila Levrant de Bretteville
    Richard DeFlumeri
    Richard Kaplan, Allied Printing
    Nina Rappaport
    Robert A.M. Stern

    The faculty, staff and students of the YSoA.

For more information and copies of this book, please write, call, or visit us at:
    Yale School of Architecture
    180 York Street, New Haven, CT 06511
    203–432–2288
    www.architecture.yale.edu